MY GREATEST
DEFEAT

Published in May 2019
Reprinted in July 2019, July 2020 and May 2021

ISBN 978-1-910505-40-3

Published by Evro Publishing
Westrow House, Holwell, Sherborne, Dorset DT9 5LF

www.evropublishing.com

Edited by Mark Hughes
Designed by Richard Parsons

Printed and bound in Malta by Gutenberg Press

MY GREATEST
DEFEAT

Stories of hardship and hope from motor racing's finest heroes

PUBLISHING

WILL BUXTON

ARTWORK BY GIUSEPPE CAMUNCOLI

For Dad
'Don't let the buggers get you down'

Will Buxton

A motorsport journalist, commentator, broadcaster and presenter, Will Buxton has had the rare luxury of turning his life's great passion into something resembling work for the better part of the last 20 years.

His first break came writing for GrandPrix.com in 2001 before a full-time role as Staff Writer at the *Official Formula 1 Magazine* became his in 2002. With the demise of the publication in 2004, Buxton toured the European Formula 1 races living in a camper van. His exploits came to the attention of the new GP2 Series, for which he became Director of Communications over the next three years.

A return to Formula 1 journalism in 2008 as Editor of *GP Week* also saw his first forays into commentary, his style and passion forging a pathway to the SPEED channel in the USA. He would become their Formula 1 pitlane reporter, moving to NBC when the Formula 1 rights transferred in 2013. In 2018 Buxton became Formula 1's first Digital Presenter, completing the circle to return to his very first home in the sport with a role within the official Formula 1 family, during a year that saw him report on his 200th Formula 1 and 500th career race.

Buxton lives in Oxfordshire, England with his fiancée Victoria. This is his first book.

Giuseppe Camuncoli

One of the most revered artists in modern comic book design, Giuseppe Camuncoli, 'Cammo', is renowned for a dark, brooding style that has seen him become a staple in the Vertigo, DC and Marvel stables.

Beginning his career by touting his work around conventions, it was for Vertigo that he made his breakthrough. DC Comics soon took notice of his talents and set him to work on the *Swamp Thing* and *Hellblazer* series, through which he made his name.

But it was with Marvel that he found his greatest notoriety, pencilling books such as *Wolverine*, *Spider-Man* and *Darth Vader*.

A proud Italian, Cammo lives half an hour from Ferrari's Formula 1 base in Maranello.

Contents

Introduction

This book was never intended to be what it is. If I'm honest, I think that's been the most enjoyable part; the fact that when I initially set out on the journey of writing what I hoped would make a good story, I had no idea that it would become something so very different from what I had originally imagined. And something that, in its writing and research, would open up so many avenues I'd never considered, whilst simultaneously allowing me to confront parts of myself I'd either not realised I'd needed to or that I had consciously dared not handle.

The original idea came on a flight, one of hundreds taken over the course of a year in the pursuit of this beautiful folly I'm lucky enough to call work. It was halfway over the Atlantic Ocean, *en route* to Barbados for some mid-season downtime with my then girlfriend Victoria.

After discovering that I'd already watched the movies on offer and that all the boxset series that I'd not yet delved into began at the fifth episode of the second season (why do airlines do that?) I made my way into the folder of regularly hidden gems that is 'Documentaries'. And there I found the fabulous '24 Hour War'.

The story of the Ford/Ferrari battles at Le Mans in the 1960s had my tunnelled focus from the first to the last of its 99 minutes. And in reliving the saga of Ford's repeated failures and consistent resilience at La Sarthe, I was reminded of a truism: the finest stories in our sport come not from victory but from defeat. These are the moments on which true greatness is built. Picking oneself up and dusting oneself off. Starting again. Coming back stronger.

That's what motorsport… well, sport, in truth, is all about.

The concept that awoke in my mind was to talk to drivers about their worst racing moment. The one that got away. The perfect weekend where everything had gone just right until, with metres left to run, their luck ran out. The race that broke their heart.

I ran the idea past a few racers. They liked it. They could all tell me, with pinpoint accuracy, not just the race but the very moment the racing Gods had sought to crush their little moments of perfection.

But one, and one I greatly admired, didn't like it. Not one bit.

'I'm worried it's going to make me sound rather ungrateful and feeling sorry for myself. Oh poor me, I lost a race, it was the worst thing, blah blah. Look, I think the basic premise is good, and I'd love to be involved in some way. I just don't think the focus is quite there.'

Back to the start, then. But not for long.

The next day I had my first interview lined up. And it was with Niki Lauda.

Niki could be a daunting interviewee. He didn't need to do interviews. He didn't particularly enjoy doing them. So if he took the time to talk to you, you had to be damned sure you'd got something important to talk about.

As it was too late to fundamentally change the concept and direction of what I thought this book would be, I went to speak to everyone I could think of in the Formula 1 paddock about Niki's career. His highs and lows. Not just *that* crash. About everything.

And then, while I was on the way to see him, recorder in hand and nerves on edge, a curveball got thrown in by a journalist who had known him for a very long time.

'You know, it might not be racing at all.'

'What do you mean?'

'You know he lost a flight. When he ran Lauda Air. Everybody died. It was the lowest I've ever seen him. He might not want to talk about it but that hit him worse than any racing defeat.'

I arrived at the Mercedes hospitality unit and sat down in front of the three-time Formula 1 World Champion. Red cap pulled over his head, the scabs and sores from his 1976 crash still raw. He sipped a glass of water and glanced up at me.

'Right. So. What are we talking about?' he asked in his clipped, gravelly, rasping yet high-pitched Austrian accent, the damage to his throat and lungs from that horrific accident still evident in every breath.

I explained the idea for my book and that I'd been talking to fellow journalists and friends, trying to figure out what that moment that broke his heart might be. Maybe Monza 1976, coming back to Ferrari after his accident and learning he'd been replaced. Maybe the deterioration in the Ferrari relationship the year after.

But then I admitted I'd also heard how much the air disaster had affected him.

'Well... they were both pretty shit!' he exclaimed, in his now much-missed, matter-of-fact, no-bullshit style. 'We can talk about both if you want. It's your book.'

'Which affected you the most?' I asked, immediately feeling both insensitive and idiotic.

'The plane crash. No question.'

'Would you be willing to discuss it?'

And that's how this began.

I decided there and then that, regardless of the subjects of my interviews being racing drivers, I would not seek to limit this collection of stories to racing. This had to be about their own hardships, their own lows. Whatever they were and from wherever they might come.

Motorsport exists within a strange bubble where nothing is really real. Sometimes, something within that world brings reality starkly into focus. Other times, real life and the real world overtake the selfish pursuit of glory that motor racing folk mark as their sole focus. That is what interested me. These stories of reality in a surreal world. The moments of lucidity, created amongst and sometimes in spite of the madness.

I would talk to the greats in an attempt to discover their weakest moments. The one time in their lives that they genuinely did not know what to do next. Be it sporting or otherwise, I wanted to show that beneath the firesuits and the helmets and beyond the heroics displayed on track, these great modern gladiators are fallible and breakable.

That they are flesh and bone.

Human.

Real.

It's a side of the racer one rarely sees. In the heat of competition, displaying any sign of weakness is a potential opening for a rival to take advantage. Few sports require such unrelenting physical, mental and emotional strength as that necessitated in motor racing. It comes, often, at the expense of all else. Human relationships suffer. Selfish endeavour becomes the primary focus in this world where nothing is really real.

Yet the humans who play this game ache every bit as much as you or I. They wrestle with life, the decisions they take and the mistakes they make. They just can't show it.

Eyes forward, visor closed, right foot hard down. Drive through it. Deal with it later.

At a time when we are being told for perhaps the first time that it is OK to struggle and to admit when we are not coping with the rigours of our lives, these stories began to hold greater resonance. With increasing regularity, those with whom I spoke opened completely. Honesty flowed as I had never expected. Mighty world champions, men I'd always seen as thick-skinned, macho, manly men, unburdening their souls.

My heroes in tears.

We all have doubts. We all struggle to find our place in this world. Acceptance of ourselves can be the hardest lesson in this life for which we have no choice but to embark without a map or definitive direction. There is no distinct destination or deadline, nor any guarantee that we will ever find that peace of mind we all crave as the solid foundation of what we believe to be a good life.

Some of us struggle with it daily. Some find the questions, the expectations and the nagging, blinding, choking fog of uncertainty too much to bare. The weight of a world that expects us to be strong can seem too heavy a burden to carry.

But if I could show that these revered sporting heroes could be open, honest and true, then perhaps it might help those who struggle the most to gain perspective and presence. To see that only in hitting the lowest of the lows could these legends find the strength to swing back, to stand back up and achieve their greatest heights.

To see that, in fragility and failure there lies freedom.

What follows, then, are the conversations that I was fortunate to share with those whom I consider to be some of the all-time greatest racing drivers across Formula 1, Indycar, Rally, NASCAR and Le Mans. Some of their stories will, I hope, resonate with you. Some may not. But I truly hope that each of us might, somewhere, find something over these pages that brings us closer to an understanding not just of the real humans that exist beneath the racing visors, but also and in turn of ourselves.

As such, I decided not to write each chapter as an individual feature, nor attempt to add my own notes of explanation to the words of the interview subject. What exists over the following pages are conversations, transcribed as they unfolded. Grammar and punctuation have been left imprecise in the hope that when you read the words of the racer, you hear his voice.

These are their stories. Their words. Their truths.

I wished to extend an invitation and for you to be the third guest at our table. To be a part of our conversation. For you to form your own conclusions and take your own lessons from their stories.

And to know that ultimately, in racing as in life, our greatest triumphs can be born from our greatest defeats.

Alain Prost

'I am a racing driver, I am a Formula 1 driver but I will do exactly what I want to do. If you accept that, I will go back into the car. If you tell me you don't accept that, then I will go home.'

Alain Prost is one of the most successful Formula 1 drivers in history. With 51 victories in the 200 races he entered, his win rate stands at an astonishing 1:4. He was crowned world champion four times, only the second driver after the great Juan Manuel Fangio to have ever achieved the feat at the time, and came home second in the championship a further four times. He finished on the podium on 106 occasions, thus in over half of the grands prix he contested.

Born in Lorette, France, in 1955, Prost was introduced to racing relatively late in life, making his start in go karts at the age of 14. But just a decade later, backed by French oil giant Elf, he was now considered the most exciting prospect in junior formula racing and was duly offered the opportunity to graduate to Formula 1. He débuted for the illustrious McLaren team at the age of 25 in 1980, finishing his very first race in the points.

He became known as 'The Professor' for his meticulous and intellectual approach to racing, but his strong will and at times single-minded focus made him a divisive character. He was fired from both the Renault and Ferrari teams after publicly criticising them and their cars. He built a close relationship with the controversial Jean-Marie Balestre, the President of Formula 1's governing body, causing some to believe he received preferential treatment from the sport's rule makers. But it was to be his now legendary rivalry with Ayrton Senna that was to place him, and the much-fêted Brazlian, into the annals of history. Their fiery relationship defined a generation of racing and is viewed today as one of the fiercest and most intense sporting conflicts of all time.

The Frenchman, however, was always guided by a deep moral compass and took perceived slights against him to heart. In 1982, with Prost in the hunt for the world championship, his Renault team had an agreement that should its driver René Arnoux find himself ahead of his team-mate Prost, he should cede position for the sake of the title. When Arnoux failed to do so at the French Grand Prix, going on to take the flag and win, Prost was visibly furious, refusing to even acknowledge his team-mate and countryman on the podium.

Such an apparent affront would recur seven years later, when Senna and Prost raced under an agreement that, such was the state of play at the McLaren team, whoever reached the first corner first would be left to control the race unchallenged. At the 1989 San Marino Grand Prix, Senna won the first-corner fight and Prost duly fell into line. But when the race was suspended and restarted from a standing grid, Prost assumed the agreement, much as the race, had been reset and that there would be a new fight to the first corner. Senna, however, believed the agreement stood from the original start. And so, when Prost got the better restart but Senna overtook him at the very next corner, the Frenchman felt an agreement had been broken.

These moments, framed by the Frenchman's unrelenting and seemingly cold exterior, would come to shape not only Prost's career, but also the way in which many in the media, the paddock, and the world at large came to view one of the most talented drivers in F1 history yet also one of the most vilified.

I had many, many difficult moments in my career, for sure. I would say I had a few bad moments that I can tell you about in terms of accidents, big accidents. But then I have two very bad moments that affected me personally. The first was in 1982 at the French Grand Prix where there is the story with René Arnoux and the second was in 1989 at Imola where more or less the same situation happened with Ayrton Senna.

They were very similar in terms of the impact they had on me.

The first one was very bad because that was maybe the first time I had experienced anything like it. We had an agreement at Renault with René, although I had never asked for anything at the time. The team had put more turbo boost on his car to put pressure on the Brabham team because we knew at the time that the reliability of their BMW engine was not so good. The team said, 'OK, we will put more boost on René but if we are first and second, Alain should win the race because he has less power and he is in the better position in the championship.' And we found ourselves in that position in the race, and he did not give the position to me. So that was more or less the situation.

The key, for me, was how this situation unfolded from a human point of view. When you have this situation, the people who made the decision need to back it up. But they didn't back up their decision and they didn't back me up. They just thought, 'We have won the race, René is the winner, and we won't talk about it.' They didn't understand that from a personal point of view what had happened was not good. They could have said, 'OK we made a decision, he did not accept the rule', and then dealt with the situation. But they only went on to do this much later. So the whole impact that it had on me, particularly from the point of view of the public and the fans, was unbelievable.

Remember this was a French team, I am French, the race was the French Grand Prix. And because I was so upset after the race and could not hide it, I became the enemy. You can't believe the impact it had on my personal life. I had cars stolen from my home, one car was set alight at my house, messages were left on my answer machine. It was something you can't believe. You can be disappointed, sure. But it went to a much worse level than you could think. I decided to leave France after that. After a few weeks, a few months, I decided I had to leave. The impact was that big.

What happened in 1989 was very similar in terms of broken promises, but the biggest impact that year was the fact that I realised how Ayrton was in these situations. He was convinced that it was me who had broken the agreement by overtaking him, and not him who had broken the agreement by overtaking me, despite the fact that it was on TV and 700 million people had seen it.

But it wasn't true. It was Senna who had not respected it.

You can have these kinds of things so you can be shocked, but on the other side all the media and then the public again, they were always on the other side.

What you need to understand is that in life, what we call in French *la parole donnée*, when you give your word, your promise, to be straight, to be honest… I have an education and an upbringing in my country which says that these things are important for me. When you have this kind of situation you think, shit! I am in an environment where something, and something which I think should be a human quality, is not important to these people. You know? So, it's just the result that they cared about. Not how it happened.

So that was really, from a human point of view, very difficult.

Then, going back to the original question, in my career I have had three or four very, very bad situations related to accidents. The first one was Clay Regazzoni in 1980. He was not a good friend but he was part of this paddock and this world. I had a broken wrist that weekend so I was commentating the race in Long Beach, and I went to see him in the hospital after his accident and, for the first time in my life, when you are doing the same job and the same sport, what I saw was really for me and for the first time a big shock.

I had many of those moments, but 1982 was really a key season for me. Obviously we had lost Patrick Depailler in 1980, but I was very close to Didier Pironi. There were the two big accidents that year that affected me very much, but especially the one with Didier because it was with me. When it is close to you, when it is with your car, when you see the accident and I will always have the vision in my head because it is a memory I cannot escape, and the vision of him in the car... you can't believe it. You stop, you run to his car and you don't know what you can do. It was really, really awful.

It was the same with the accident that killed Gilles Villeneuve that year. I drove past the scene. I saw him, in his seat, on the side of the track. That is the kind of vision you cannot translate because it really is something you don't want to see. You know that it can happen but when you see it with your own eyes it is something really bad. I came back to the pits, to the garage, and my team manager Gérard Larrousse and I went up into the motorhome together and he said, 'You need to go back to the car as soon as possible.' I told him to leave me alone for ten minutes.

When he came back I said, 'Listen Gérard, from now, from today, I am a racing driver, I am a Formula 1 driver but I will do exactly what I want to do. If you accept that, I will go back into the car. If you tell me you don't accept that, then I will go home.'

That was 1982. People sometimes don't understand what it is like to be in the car, when visibility was bad like in the wet and we were aquaplaning that you cannot control. They don't understand it is your life. Your decision. That's why I said, 'Shit! I do what I want. I do what I feel.' And that really came from 1982, because of what I had seen with Patrick and Gilles and Didier.

Of course Ayrton's death in 1994 was really a shock. I can see the accident of Ayrton so clearly because it is like our lives, our careers and everything have almost become one, together. I see it very clearly.

But the other big accident that really affected me was 1986 with Elio de Angelis, in a test at Paul Ricard. Then it was worse than everything. He had the accident, I was there at the track and I was the first one who arrived. He was inside the car, the car was upside down and he was moving, but I could not get his belts off. The fire burned all around but it was not the fire that killed him. It was the smoke that he inhaled. And when you have this kind of thing, you feel so bad that you do question it all. You ask, 'Should I continue? What should I do? How can I go on?'

In fact, I went directly to England and I don't know if I went to see Bernie Ecclestone [F1 supremo] or Max Mosley [FIA President] first of all, but we stopped the test and we started to then have the regulations for private testing with marshals and helicopters and medical facilities where before we had nothing. You had to use the situation for a positive, otherwise perhaps you'd have to have stopped immediately.

After seeing so many of these accidents and within such a short period, did you ever hit that moment of saying you would not put yourself into that situation again?

Honestly, only in 1982. I don't know why, but 1982 was a very tough season for many reasons and sometimes you realise, OK we are all human. I can say that I am sensible. People, if they know me, they will say I am sensible. So I've never said I don't care. You always care about things. But if you have the situation I was facing at the team, plus the accidents that happened to friends, that very quick meeting in the motorhome really determined the direction of my whole career.

And that was it, then? It has to be your way.

I will do what I want. I will do it my way. You know? Whether it was with Renault, McLaren, Ferrari or Williams, I did it my way.

Do you think teams found that difficult to deal with, because you had a tricky relationship with a number of teams, particularly in the manner in which your careers with them ended?

That is maybe a question for them, but I don't think it was difficult. When I stopped in 1989 with McLaren, everybody came to see me and it was OK because they understood my reasons. The relationship with Ferrari, well you could write a book on this by itself because it was really something. It would be fun to really go into that today, to look back. Really, that situation had absolutely no relation with my way of working or driving or thinking.

But I never saw a problem because of my way of working or in setting up the car. People understood that. Even in testing my approach was very different and was sometimes quite difficult for people to understand in the beginning. I knew where I wanted to go.

But I knew the risks I was willing to take. Some people are different. Some people don't want to talk about the danger and the risk. If you look at Ayrton for example, he never wanted to talk too much about risk or danger. Then suddenly he realised and was finally able to talk about these things two or three months before his accident.

Depending on what you experience or what you see, how you see it, it's very strange, but it's human. If you have an accident or you hear that someone has an accident it is one thing, but if you have the accident with the same person you react differently. When you see the blood on someone else, or when you feel the pain yourself it is really very different. That is why the drivers of this generation today perhaps don't understand. Obviously we had the accident of Jules Bianchi [during the 2014 Japanese Grand Prix] which was awful, but other than that you don't have this kind of thing very often.

Looking at 1982 and the situation at the French Grand Prix that you talked about at the start, you were still very new to Formula 1. It was only your third season. How hard was it to be in that position, to feel so let down by the team, the backlash at home? How did you deal with it? Did you think about quitting?

Yes, I was thinking about it. And I cannot say that I found the answer quickly. It took a long time. But even today, I very often think about that situation. At the time it was very difficult to deal with it, but you have your professional environment and your personal life. When your profession affects your personal life, that is the worst. So how can you go on? Well, you just have to close your eyes, be a bit stronger. But it was very difficult, it was very tough.

But stopping Formula 1 purely because of the fan reaction at home? No. That would have been a nonsense. But when you add it up with the team situation, with the accidents, then it becomes too much. My son Nicolas was one year old and so you think about everything. It was tough, yes, but I just had to continue my own way and follow my road.

Did it change your opinion of what Formula 1 was?

My opinion of people? Yes. But not Formula 1. Because Formula 1 is competition, it is sport, it is racing. I think it was tougher outside the sport than inside.

After experiencing the difficulties at Renault and the personal injustice that you felt had been handed to you, at what point did you see things start to unravel at McLaren and in that relationship with Senna?

To be honest the problems only started with Ayrton in 1989 after Imola. Before then and all the way from the start it was very intense but always fair.

But you had suspicions that Honda was favouring him over you.

Yes, but it was different. You can write a book about that situation, too. For sure I was not very happy about the team in 1988 and 1989, because at the end of 1988 I went to see the head of Honda, Mr Kawamoto, and he recognised that things had not been fair and promised me that things would be different in 1989 and I just needed to understand how things had been for 1988. But 1989 was even worse.

To give you an example. When we are talking about feeling right, feeling well, you must understand that the psychology of a racing driver is so important that when you see that the approach of the Honda people was much closer to Ayrton than to you, even if you cannot see anything in the details, but your feeling is not correct, then you are losing motivation and that cannot work well.

When you see an engine, and written on the engine is 'Special for Ayrton', and everyone saw it, even journalists, and I saw it and it was not the first time... you think, what? You do that on purpose to put me down? Maybe the engine was the same. But you don't know. So these kind of things cannot be positive.

You cannot be angry as it doesn't make you quicker. It's just a negative and it can only ever be negative. That's why I didn't feel right at the team. It was a tough moment. Maybe not the toughest of my racing life, but it was a tough time.

So to then have that gentleman's agreement reneged upon in your eyes at Imola, with all of that in the background, did you just decide there and then that you and Ayrton were done?

No. No, no. That was very simple in 1989. I continued. I did my job. It got worse and worse, race after race, and then in July before the French Grand Prix I made a press conference and I announced that I would stop. Ron Dennis had come to see me maybe one week before and had said he wanted to continue, he wanted two more years with me, and I asked him why I should continue, just doing the job for Ayrton when he's in Brazil for the whole winter and I'm doing all the testing and then the situation I have here is no good?

So I didn't tell Ron everything, but maybe the day before I did the press conference I told him that I wouldn't be continuing with McLaren. And I swore then, and I swear now, I never, ever, had any contact with another team before I made my decision. That's the way I have always been. The first decision was to say I cannot continue like this. And I was ready to stop. Completely. I was ready to stop Formula 1. I would have preferred at the time to stop racing altogether, even with the best team in the sport, than to continue in that way.

Is that how you got through those hard moments, then? To have that faith in yourself to be able to say you're willing to give it all up and walk away rather than to carry on with something you don't believe in?

Yes. Absolutely. Because I knew that I could make a decision and that whatever the consequences it had been my choice on my terms. People can criticise me, but if I know inside that the decision was mine then I will feel happy.

Do you think history judges you unfairly?

Completely. For sure. But it's part of history, and part of the story of Formula 1. Very often I can see it on social media, what people say. And I smile. Because it is the way it is. On the other side, maybe I haven't done exactly what I should have done, maybe my personality, my character was not the right one for this environment, maybe my culture or my nationality stood against me. You don't know. But it is history. You have to accept that.

And it is exactly the same situation as people who ask, why did you put Ayrton in the team in 1988, because I had the possibility not to accept him back then. Then, they say, you could have been a six-time champion or more. But I never look at it that way. I had no predisposition to be a racing driver. I have done everything by myself and today I am still here working in my environment and you need to see the whole story to understand it. I have seen a lot of very good drivers and very talented drivers who deserved to be world champion and never were, or a world champion who maybe deserved it less, but it is all part of the history of our sport.

If people say that the way I am viewed is unfair, then I am pleased to hear that. But I really don't have any problem with my role in this story. I promise you that.

So you wouldn't have done anything differently?

For sure not. Because when I make the decision it is a decision I wanted to make at that moment. And I never looked back. Never.

Alex Zanardi

'Alex, you will never, never complain about what happened to you because what are you missing? Nothing... You only have to find the direction you want to take in your life.'

T he words legend and hero are bandied around in sport to the point where, often, they risk losing all meaning. But not in the case of Alessandro 'Alex' Zanardi.

Born in Bologna, Italy, in 1966, Zanardi began karting with a contraption fashioned from spare parts that he'd found. But he excelled, quickly moving up to Formula 3 and then Formula 3000, winning his very first race. His ascent took him to the pinnacle of motor racing that same year as he made his Formula 1 début for Jordan at the 1991 Spanish Grand Prix.

He contested only sporadic races in 1992 before joining the once mighty Lotus Formula 1 team as the outfit endured its death throes throughout 1993 and 1994. Despite much promise, his Formula 1 dream never truly delivered and so it was that he sought refuge in America and Champ Car. And it was here that he flourished. A two-time champion, Alex Zanardi quickly became one of the most popular and successful drivers in America.

But despite his new-found glory, the lure of Formula 1 and the perception of an unfinished chapter remained. With an offer on the table from Frank Williams, Zanardi leapt back to Formula 1 in 1999. But the Williams team he found was far removed from the one that had won World Championships in its recent past. The dream became a nightmare, his three-year contract ended by mutual consent after just one.

He returned to Champ Car, but in 2001 experienced the moment that changed his life forever. Exiting the pits at the Lausitzring in Germany, he lost control and slid across the track into the path of another car. In the resultant crash, Zanardi lost both legs and almost three-quarters of the blood in his body. Only the incredible reactions of the medical team saved his life.

And it is here that the story of Alex Zanardi truly begins. Frustrated with the prosthetic options that lay in front of him, he started to build his own. A racer still at heart, he used his knowledge of engineering that went all the way back to his first home-made go-kart to help teams design new technologies that would allow him to get back behind the wheel of a racing car. And to win.

By far his greatest challenge and achievements, however, came not on the race track, but on the roads. Handcycling became Zanardi's passion and duly gave him his greatest moments of glory. He won the Venice, Rome and New York marathons. In 2012, at the London Paralympic Games, he won two gold medals and one silver. Four years later he returned at Rio. The result? Two further golds and one further silver. In World Championship competition he has won eight gold medals and two silver. Thus far...

Because, incredibly, he's still racing. In 2018 he made his début in the DTM. In a one-off appearance in a specially modified car, on home soil in Italy and in one of the most competitive championships in the world, he finished fifth. Aged 52.

Hero. Legend. Words that are overused. Yet in Alex Zanardi's case, words that fail to do the man and his achievements even scant justice.

I think the perfect life is the right combination between good moments and bad ones. If you never hit a bump with your tyres, you're never going to appreciate a smooth road.

What was the darkest moment of my life? I can tell you, honestly, I don't feel any direct responsibility for what happened to me in relationship to my accident. Bad luck is bad luck. It's as simple as that. But thanks to what I did, I got out of those problems and not only that but actually I was able to change what happened into probably the greatest opportunity of my life, because all the things I'm doing these days are directly related to my new condition. So, I can't really say that what happened to me was a bad moment.

And on top of that, I came so close to losing my life that eight days after my accident when I woke up from the coma I was simply joyful. That was the only feeling, above everything else. I was just so happy to be alive that everything else came second. You know, the fact that I lost my legs at that point was the least of my problems. I was just very, very happy to be alive.

On the other side, the poor season I had in 1999, the bad season I had the following year doing nothing and the even worse one I had in 2001 with Mo Nunn racing in the United States, were the direct result of me not being able to see clearly what I really wanted to do with my life. Because, had I been able to understand clearly what I wanted to do in my life, I would have made a clear choice and instead, I didn't make one. I decided to drive, simply because one side of me was telling me that I was too young to retire. But I was not acting like I wanted to drive because I was not committed. I could not find the way to act and to use my talent.

I would say that up until the end of 1995 I had some decent ups but nothing very high in my racing career. So, if it would have ended with me never meeting popularity and success and so on, so what? My story would have been the same as many drivers who tried to make it, came close but never really had the great opportunity. God knows what I would be doing today.

But then 1996 changed everything because I met success in the United States with Ganassi Racing, and since then everything I was doing was elevating expectations. I thought that to continue at that level would have been as easy as winning races had been in America, when I had all the ingredients to do it right. But I didn't have the knowledge back then of how simple it is to reach that level by just making the right choices when you can.

And in 1999, I made the wrong choice. People said you'd be crazy if you would not accept Frank Williams's proposal to drive for him in Formula 1. Because this is what you wanted to do since you were a kid. And why shouldn't you do that? Why should you stay with Chip Ganassi in the United States and keep driving in a continent that is so far away from where you were born, from what you were dreaming of as a kid?

In my life I have learned that if you have the ability to decide you should very accurately set out that mental process in order to make the best choice.

The concept itself is simple. If a lot of people are running in a particular direction, well it's very likely that down there there's something interesting that everybody's chasing. You may yourself enter into that chase and get very passionate for what you find along the way in order for you to finally cross that line, possibly ahead of others, and eventually do that thing that everybody is excited for and wants to do. But you should ask yourself whether you really want to go there or if you're just going there because everybody's running in that direction. Do you understand what I mean? And this is a question that ultimately, in my life, I learned to ask myself.

It is exactly the question I asked myself at the end of 2009 when I was driving for BMW as a professional race car driver in touring cars, in spite of what had happened with my accident. I was getting paid, I was getting decent exposure out of what I was doing and therefore very often people would stop me to say, hey Alex, it's so cool that you won in Brno with BMW, and so on.

But it was at that time that I discovered handcycling. I wanted to investigate it and to a lot of people, some of them outside observers and some who were quite close to me, it didn't make a lot of sense to them that I was thinking about quitting motorsports in favour of this new activity that I was wishing to investigate and to see where it could take me. But it was important for me. I wanted to do it. So, although everybody would have run in a different direction, I decided to stop and take an alternative road that was interesting for me.

So why did they all question this? Well, when you are in your mid-20s you are certainly much better equipped to take part in a sporting activity like the one I do today purely from the sense of strength and resistance. But there are other things that play a very important role, one of which is the preparation you are capable of organising in order to show up to the event completely ready to compete.

Now, in order to do those things you could talk about dedication, you could talk about commitment, you could talk about whatever you want, but ultimately you can only do what you really want to do. Everything else is very, very much related to the word ambition. And ambition is a strong thing. But it's not as strong as the word passion. If you are passionate for something, boy you wake up in the morning and the first thing that goes through your mind is, how can I be better? What can I do today?

And it's not a question of sacrifice, that instead of going out with your friends you work out in the gym. You know? It's not about spending time talking to the engineers when you could be somewhere else.

You're not dedicated because of your ambition to become the number one driver. You are dedicated because you'd rather be there, playing with your passion, with your activity, than being somewhere else. And it is very, very important to understand when you sign a new agreement with an organisation, when you accept a new commitment, whether you are doing this because you are very passionate for what you're about to do and you really want to do this, or whether it's just because everybody says, hey, you'd be crazy if you turned it down.

Then there is also another scenario which is to say, OK, I have to do this. I have no choice. And if you have no choice, you really have to try to develop a particular passion for this thing because this will help you to do it much better.

This was the case with my accident and my recovery, for instance. How did I develop a passion for it? Well I'm a very technical guy and so I was able to find a similarity between the mechanism of a prosthetic knee joint and the suspension of a race car. This was, for me, the starting point to develop this passion and to pick up the knowledge that let me speak the same language as the orthopaedic technicians, as the physical therapists, and to form a team around me. Quite rapidly I developed a passion where it became fun for me to cover that rehabilitation course. And I developed a friendship with the people that were my team at the time that survived beyond me completing the rehabilitation.

This is what I know today. OK, I didn't know that at the time, but luckily I found myself in situations where the only thing I could do at the time led me to become immediately very, very passionate for my task. And that's why, not knowing this, I ended up being able to deliver the best I had.

So that choice to go back to Formula 1 and drive for Williams in 1999, which you said was your lowest moment, was that driven by ambition or passion?

It was driven mainly by ambition. I think if I could go back in time, I could easily change that. What I mean is, if I could go back, the man I am today would know how to turn that situation into something very passionate in order to be a different person. Not so much a different driver, but a different person for my own interest on top of everybody else's interest. So I know now how to make it work. But back then, the fact that I was coming from a very successful period of my life, this was the biggest down point, in not allowing me to understand then what I understand so clearly today.

It is not so much a question of listening to that particular person who tells you, 'Oh you should do this', or listening to the other tells you, 'Oh you should do that.' You have to know for yourself what you have to do. It's as simple as that. It is not a question of having the right mentalists next to you or having the right training or having the right engineer. It is a question of using the instruments you have surrounding you in order to simply deliver the best you can. And my best for sure is not and would never have turned me into the greatest driver in the world. But my best has been plenty sufficient to win races when everything else was right. So, there's no reason why I couldn't have had a completely different history, you know, in making that particular choice work.

It's not a question of how much talent you have, but whatever talent you do have, you have to use it for Christ's sake.

After I'd won those two titles in Indycar it was clear that not only was I sufficiently talented but also that in the right situation I would've been like a machine-gun in delivering what I could. My problem, if you can call it that, is that everything happened magically in 1996 for me in that environment that was absolutely perfect and I didn't take that into consideration. I thought that I could do exactly the same wherever I went.

So did success in America come too easily for you? Was there ever an element of you thinking that this was all just a piece of cake?

To a certain degree, yes. After so much struggling in my life I got used to doing things in Indycar in such an easy way that I began taking for granted that wherever I went, just by turning the wheel, I would magically see the right number on my dash telling me that I was faster than anybody else. But it doesn't happen this way.

It is not a question of being sufficiently respectful of your opponents, because that was never the question. It was rather a case of over-evaluating myself, thinking that I could be capable of just showing up whenever it was time, sitting in the car and magically doing the job. And not only is that not the case, but it was completely the wrong focus.

The path to creating the conditions that enable you to actually sit in the car and deliver should be the most important part. The most desirable aspect of it all is the journey, not simply crossing the line ahead of everybody else. It is the journey that should interest you and make it fascinating for you. It should be about executing the project, rather than cashing in on the result.

Do you think you got to Formula 1 too quickly the first time around? Were you ready for it?

Look at Max Verstappen. What is he, 21? He's incredibly mature behind the wheel. Certainly I did not have the same talent as him. When I was 24 I had not reached half of his maturity, but nevertheless in Formula 3000 in 1991 I had fantastic equipment, I had a great organisation behind me with a real family environment, and I don't think I made a single mistake all season, other than that race at Hockenheim where I did all the mistakes at once. But at least when I had my crazy day I got it all done in one.

But I drove a very clean championship, taking advantage of the opportunities I had. Maybe the duty of a good team manager is to identify talent in a young kid and to make sure that you give him the right environment to make his talent shine rather than making it too difficult for them. Had I found that situation in Formula 1, that opportunity, then maybe I could have exploded, from this point of view, immediately.

Eddie Jordan was my mentor initially in Formula 1 as I made my début for his team at the end of that brilliant year in Formula 3000 in 1991. In my second ever Formula 1 race, in Suzuka, before the gearbox had a technical problem, I had come up from 13th on the grid to fourth place and, I mean, I was making ground like a rocket. The car was flying and I was going really well with the lap times I was doing. Potentially I could have finished in third place in my second race ever in Formula 1. For sure if that had happened I would have been granted a good number of opportunities before my mistakes or my failures had been too much to make my star fall. But I have to admit that in the enormous luck I had in having that first opportunity, it kind of levels out a little bit with that small misfortune of not being able to really complete what was potentially possible and for retiring from that race.

Then we went to Australia and again we were really fast, making some more mistakes, but then ultimately in the race still coming back in this torrential rain we had until the race was suspended. So what I had done in those first three races still lit a lot of interest around me as a race car driver. But yes, ultimately, my Formula 1 story could have been written in a different way from the very, very beginning.

Unfortunately I had no seat for 1992 and staying away for basically one full year in that time of my life did not help. When I finally came back with Lotus in 1993 it was a little bit of a déjà vu, from this point of view, with me being very anxious to have a podium finish, not simply a few points, and in fact I was very close to doing that. But I just wanted it too badly. And so I kept making mistakes.

I remember in my very first race with Lotus I crashed with Damon Hill. He was driving for Williams, I was fighting with the handling of this Lotus, and I passed him three or four times and he was always passing me back on the straight. So at one point I got pissed and I was not really trying to do anything to pass him, I just completely lost my concentration on what I was doing, missed my braking point and I ran into poor Damon taking him off as well with me.

At that point of my life I was suddenly very vulnerable, psychologically speaking, but I still believed that I was potentially also capable of winning races already. Then 1994 and '95 were two very, very difficult seasons so by the time I had my opportunity with Ganassi in 1996 I was experienced and I'd had a lot of time to think about all the mistakes I had made.

I think as far as speed is concerned I was the same driver as I was before, but I was very humble as well because I had been beaten a lot by life in general, so I didn't want to waste the next opportunity that came my way. Overall I was really prepared to deliver and on top of that I found an environment at Ganassi Racing where everybody was treating me as a family member and everything was perfect. Everything was right.

But in those three years between 1996 and 1998 as a result of winning a lot of races, my ego grew a lot, to the point where all the fantastic treasures of experience, of positivity, of the capability to organise your list of priorities every day, of keeping your eyes on the road, not getting distracted and staying focused, they had all vanished. And I thought, hey, I'm Alex Zanardi. I'm going to go and drive for Frank Williams and win the very first race.

Actually, let me rephrase that. That was certainly not my attitude. It's never been my attitude. But deep inside, if I reflect today, then I can see that confidence and that ego in my approach. It was not the one that I should have had. Although at the time I did not see it, today I can recognise that I got carried away.

As an Italian, I imagine Formula 1 was always the dream. Given that Champ Car was not Formula 1, was there something about racing there that maybe took the pressure off? Because it wasn't the ultimate dream and the ultimate goal?

No, that was not the case for me. Whenever I'm racing something there's a big difference in the preparation between, I don't know, the Paralympic Games and the local race I'm going to do because they've invited me and so at the last minute I say OK I'm going to go in. But then when the light goes green there's no difference. I mean, I will hurt myself rather than give one centimetre away to my opponents. This is the way I am. So the pressure I put on myself would be completely identical.

It's just the capability of dealing with the pressure that is different. If you know that you are as good as you can be and you are surrounded by an enormous amount of talent in all your opponents, then this is actually the greatest thing in the world. Because to race on your own and to win, well where is the joy in that? You want to challenge the best and try to find a way to get closer to the front and maybe one day find yourself at the top. And when you finally end your days of glory then it's very, very special because you know that you've been able to beat the best.

I never felt what I was about to do when I signed with Ganassi was easy. I actually thought it was even more complicated because not only would I have the opportunity to race and compete on permanent road courses or street circuits, something with which I was quite familiar, but I also had to race on ovals, which was something that was really mysterious. So when I managed to win my first race on a superspeedway, well I was really very proud of this.

And they loved you in the States. You became such a hero so quickly to those guys. How much did you enjoy being there, racing those cars, the fanbase, the whole atmosphere of what Indycar, Champ Car, was at that time?

What you get is an incredible multiplier of how good you can be. Of course if you tell a joke and you are considered an idiot by everybody, then the joke has to be really funny to make somebody laugh. But when everybody thinks you're a hero you can tell even the worst joke in the world and everybody is going to laugh like it is the funniest thing they ever heard.

And in those days for sure I had a lot of lights on me because of the results I was getting. Then I think I am someone who is also quite entertaining because to be synthetic certainly is not my best quality. When I had things to say, people wanted to listen to me. I'm certainly more of an entertainer than Kimi Räikkönen for example, even if he is a much better driver than I ever was and maybe more profound than me. I don't know. But in those days I was considered one of the protagonists of the show because of the results I was getting. And whenever I was winning the race in those press conferences I was getting a lot of questions and the more I would talk the more questions would arrive.

You know, I think to a certain degree it was also a way for me to express my gratitude to the fans because I wouldn't have been able to do what I did, which is to turn my passion into a profession, which I think is the greatest privilege you can have in your life, if it wasn't for the fans. So whenever I was talking to a journalist it was my access to the fans and a way to express my gratitude and that's why I never felt in a hurry to answer a question because I knew that I was answering the curiosity of my fans. This is also a very American way to communicate. But I believe it is something that was quite naturally my attitude.

Did you find it hard to leave that behind to go back to Formula 1? As you said, you had such a great fanbase out there, a lovely family atmosphere at Ganassi, and it was all good. Was it hard to make the choice to leave and go back to Europe?

Nobody forced me. It's ironic because actually when the phone started to ring at the very beginning of the 1998 season everybody knew that my contract was expiring with Ganassi at the end of the year. So a lot of people were in the market for a driver and I was, I guess, the natural option for many American teams and for some Formula 1 teams as well. And I have to say that when Frank Williams rang, it was very special for me because I always looked at Frank like an idol.

Ayrton Senna had driven for him in 1994, the year he was killed, and Senna was my hero from when I was a go-kart driver. He was the guy I wanted to become. He was the type of driver I wanted to be. When Ayrton passed away, I have to admit I thought of phoning Frank to offer myself for the job. Which is stupid and ridiculous. Why would he take me, Alex Zanardi? A guy with a few races in a Jordan and a Lotus who had crashed into poor Damon?

So when Frank rang and asked me whether I was interested in starting a negotiation to drive for him the following year, it was like — wow. Yes. Saying no was not an option. I mean it was clear in my mind that it was just a question of dealing with the numbers and trying to make it look good from many different points of view.

The reality, as I see it now, is that I was interested in driving for Frank Williams but I never really stopped to ask myself whether I was interested in driving for the team. Not just for him. Whether I really wanted to drive for his team, whether I really wanted to drive Formula 1. I never really asked myself that type of question.

Is it one of those things that we form in childhood maybe and it keeps going into our adult lives, those dreams that we have as kids that end up steering the direction of our lives because of some fantasy that we create in our minds?

Yes. For sure. Because whatever we dreamt of in the past can certainly affect our decisions in the present and in the future. No doubt about that. But the more we live, the more experience we gain and the more we develop the capability of making the right call in spite of all the things that could potentially affect our decision.

Romance and passion are very closely linked. Earlier you spoke about needing passion in what you do, but if you're caught up with the romance of something, does it become difficult to determine if it really is your passion? That perhaps a romance built on the foundation of a childhood dream, a fantasy, blinds your decision making?

You touch on a very interesting point. You should really ask yourself, OK this is what I'm dreaming of here, but is it really what I am choosing? Because if in my mind what I'm dreaming of is to go with this organisation, well let me find out whether this organisation can really provide me that dream or if it simply is a dream. Is the reality what you want? Is the dream only a dream? Is the reality completely different to the dream you may have created?

Although back then a lot of people might have said, 'Look, Alex, you are completely stupid to even ask this question, when is this kind of thing going to happen to you again?' At the same time I know now that I really should have said, 'Thank you very much but let me go on with what I have.'

As I've told you, going against the perception of what I should be doing is what I did at the end of 2009. Everybody was saying 'OK Alex, but with all due respect you are driving touring car racing. OK, it's not Formula 1 but it is a well-exposed championship among the worldwide fans. Everybody acknowledges you're doing an amazing job even with your physical disability. You're getting paid. You have a team all working for you. Why should you leave that just to find more time to play around with this handcycling thing? It doesn't make sense.'

And to a degree they were right.

But three years later, at the London 2012 games, I was coming back from Brands Hatch, which is where our competition was held and where I had won my medals. I was going back to the Olympic Village and the trip took about an hour and fifteen minutes with the bus ride and I simply could not follow all the phone calls that were coming in.

There was over and over this call coming from a number I didn't know with 06, which is the code from Rome, with another three numbers, which is a strangely short telephone number and I didn't know who the hell it was. So I kept answering calls and calls and calls from people I knew and all the time this other number was coming up and I kept saying, who the hell is that idiot that keeps calling me with this strange number?

When I arrived to the Olympic Village I went to the Italian team house and all the members there basically approached me saying, 'Where the hell were you? Our President Giorgio Napolitano was trying to call you! He wants to congratulate you!'

The reason I wanted to make this point is because when I made my decision to leave racing and focus on handcycling, I had no idea of what it would mean to my country and how romantic it was.

OK, when I had my accident maybe I wasn't on the same level as someone like Michael Schumacher as far as the perception that people had with my success and so on, but I was a successful race car driver. I was a successful athlete who had made maybe not a fortune but a lot of money out of his profession, so I was seen as somebody who had perhaps something of an enviable life. And when something like this happens to you it is inevitable that deep inside, maybe not even in a conscious way, you think someone is testing you, saying, 'OK, you've lived a very privileged life and now I want to see how you manage. Now that you are in a hospital bed, now that you are in a situation like this one, how will you react to it?' And my reaction was the one you have seen, the one you have witnessed, the fact that I gradually turned what happened to me into an opportunity.

And that was London. Winning. Raising my bicycle in the air. That was the moment where people said, 'Fucking hell! That guy! You simply cannot keep that guy down. Whatever you do to him, that guy will come back.'

That was amazing. I know the perception that people have looking at my story is much more simple than what I know of myself and what I went through, but I would certainly join the club with the ones saying, 'Bloody hell, that guy!'

All of this is to say that when I took that decision in 2009, it didn't look like being the great opportunity that it ended up being. And when I won at London 2012, something so special happened for my country that I don't think I would have been able to replicate even if I had won the Italian Grand Prix at Monza.

That decision to leave racing in 2009 came exactly a decade after your fateful move to Williams and back to Formula 1. Did the fact that you had the experience of making such a big decision for the wrong reasons help you to make a choice ultimately for the right reasons?

Yeah, that is the better way of putting it. I made the decision for the wrong reason. It was not the wrong decision. Because I think that, as I said in the beginning of our conversation, I could have made that decision work and produce success. Maybe not as well or as easily as it happened in the United States with Ganassi but I took the decision for the wrong reasons.

Why didn't it work in '99? Because you had a three-year contract and while I know there were a lot of issues in that first year when the car wasn't great, you also had some stand-out performances. Why did it all fall apart after just one year?

The key is that you should always work in order to keep the speed more or less steady and at a decent level. Most of the time it was completely insufficient but some of the time it was excellent. Not decent. It was excellent.

And there are reasons why it didn't work, for sure. I could talk about it for hours. Technical aspects were not considered in the right way, for example, but for me to go back over all of it now would just sound like good excuses to justify myself. I don't want to point fingers because at the end of the day my team-mate, Ralf Schumacher, scored 33 World Championship points that season. I didn't score any.

So yeah, I could talk about, you know, the technical failures I had. I could talk about the problems I had. I could talk about the choices that some of the key people took on my behalf to organise the technical structure on my side of the team. But in reality nobody ever denied me the capability of affecting those decisions. I could have said, 'Hold on a second, I disagree.'

Why didn't you?

Because I am a human being. Now, if I could go back in time, I would know what to do. There was one point, after the fourth race, where I had a conversation with Frank's right-hand man and the team's head of engineering, Patrick Head, and I told him things which I strongly believed. Had I told him exactly the same things two months before, even two races before I think he would have said, 'Right. OK, let's do it.' This would have been his reaction. But because I left it too long his reaction was simply to say, 'Hmm, Alex. I understand what you're saying but as hard as it may sound for you to listen to this I have to tell you that if I look at the sessions, whether practice, qualifying or races, Ralf, with roughly the same equipment, is able to outperform you by five tenths of a second. So I don't think the problem is in the area you are suggesting.'

When somebody shows a total lack of confidence in your basic capability of giving the contribution that is needed to make the package perform, it's very hard to restart. It had gone too far. And for sure at that point I was simply too weak to talk.

Maybe the opportunity was still alive from a certain point of view. It was not completely over. But that made me feel even weaker than I was the day before. And I was even more confused than I was the day before and I was even less confident that I was right in saying the things that I just said to him in comparison to the day before. So it was a question of working really to gain a few centimetres and then something happened to make you gradually lose metres.

I think a lot of people would find it so difficult to understand that Alex Zanardi, this great Indycar champion and a guy who we know today has the heart of a lion and who can do anything, that he would be too timid and not have the confidence to tell his truth. How did the situation get so bad that it became impossible for you to be able to say these things?

Well, first of all we could live a thousand lives and still die as ignorant people. A thousand lives would not be sufficient to learn everything we can possibly learn. But in comparison from when I was in my late 20s or early 30s, today I'm in my 50s and I am a completely different person.

Today I'm not as well equipped as far as my muscles' capability to deliver energy, but incredibly more equipped from the standpoint of my mental strength and the capability of knowing not necessarily how to deliver something magical, but how to deliver absolutely everything I can. It's as simple as that. Because sometimes you're much better than the others simply because you are approaching your 100 percent, while they are just delivering 25 percent of what they could.

Take the Ironman, for instance. That is a perfect example of a discipline where your mental strength is incredibly important and knowing what you have to do, which is just what you can, will lead you to the equivalency between your potential and the performance that you deliver.

If you start the race when you are in your 20s or whatever, you think, OK, roughly my potential is to finish the race in 12 hours. If you start the race and you go after a guy who has a 10-hour potential in his body, then for the first four hours you will stick with him thinking, 'Oh shit I thought it was going to be much tougher than this. This is a piece of cake. It's a Sunday afternoon ride.'

But then when you crash, you make a noise that everybody will hear from the finish line and you will still have 120 kilometres in front of you between the cycling course and the running portion, which is 42 kilometres on its own. So the result is that not only do you fall away from that guy who is doing his race calculated on the 10-hour mark, but you can no longer finish your own race. Your target of 12 hours is gone and now you are looking at 14 or 15 hours and the rest of it is not only torture but a torture that would last another six or seven hours if you're strong enough to even make the finish.

So it's not that today I'm stronger. It's that I know what my value is. I know what I'm capable of. I get decent results in some of the things I do because I'm smart enough to say 'yes' or 'no' in accepting or not some of the challenges that are offered to me. And so today for me it's very simple. Again, I could have carried on driving with BMW but this thing, as stupid as it may look, for me is more important.

So I do this and because I do it to the best of my ability, because I do it well, actually this stupid thing will provide me also an exposure and a love and an affection from people watching that is superior to the one I would get if I would do something that from the word go seemed to be more popular and more intriguing to people. The reality is that if you don't do something well, it will not grant you anything other than a bitter sensation because you won't enjoy yourself in doing it.

So how do we as people, and I know it's different for everybody, but how do we find the difference between our passion and our ambition? How do we figure out which one's which?

Well for every one of us it's different and for sure we have to accept the idea that through the course of our life we will make mistakes, some of which were avoidable and some of which were inevitable. But if I was to use a cycling metaphorical expression, I would say that arriving on the starting line when somebody lines up next to you, the act of putting your wheel even only one centimetre ahead of one of your opponents is what can be named ambition. It can make you win a race that you wouldn't have won otherwise. But the only thing which will make you get to the finishing line, that will keep you going through the final miles and keep you pushing in that final sprint, is passion.

When I crossed the line in London for the second time, I realised how passionate I had been for that particular project because I only felt sad. I was crossing the line. I was finishing that chapter of my life in a way that couldn't have been better. I couldn't have dreamt it that nice because I was winning the race again. But at the end of the day it was the end of the chapter and from the following day I knew I would have to find something different to do.

Of course it was better to finish ahead of everybody else than finishing behind, but it was still the finish. And all I could think about when I passed that finishing line was every day of those past three years searching for small improvements, all the mistakes that I had made, the climbs up the hills, all the sweat. It had been my sole interest. London 2012 was the horizon and it was probably one of the best chapters of my life.

If I think back it was such an enjoyable time of my life, preparing for something like this, not knowing that crossing that line would have also granted me the glory I had, which was also a great reward. But I was not expecting that. It was an added value, as was winning the gold medal. I'm very proud of that. But it's an added value. The real value was all the time that I spent in the wooden shed I have in my garden where I keep all my stuff, training on my bicycle and then whenever I had nothing else to do, lying next to my bicycle looking at it and asking myself how I could make it better and how I could couple it more with my residual talent.

This is a very interesting point in paracycling and many Paralympic sports, where you use a particular aid that has to be adapted for your needs. My needs are certainly different to the ones of my opponents who may have longer limbs or may have one leg, maybe two legs. So it's a very interesting challenge from a technical point of view. And this is why I think I've also been able to stay alive, from a sporting point of view, in spite of my age because if I would want to challenge my younger opponents just on the ground of strength and resistance I would've lost the instruments to compete at that level a long time ago. But I am smarter, so I know how to take care of the small details so that when you put everything together they make a big, big difference. Just three days ago I was in the wind tunnel in Parma with my friends from Dallara, testing some new solutions that I have designed and the numbers are certainly in my favour I have to say.

It's amazing because I was actually testing all the different bicycles I've used in the recent past, starting from London 2012 to Rio de Janeiro to the one that I used most recently in the Ironman which is a special development, and also another one that I've just created recently, and the difference between the beginning and the end is amazing. It's something that I could not find through just training. Even if I would be like Dorian Gray and never get older and even if I would train for two thousand years, I'm sure I could not find that advantage in training better. So yeah, maybe I have a chance to stay alive for some more seasons.

Where does that resilience come from in you? Not just to keep going into your 50s, but to bounce back from the disappointments, whether it was making a success in America after the Formula 1 dream ended the first time, whether it was coming back from your accident to make a success of paracycling...

Where does that strength come from inside you?

As I said, you know, we are human beings and we are capable of great and terrible things. I'm the same. I've been arrogant enough to believe that I could win without effort as I just confessed to you. But I am also someone whenever he is down, who always stays curious to try to find the right inspirations, also in others. And I tell you, we are surrounded by inspiration.

I always tell this to kids when I go and talk to them in schools. I say kids, you know, I've lived a very special life. And sometimes when I tell you about inspirations and so on, you may say, 'OK Alex, we understand how important it is to develop a passion for what we do but hold on a second you're talking about competing in the Olympic Games, driving beautiful BMW machines. We are dealing with mathematics and literature at school. I mean we're dealing with different instruments, it's difficult for us to develop a passion for that.' And they're right.

But if I would not have been able to apply the same principles at the beginning of my rehabilitation, where my task was completely different to what I was used to, and had not much to do apparently with what I knew was my passion, I wouldn't find myself where I am today. The functionality of a mechanical knee joint on a prosthetic leg and the similarities it had to the mechanism of the suspension of a race car started this new passion for me.

Sometimes on our own we are not sufficiently strong enough to overcome adversity. But sometimes you don't need a particular adversity. Even a simple problem. It may seem too big for us in that given day to move on, but we must use that day as an opportunity to do something, to do just one little thing that will lead to a starting point for the following day. And we should always search for inspiration in others.

I remember one day when I was recovering from my accident that I was in the rehabilitation centre and I bumped into this gentleman who came and offered me a coffee. He was talking about Ferrari and racing, typical stuff. When you meet Zanardi you talk about motorsport.

A few hours later, true enough, I saw him holding a little girl in his arms. And she had no legs. He was looking out of the window and he was crying. I wanted to comfort him and he said, 'No Alex, I'm just very, very happy. That's why I'm crying.' And he said, 'You know, my baby was born with no legs and when I came here the first time the orthopaedic technicians, they told me I would have to wait, that she will be four years old before they would give her legs because there would be no point to build her a pair of prosthetic legs if she could not hold her balance and stand.

'Well today was the day that she would get her legs. But when it was time to get her standing the technician looked at me and said 'Where are her shoes? I need a pair of shoes for her to stand in her prosthetic legs.' So I had to rush out to the shop and I didn't know the village, I almost got lost and so I was panicking. But finally I found the shop and I bought my baby girl her first pair of shoes and I have to tell you, I'm the happiest man on this planet.'

I was touched by this gentleman, you know? So ten minutes later I found myself on my own in front of a mirror and I looked hard at myself and I said, 'Alex, you will never, never complain about what happened to you because what are you missing? Nothing. You've got money in the bank so it's not going to be a problem for you to feed your family and worry about the things you want to do. You only have to find the direction you want to take in your life. OK, it's going to be a question of readjusting things a little bit to get used to this new life, but from then on you know you will have plenty of opportunity and you must then just make sure that when you make a choice you make the right ones.'

And since then, I think I have done.

I think this has always been part of my attitude, but even more so since my accident. Looking at others and searching for inspiration. But now, from that point with that gentleman and his daughter onwards, instead of getting bent up over my personal problems, I have developed a capability of becoming more open to life and looking for motivation, searching consistently for inspiration in others.

I have to say it's amazing how much you can learn every day from everyone.

Ari Vatanen

'It is hard for us to accept that we need defeat... What you see as a setback, I may see as an opportunity. But it will only look that way to you when you can see it with your own eyes.'

B orn in Tuupovaara, Finland, in 1952, Ari Pieti Uolevi Vatanen is widely regarded as one of the greatest and most fearless rally drivers of all time.

In 1981, driving for the private Rothmans Rally team against the might of the factory outfits, Vatanen won the World Rally Championship — the only driver to have done so in an independently entered car. He commanded the Paris-Dakar Rally, winning the monstrous intercontinental race four times. The Finn's run to the summit of Pike's Peak in 1988, dubbed 'Climb Dance', remains one of the most visceral and enthralling pieces of driving footage ever captured, as he set a new record time to mark Peugeot's first-ever victory on the hill.

Vatanen made his World Rally début at the age of 22 in his native Finland's 1000 Lakes rally, his early showings on the scene proving impressive enough to bring him to the attention of Ford, with whom he made his full-time British Rally Championship début in 1976. He won the title in his rookie season, repeating the feat in 1980, the same year he won the Acropolis rally, his first WRC victory.

By far his greatest successes came with Peugeot, under the team direction of Jean Todt, who would later go on to oversee the dominance of Ferrari in Formula 1 in the 2000s before becoming President of the sport's governing body, the FIA. Vatanen ran for the same office, campaigning against his erstwhile boss and friend, having left motorsport in the 1990s to concentrate on a career in politics that saw him elected to the European Parliament.

The Finn remains best known by far for his uncompromising courage behind the wheel, yet with such bravery came the risk of tremendous peril. Vatanen had some major accidents over the course of his career but none matched the impact of the crash he suffered during the 1985 Rally Argentina.

Fortunate to escape with his life, in convalescence Ari Vatanen was thrust into the depths of despair and depression, his broken spirit taking him to the very edge of his sanity.

———————

I don't remember the crash itself. No, no. I remember going to the start line. I remember the dirty building on the left-hand side. And that's it. Then nothing. Nothing for several hours.

The next thing I do remember is that I didn't know where I was, all I knew was that I was in incredible pain. I'm in just incredible pain everywhere and I can't breathe. I remember a weight that felt like 1,000 kilos on my chest and I just could not breathe.

Did I know that I was dying? No. I knew only pain. I did not know where I was. I had multiple internal injuries and bleeding inside, my chest was broken and my lungs punctured. Left knee was totally crushed. Apparently the colour had gone from me and I looked like I was dead already. No more blood pressure. Little respiration.

The accident itself happened in a straight line, on a kilometre-long straight. There was a dip that was not there on the recce. It was a very little country road that few cars used, and there was an unusually long time between the recce and the rally itself. There had been a lot of rain in that time in that region and the flow of water had created this dip in the ground.

A few cars had been through before me, but whether I was one metre more to the right or one metre more to the left, I do not know. When I hit that dip the back of the car went up and we barrel-rolled end over end down the road. It was like an aircraft accident. There were bits and pieces everywhere. Everything that could come off the car came off the car, but the cockpit itself, the roll cage, was relatively intact.

The wheels were partly off and the suspension was off but the cockpit was OK. Except for two things.

We had a Sparco seat that was ridiculously fragile. Even today I will still avoid Sparco equipment or if I am in a car with their seat I will always put tape over the name. The seat broke in half on either side of my hip. It broke in half where there are holes for the seat belts.

My co-driver, Terry Harryman, had relatively minor injuries because he stayed in his seat. Although we kept on rolling end over end for a such a long distance, we did not have a sudden stop by crashing against a wall or tree.

Also we used a crotch strap already in those days, but for some bizarre reason for that rally the crotch strap was not installed in my car. What happens when a seat breaks and there is no crotch strap and the car tumbles like that, is you get thrown around like you are in a washing machine. And that explains my horrific injuries.

We had a surprising rally driver in the team for that rally — Carlos Reutemann. 'Lole' had a huge following in Argentina and he was literally worshipped by people during the recce. I took him in my car on this second stage during the recce and did a couple of extra runs to show the Formula 1 star 'how the rally car is driven'. So I learned this section much better than any other stage and I felt very good and confident at the start line.

When the other Peugeot drivers, Timo Salonen and Carlos, had finished the stage but I was missing, our team boss Jean Todt sent our service helicopter and mechanics Carlos Dos Barros and the late Patrice Caillon to look for me. They found me lying on the grass and I was very, very badly injured. My leg was in an awkward position and I only know this because I have seen a terrible photo. There is blood coming from my anus. You can imagine how bad it looked.

Carlos Dos Barros told me afterwards that I just kept groaning: 'No more rallies, no more rallies...' The helicopter had no medical gear, but the sump shield had come off the car in the accident and they used it as a stretcher to lift me onto the helicopter, which flew me to a nearby little hospital. The pilot had flown planes in the Falklands War, and had to land on a railway track because there were so many wires around the building.

The situation was really quite desperate. The internal bleeding was so bad and my blood pressure was so low, really below almost any medical criteria, that they were scared to try to get me to a big hospital in Córdoba. They wouldn't fly with me in that condition. Jean Duby, the team's doctor, had arrived in the meantime to the hospital. He realised that I was going to die if I stayed in the little hospital. But my blood pressure was too low for the transport.

Duby turned his back and took a false blood pressure measurement to get local doctors to allow me onto a military helicopter. Our own helicopter had gone to look after Carlos and Timo. Duby told me some time later that during the transport he had seen me lose all colour and told the pilot to go lower and faster to get oxygen to me. That is when I had my first recollections, and the terrible weight on my chest.

We arrived at Córdoba at the last minute.

Do you remember much of it?

Not a lot. Jean Todt would come to call the place where I was 'The corridor of death' as I was on a ward with people who had been shot, stabbed and were in a terrible state. It was a trauma unit for a huge area and he found it very difficult to be there. The doctors asked Jean to talk to me just to see if I would react to him.

But while I was there, there was an amusing anecdote. At the same time Argentina was hosting the World Council of Churches, so the Finnish Archbishop, John Vikström, was in Buenos Aires at the time of the accident. I'd never met him. But when he heard that his countryman was in a critical condition in Córdoba, he took a plane to come and see me. Respect.

Although I was critically injured I was able have some kind of conversation with him. I realised the Archbishop had come to see me so I thanked him for that, and then suddenly I realised that in Finnish, like in French, there is a polite way and a familiar way to talk to someone. Well I had been using the very intimate way of talking to him in Finnish. Like your friend. So I apologised for being that way. So it was very funny to me that as a dying man I was apologising to the Archbishop...

There was a hospital in Buenos Aires that could have operated on me but it was considered safer to do it in Europe. So once I was stabilised they flew me to Europe and it was the most horrible trip because of my injuries. I was in a little private jet and my face was pushed almost up against the ceiling, it was 20 centimetres above my face. I was supported from all sides on the bed, under heavy sedation but in incredible pain the whole time.

We were flying for a long, long time and then I remember that we landed. I'm sort of half conscious, half not conscious. My sense of time was blurred. I asked if we were in Europe. But no, we were only in Brazil refuelling. I was in absolute despair that this terrible pain would continue forever.

When we finally landed in Paris, Peugeot wanted me to be operated on there, but my wife Rita insisted that I was operated on in Helsinki. Kalevi Österman, who would operate on me in Finland, came to Paris with Rita and Rita's brother Raul and it took a day to find a new plane to take me to Helsinki.

In Finland I stayed in the hospital for three months. I was too weak to be operated on immediately, but at the same time my body was holding more and more liquid and I was puffing up and becoming like the Michelin man.

Despite my sedation I was awake most of the night before the operation, Rita being with me in the room the whole night. My pulse was 140 all the time.

When they operated to fix my left knee, which was completely broken, diagonally, like it had been stripped completely off the rest of my leg, like someone had taken an axe to me, the result of that operation was something so elegant and beautiful. It took seven or eight hours to get my leg together. Dr Österman did an incredible job.

But after the operation the worst scenario the doctors had been afraid of, materialised. My lungs stopped working.

My blood didn't get oxygen any more. I was in a big orthopaedic hospital, but when things became critical on the Friday evening I was taken to the University hospital's intensive care. Honestly, I was not in this world any more.

To make matters more complicated the chief anaesthetist, Aarne Kauste, had already left to go to his summer house. That's what we do in Finland in the summer weekends.

So he has got this summer house 100 kilometres away from Helsinki and they called him and said this rally driver is about to die. So he gave some advice to the doctors and started driving back as he wanted to be there in person.

That night, between Friday and Saturday morning, was incredibly critical. I don't know if in medical history many have had such low oxygen levels. Normally it is 97 or 98. If pH goes down and oxygen levels drop to 50 or 60 then you are in big trouble. But mine was around 20.

Poor Rita had already lost her first husband in an aircraft accident after just one year of marriage. And now here I am in this mess. And so she was called at about five o'clock on Saturday morning with her brother to see me because I was absolutely critical.

But then slowly, slowly I started to stabilise.

Even then, there was no guarantee that the old Ari would be back. All the signs were that I had suffered brain damage when my blood pressure had dropped so low. They did not know if, when I was awake, I would be the same person again. The tests showed very low brain activity.

Rita asked how life would be with me, if my brain was as damaged as they believed.

'It depends how strong you are,' Dr Kauste replied.

But something incredible happened. I was visited by our friend, Pastor Olli Valtonen. He anointed me with holy oil on my forehead and while he prayed with Rita, I awoke suddenly. I was fine. I knew everything. The doctors asked me who I was, who my wife was, to count backwards from 20. And I became frustrated because the questions were so silly.

We can make of this whatever we want. Whether their original reading had been wrong or whether something incredible had happened, the damage that they believed had been done to my brain was not so.

I had been saved. And eventually my body would recover.

The consequences of the accident ran far deeper than physical injury. When you started to convalesce, when you started to recover... how hard was it for you? When did the difficulties and the depression begin?

Very soon. There were countless little moments.

Maybe two weeks after the operation in Finland, I was taken to have another X-ray. There were hundreds of them. They had to take my left leg out of the plaster to get a better angle for the X-ray and I realised that I could not move my left ankle. Not at all. I wanted to pull it towards me but nothing happened. There was no connection between my brain and my left ankle.

So, you know, my heart stopped. My heart stopped. Because I was not any more a driver. I was no longer thankful for having escaped death or even the shadow of death. My left leg wasn't working so I couldn't drive. I couldn't use a clutch.

The fear invaded me completely. It froze my body. It took over the whole of my inner self.

So from then onwards it was downhill. All kinds of fears started to come into my mind and I was absolutely like a shivering dog. I was like a leaf on a tree. The slightest breeze and the leaves start vibrating. I was like that. I had no strength any more. I was completely overcome with fear.

I realised that there were lots of X-rays, and I heard nurses who said, 'You know we must take care of Ari because we have to take so many X-rays from him and we have to protect him from radiation.' So I started to think that I was going to get cancer. And soon it becomes a fact. Yes, I am going to have cancer.

All I was thinking and asking was, come on, can't you protect me more? Do we have to do another X-ray? I started to resist. If I said 'No, I think this is enough', they would say 'Come on I know you are in a vulnerable state. We have to face it, it's for your own good.' And I would say, 'No, I won't have one. I will get cancer.'

That irrational fear started to occupy my mind totally. And there is nothing rational about it. That's how your mind is. But your mind, your mental state is a line drawn in water. Who is well and who is unwell? It is almost impossible to tell.

Your mind has got a dark side to it. But of course in my case it went to extreme lengths. What happened to me is that I became like a piece of dead wood floating on the river. Totally no rudder.

I was floating to wherever those fears would take me.

I was completely sure that I was going to have cancer. And I'll never be driving again; my left foot is not working. I had no future.

I was extremely fragile.

And my body was still very, very badly damaged.

My back was broken so badly. My vertebrae still, now, stick out. My rib cage juts out from my body. That's how broken I was. Even today people get frightened if I make them touch my back. There is a big lump but it's not meat. It's bone. It's a bone lump sticking out.

Then I make them touch my lungs. Well there's a big lump sticking out and that's not meat, that's deformed lungs.

The fact I am alive is a miracle.

In my back I had an unstable fracture. The vertebrae had turned 30 to 40 degrees out of position. I was very close to being paralysed but not quite, so they had to wait until this fused into its new position. So that was two months of not moving.

I was very, very weak. Then they made a plaster cast for my whole upper body. From my waist up I was in a plastic cage to support it. My left leg was completely cast and my ankle didn't work anyway. The only parts of my body that I could move were my arms, my eyeballs and my right foot.

I imagine it must have been easy for your thoughts to run away with you while you were incapacitated like that.

Your mind takes you to dark places. With my body broken, cancer looming and with my belief that I was no longer a driver, this thing that had defined who I was and what I believed my place in the world was, I slipped into a terrible depression.

And then Rock Hudson died. I'd never heard of him because I wasn't really into celebrities so much. I know Elvis and Paul Anka and Clark Gable, but not Rock Hudson.

I'd never heard of this actor and I definitely didn't know about AIDS, this new disease that had killed him. But when I looked it up and started reading, I thought that I had all the symptoms. I remember I looked at my tongue in the mirror. When have you ever looked at your own tongue? But I looked at it and it was the colour of an AIDS patient and so I thought, 'Yes. That's it.' Horror overwhelmed me.

I'd been transfused with plenty of blood in Córdoba and of course back then in those countries you would get paid to be a blood donor. So with AIDS not being known in those days I realised it was entirely possible and probably quite likely that infected blood from a drug user or someone who wanted some quick money would have been given to me in the many litres of blood they had used to save my life.

The demons in my mind created it and then cemented it. There was no question. I had AIDS. And if I was in a freefall before, then now it was multiplied by 100. And that lasted from November 1985 until August 1986.

Did people notice the change in you? Did they ask you to seek help, to seek counselling, to talk to somebody to make you realise that the things that you believed from the cancer to the AIDS to the depression you were going through to try to get you out of it?

First of all I didn't really speak. Of course I went to see doctors. And they gave me AIDS tests which all came back negative. I told them, 'You are lying to me.' I was living near London and so we went there, to Harley Street, which is where the best doctors are. AIDS was still relatively unknown and so we went to see the best doctor on Harley Street.

In my sick mind I thought everybody knew that I had AIDS. I thought everybody was lying to me, that everyone was following me, that my illness would make a good story for them.

Wherever I looked I thought I saw newspaper people. I thought they were spying on me. Whenever I looked at people they looked away, which I took as proof that they were press following me and that they felt awkward because I knew who they were and what they wanted, when in reality I was so ill that my eyes were popping out of my head and I looked terrifying. Of course they looked away. But I interpreted that as proof that they were Fleet Street guys spying on me.

No counselling can help you when you are like this. I was convinced the doctors were lying. The doctors told me over and over again that I was fine. I said 'Mr, please why are you lying? Why are you lying?' And my reasoning why I thought they were all lying is because there was no cure for AIDS anyway. So my reason in my sick mind was that the doctors think, because there's no cure for it anyway, it's better to keep him in a place where he doesn't know.

I was begging them for the truth, just for them to be honest to me about the AIDS then at least maybe, you know, we can protect the rest of my family because at that time I was convinced that if I'd hug my daughter, she'd have AIDS too.

I was so sick in my mind.

It must have been a terrifying ordeal. Perhaps even more so now to look back and realise the depths of the illness that had taken you down to that point.

It proves what can happen to you. In this incredible puzzle of life, while it can all come apart easily, the right pieces can and do come back together and you actually can be cemented together again as a human being. And so far from being a sad tale, it's a very encouraging story. Yes, this can happen to you in both good and bad ways, and in the end it's totally normal because that's how life is. And yet even at the worst you can recover from it.

I woke up eventually from that incredible ordeal. But it took a long time.

Can you imagine what life was like with my family? My wife Rita, my kids were so small at the time, but I kept on believing I had this illness and that I would have passed it to them. Any contact, even if they took food from my plate or used the same spoon, it was too much for me.

I was shouting at Rita, asking her why she filled the car up with petrol because I was sure we would be dead before the tank was empty. That was the truth in my mind.

Life was surreal for Rita. Afterwards she said that had she not gone through the death of her first husband, she would not have had the strength to hold the family together after Argentina.

The puzzle of life is far beyond our comprehension. What I am today, with all of my shortcomings, I am a combination of whatever I have experienced up until now. Have I always been able to draw the right lessons and learn the correct things? Very often not. But life has given me these ingredients and they have created the person that I am today. They are all a part of who I am.

What appears to be a defeat today is only a thought in your mind. Tomorrow or in a month's time or in a year's time or in five years' time or in ten years' time or maybe after you're not here any more, in fact, that defeat will turn out to be something different than you ever imagined. Something new comes out of every incident in your life.

Life takes a ricochet to a new direction from our success and failure. We'll never know what is around the corner.

It is hard for us to accept that we need defeat. We need setbacks. We are not omnipotent. I have learned the most from those who have cried a lot in life.

But we also have to remember something that is said in every language. Whether English, French, Finnish, Japanese, everyone knows the phrase that beauty is in the eye of the beholder. And this is key. Because what you see as beautiful may not be what I see as beautiful. So the same is true with all things. What you see as a setback, I may see as an opportunity. But it will only look that way to you when you can see it with your own eyes. Not when somebody tells you. Only when you, yourself, know in your heart that the thing you saw as a defeat has finally become beautiful. Only then do you know.

You know people always ask is a glass half full or half empty? That's another classic statement.

Well, if the glass is at least half full then I've already learned something in life.

But you know if you have gone through the desert and you have no water at all and you are really being thirsty, then even if one tenth of the glass was full of water and nine tenths was empty, you would be very grateful to have that small amount of water. Most people might look at how little water is in the glass and say how dare you give me so little? I deserve more!

But who tells you that you deserve more? Who gives you this born right that you deserve more? Nobody. Everything we have is a gift from God.

Only if you have been really thirsty in life, will you appreciate that little sip of water. So therefore your life becomes much more gratifying to you, because the beauty is in your eyes. It's all relative. It's all subjective.

As strange as it sounds, we should be thankful and grateful for the setbacks in life because success is very dangerous for man. Very few people can handle success. Very few people have matured enough in life that they can handle success. Any one of us can get derailed if we get success after success. An idea that you are better or higher than someone else can creep into your mind, changing you without you even noticing. We forget how mortal we are.

Anything can happen to us. Maybe the doctor comes back to you with something wrong with a blood sample. Perhaps the police call to tell you that your daughter has been in an accident. Suddenly whatever you thought five minutes earlier, you realise it's all on the scrap heap. If you get carried away with success you have one day to stand back and realise that it is not real.

Life goes on. We cannot escape its scrutiny.

Can I ask you how you got to that point? What you were saying about the empty glass seeming full to the man in the desert is something very positive. And yet when you were in hospital and when you were recovering, it seems as though all you had in your head was negativity, brought on by this deep depression that had taken you. The illness made you believe so many terrible things, be it cancer or AIDS. How did you finally wake up to the sip of water in the empty glass as being positive?

I cannot unravel it. I cannot scrutinise why. That fear existed for months and through the whole following spring and summer.

Occasionally I had a moment where I would think, perhaps I don't have AIDS. But it only lasted for a few minutes until I fell back into the darkness. Despite everything the doctors said, my depression convinced me they were all in a conspiracy against me.

I watched my two daughters Ria who was five years old and Tua who was just three, taking their afternoon nap. The idea that they would soon die would tear my chest apart. I went to stand on the balcony of our house. And even though jumping would have brought an end to the suffering I endured and the demons in my mind, I always had as a clear sight that I did not have the right to do it.

In June 1986 I went to see an Egyptian-born psychiatric doctor in Berkshire and I started to tell him my usual story of how I have AIDS and this and that. And he just smiled, shook his head and said, 'Ari, I can send you for an AIDS test tomorrow in New York. I can send you the day after to Tokyo. I can send you anywhere in the world in complete secrecy but no matter how many times the results come back negative, you will not believe it. We agree to disagree.'

I'll never forget those words. 'We agree to disagree.'

I went to Finland for the summer, hiding away because I was convinced that everyone knew about my condition but were too polite to speak about it publicly. I thought that some perhaps were just waiting to read it in the papers, whether it was the article saying I had AIDS or the one that would say that I had died.

Anyway, my brother-in-law and best friend Raul Holmborg was flying helicopters as part of his profession and the 1000 Lakes rally was being held in the August. He asked me if I wanted to go along to watch. Well that was the sort of thing that I had not done since my accident. I couldn't face people, I just couldn't. I spent all my time in the corner in my house and I didn't want to stop hiding.

I was just hiding and not moving. Hibernating.

Anyway he decided that we would go. But I told him I cannot. I absolutely cannot. I'm afraid. I cannot face people. But he told me not to worry. 'It's remote fields in the forest. Nobody will see you.'

And so he managed to persuade me to get in the helicopter, but on the condition that we don't go to public places at all. So I took all my Valium, and I was having 20 or 30 milligrams a day. The Valium sedated me, and then I'd take another pill to keep me awake. I was like a zombie, just ticking over.

In the end he flew us to a hotel, Laajavuori, one that I had stayed at for every 1000 Lakes since my very first in 1974. And as we came in to land, I remember the ground coming closer and closer. And when we were no more than two metres off the ground, I felt a huge shudder inside me. That feeling in your stomach as though I'd just been stopped from falling off a roof. I breathed in and my body shook. And I woke up.

That is the only way I can explain it.

When you are in the middle of a nightmare and you are so terrified, but that shock wakes you up and you realise it was only a dream. Imagine that relief, but 100 times higher. Because I had not woken up from a dream. My nightmare had been my reality. It had been my life.

But two metres off the ground, with my eyes wide open, my brain suddenly awoke. And my nightmare, my living, breathing nightmare was over.

Of course I don't have AIDS! I am OK.

You cannot believe that sense of relief. Very few people have experienced that kind of genuine, overwhelming emotion. Yes! You are alive. And no, you are not going to die tomorrow.

That's incredible. So was it literally that moment that you arrived back at a rally? Because if we go all the way back to the moment when you started to have the doubts about your health and the moment when the demons set into your mind, you distinctly said that your descent into this depressive freefall began when you discovered your ankle didn't work. That was the point at which you didn't feel like a driver any more. And so the moment, then, that you return to your world, to your comfort zone, if you like, of being a driver and back in the surroundings of the rally world again... suddenly you snap out of it.

When you put it like that...? I had not thought of it in this way. You know, it just clicked. That is exactly as it happened. And you know what? The helipad was barely 50 metres from the hotel, and of course everybody was there. And the fans, they had not seen me for a whole year.

They knew that I had been in a critical condition around the time of the 1000 Lakes in 1985 and so nobody had seen me except for in articles.

But it took me an hour, maybe even more, to limp that short distance from the helipad to the hotel. There were just so many people. They were all cheering and shouting. And I could not stop smiling nor talking. I felt like I was a piece of sunshine. I was alive again.

It was as if I had been on Death Row in America. I had been strapped into the bed and they were preparing my lethal injection for midnight. And suddenly at five minutes before, the red telephone rings and the Governor has granted me clemency.

That's what happened to me.

All of a sudden I realised that the whole ordeal, everything from the past year, it had not been true. I climbed out of the black hole and into sunshine. And I saw life in its true beauty and real colours, not the twisted, surreal and murky colours it had been.

I called Rita, who had already gone back to the UK with the kids, and told her with the voice of a lottery winner: I'm well, there is nothing wrong with me, the nightmare is over! She did not believe me at first. Of course she knew all along that the problem was in my mind, but she was puzzled of this sudden change after nine months of such a terrible ordeal.

My new lease of life made me to look over the life I had lived and I realised how wrong I had often been in my attitudes. My dear colleague and neighbour in Cookham Dean, Markku Alén, had a big Mercedes but I thought that we must not show off and I settled for driving a Peugeot 505. What a false modesty.

So on my first call to Rita from the 1000 Lakes rally my message basically was that I'm not dying now and we'll buy a big BMW!

I was myself again. I was so happy that I kept on speaking to everybody. That weekend back at a rally was just incredible. And then on Sunday evening there was a party, because in those days we still had good prize-givings and dinners. We went to the party and there was music and I was dancing on Sunday night until three or four o'clock on the Monday morning. Well my left leg, which was far from being healed, was so swollen on Monday morning but I didn't care because for months I had just been dragging my foot behind me.

I was dancing all night for no other reason than for the first time in a year I felt alive. And the other drivers, at that moment, I think they all knew that either he has recovered or poor Ari has gone completely crazy.

In next to no time I was testing a Peugeot in the Sahara Desert, preparing for the Dakar.

You were back in the car that quickly?

Oh yeah. Exactly.

And it was Jean Todt who got you back in the car. How important was he in your rehabilitation?

Very. It was not known if my left foot and leg would work, so he had asked the great Peugeot engineer Jean-Claude Vaucard to design a rally car with an automatic clutch.

Jean managed to persuade Peugeot to pay me the same salary as I'd had for the previous year.

A few weeks after the 1000 Lakes rally, Peugeot invited me to drive the 'zero' car at the San Remo rally, the car that goes out first on the course but doesn't actually compete. It is like a course car, driven for the organisers, just to check the course and the timing loops, things like this.

Well, soon I was sliding about, throwing the car around. The car was an extension of me again. It was the most wonderful feeling. I also found that I could operate a manual clutch. The old Ari was back in every sense of the word. But in my joy I went too far and I got carried away. I put the car into the ditch, although thankfully on this occasion only the number plate fell off. How embarrassing.

When did you know that you were back?

At the start of the Dakar. It was December 31st, 1986 and my morale was maybe the highest I can remember. You have to understand, I had been to the very depths of despair and yet here I was, not just awoken from my nightmare but reborn.

But my confidence was not shared by everyone. To even finish the Dakar takes resilience and self-control. I knew I had the first of these but people doubted I had the latter. I was known for my make-it-or-break-it style. Experienced drivers said I wouldn't make it more than a few days, maybe not even to Algeria. Well, I decided that I would show them all what I had finally learned.

The Paris-Dakar rally in those days was truly a run from Paris all the way to Dakar. It was a 13,000-kilometre trek where you need luck and speed. I knew that if I was to have a good result and bring Peugeot the rewards they deserved for trusting and believing in me, I would have to be careful and mindful. The first stage, prologue, was near Paris and incredible numbers of people had come to watch the first attempt of Peugeot to conquer this great challenge. Prologue would determine the starting order in Africa so I'd take no chances at all. The prologue was less than 10 kilometres long and there was 13,000 kilometres more to do.

But disaster. After a few kilometres the front right wheel collapsed in on itself. I thought, this cannot be true. I have not hit anything. I was being so careful.

Rita was standing in the heavy rain and heard everyone saying, 'Oh here is the same old Ari. Back from the shadow of death and already he has hit something. He has learned nothing. He will never change. Day one and not even 10 kilometres completed of 13,000 and his rally is over.'

Rita said to herself at that moment that she would never ever go to see another rally.

But I saw the faces of the spectators. And I heard their cheers and encouragement for us to keep going. My four-wheel-drive car was now a three-wheel-drive car. We could keep going. The biggest problem was that the steering was now so damaged that the car would only turn left. At right-hand corners or hairpins, I went straight, turned the wheel left and reversed, then went straight and repeated this until I had got around the corner. You can imagine how long it took to turn around just one corner.

I looked in my mirror and saw people hanging on the back of the car. I was confused but then I realised they were fans who were acting as a counter-weight trying to balance the car. Just to help me. It was unbelievable.

We made it to the service park and Jean Todt came to see me. I could not grasp what was happening. With a lump in my throat I told Jean that, for once, it honestly was not my fault. And in the end, we discovered this to be absolutely true. The circlip, a suspension ball-joint locking device, was missing. That is why the wheel had collapsed.

I had done nothing wrong.

That was the last day of 1986 and I decided to put that day in the diary with the rest of my nightmare. Tomorrow we would start a new year.

With the finishing time of that first day determining our starting position, I began in Africa, January 1st, 1987, in 282nd position. Every car and lorry was in front of me making terrible dust clouds. In Algeria the terrain is rough and rocky and you have to stay on narrow roads to avoid endless off-road traps. Until today I do not know how we managed to get past all the competitors in front of us.

But three weeks later, on January 22nd, we won the Paris-Dakar Rally.

The time around Paris-Dakar was simply unreal. At the start line I had to pinch myself that it was really me. It was like a second life starting. I cannot describe my sentiments when I arrived as a winner to Dakar and I saw Rita. Is this a dream?

Yet life soon reminded me how small we are. I liked my co driver Bernard Giroux a lot. A few months after we won the Dakar together, he died with Formula 1 driver Didier Pironi in a boat race in England.

Winning the Dakar must have been an incredible feeling for you, and for your family. How different were things with Rita and with your children now that you were out of the nightmare? To have gone through all of this with them?

This is a very important question and is probably not one I can do justice to answer. They suffered terribly. Their husband and father was totally out of this world and for them it was terrible, just terrible.

For Rita, having to hold the family together... she was incredible. The aftermath of Argentina was a devastating time.

But as she says today, these experiences have helped us to keep our feet at least occasionally on the ground. We are not floating all the time.

She is incredible. Imagine having lost her first husband, having almost then lost her second husband and yet she was the first one convincing me to go back to rallying. But she knew that rallying was my life, our life. The motor of your life is your passion and she knew that for me that was rallying.

But every now and then I awake to the reality of how lucky I am to have her, to have my family, and to still be alive. And that, just a few years later, our son Max came into our lives.

Life has unfolded in front of me in an incredible manner, one filled with excitement and privilege. I consider myself truly fortunate to have experienced all that I have and in many ways I am thankful to have been through something as bad as I have, for the perspective that it has given to me.

Life, I have come to learn, is like a Finnish summer. It is at best so short and fragile. Every day, rainy or sunny, is precious. When you realise how mortal you are, it is the most fabulous gift. It liberates you to live your unique life to the full.

Bobby Unser

'Getting hurt didn't bother me. Having my brother get hurt bothered me... There was nothing we could do about it, but I was a lost fool... But something inside of me said I've got to keep driving a race car.'

Bobby Unser is one of the most successful American racing drivers of all time. In a career that spanned five decades, 'Uncle' Bobby held land speed records, was crowned Indycar champion twice, won the Indy 500 in three consecutive decades and became known as the King of the Pike's Peak hillclimb, winning on the perilous mountain road a record 13 times.

In a rapidly changing and evolving era of motor racing he was the master of all, with a command of his craft and a deftness of touch that would form the cornerstone of a family reputation and a legend that has echoed through time.

Robert William Unser was born in 1934 in Colorado Springs into a racing family. His uncles Joe and Louis had first taken the Unser name into motorsport, Louis having already created an aura around the Unser family name at Pike's Peak. Dubbed 'The King of the Mountain', Louis wrestled with the course into his 70s, eventually only stopping when the organisers forced him to. But it was to be Bobby, his twin elder brothers Jerry and Louis and their younger sibling Al who truly created the legend of the Unser family name. It was to become a name that would go on to dominate American auto racing into the next millennium with Bobby's own son Robby and nephews Johnny and Al Jr carrying the torch.

But despite the depth of talent and passion for motorsport that exists within the Unser family tree, theirs is a story beset by tragedy. Motor racing was perhaps never more dangerous and its heroes never more daring than in the immediate post-war period, but the perils of the sport were brought home in the most devastating of fashions in 1959 when Jerry Unser was killed in practice for the Indy 500.

Bobby questioned his continuing participation in racing after the death of the elder brother whom he admired and adored, leading him to make a key decision that came close to costing Bobby his own life just weeks later.

———————

I don't dwell on bad moments. I've had a lot of wrecks, of course. Any race driver that excels will have had plenty of those. But the most important and hardest moment of my life was losing my brother Jerry. It was a very big deal. But being able to continue on after that... I've had many thoughts about that.

Let's start at the start. What got you and your brothers interested in racing?

Well, since we were really young my dad had a trunk upstairs above the garage filling station out here on Highway 66, which was where we made our living for many years. Tourists had to make it from California to Chicago and they'd have to take the 66 and so in amongst all of his things there was this trunk and we'd go in there to look at Daddy's racing pictures of Pike's Peak. So it was no surprise that we became interested in it.

They used to have baseball-style cards for all the Indianapolis cars and drivers. Hell, we'd select our favourites and we could remember all of them. It got us attracted to motor racing and I think that was the first thing we knew about racing, except for driving up to Colorado Springs which is where, technically, myself, Jerry and Louis were born. We weren't born here in Albuquerque. And so we went up there one time and I can remember the first trip we ever took up the highway to Pike's Peak, the only problem is that I was so young I can't remember what the year was. All I remember is that it scared the hell out of me. I remember that. The big drop off the side.

We were a very poor family, but Daddy and Mom somehow managed and we'd all have a vacation once a year. This one time we went to Colorado to go and see my Uncle Louis. My Uncle Joe had already gotten killed in a race car, testing it for Indianapolis up on the Denver–Littleton–Colorado highway. In those days there wasn't much pavement. Everything was still dirt and gravel.

But my Uncle Joe died testing the car that he and Louis were going to take to Indianapolis. We knew how he'd died, but given that he'd died before we were born and being so young I don't think we really knew what it meant.

So growing up loving racing, but in a family where death in the sport was very real, was there always this knowledge in the background of its underlying danger?

Yeah, and I think it all happened from that trunk. I think largely it happened because of my Uncle Louis. He ended up winning the Pike's Peak hillclimb nine times, which would become my aim for record achievements. When I was very young I told him that's what I was going to do, and that's what I eventually did. I have 13 wins at Pike's Peak. In total our family's record up there goes into the 30s!

When you were looking through that trunk, who was your hero?

Well, it wasn't just one. Things change as you grow up. You didn't really know them, you just looked at them and thought this guy had a pretty car or a good helmet. But, we had the filling station right there on Highway 66 and one day the great Tony Bettenhausen pulled up. He became a regular. And every year he would buy a brand-new Cadillac. Didn't matter how many miles he had on the other one. I remember airplanes weren't all that plentiful in those days. People didn't have private jets or anything like that, so Tony would drive to the races. He didn't run many smaller races, just the big ones. And every year he'd have to drive right by our place which was a garage, wrecker service and filling station, and he'd make a point to stop by as he was coming by and going back home. And every time he stopped by, he would always take me to dinner.

Isn't that weird? I never figured it out. He got himself killed before we got to know each other really, really good, but he knew that I was a race driver, running local races and winning almost all of them and so he'd stop by, fill up with gas, go get a motel and he and his wife would pick me up and we'd go to dinner. I never could figure it out. I had my brothers, my father and my mother, and he became a good family friend but for some reason he singled me out.

Do you think he saw something in you?

I guess so. Why else would he be here? Why wouldn't he stop at somebody else's gas station? I wasn't old enough or smart enough to figure it out at the time. But I'm damn sure he must have.

So when did you first step into a racing car?

When I was 15. It was a super modified and the driver didn't show up one day and I talked my Dad and Mom both into letting me drive and they both separately agreed. The next year, by the time I was 16, I'd won the whole South Western Championship. Against grown men, you know? Not kids. Who knows why I took off so good, I damn sure never figured it out.

My brothers were racing at the same time, albeit in different cars. Jerry even drove for the Ford dealership here in town. I drove for them one time. We were just drivers. We'd drive anything and we'd often have three cars running at once.

Did it get very competitive between you?

Oh yes, but it was always very good-natured. We were very close. We did everything together. If we went to a dance and there was a fight, it was a fight with the Unsers. If we went any place it was the Unsers. All of us. We were very close kids. The whole family in fact.

We used to catch wild horses, never touched by a human being before. We had donkeys that we rode as kids but we sold the donkeys to buy a Model A Ford. My dad would give us a gallon of gas a day. We weren't allowed to drive it anywhere with pavement, just on the dirt and there were hundreds of miles of those roads so that was easy enough. That's how we learned to drive. We were really active young kids. We were always camping out, doing a lot with the boy scouts. We were good kids. I mean I'm not going to tell you we were angels, I won't go that far. But we weren't bad kids.

And, of course, we were brothers. We'd get into fights with each other all the time, constantly. But we were together in everything. Even when we were racing.

You have to remember we were kids going up against grown men and some of them would get jealous. The Unser boys were winning most all the races and so sometimes they'd pick on one of us. Well, then they'd have the group of us to deal with. We'd be on the counter-offensive. It went that way all the way through life.

Al ended up with tremendous records, I did too, Jerry got himself killed and Louis ended up with multiple sclerosis, so he ended up being a very, very famous engine-building mechanic and tuner with his own shop. There was a time when if you didn't have a Louis Unser engine, you didn't have a good engine.

Like the last time I won Pike's Peak, in my own car. I called Louis. I had just won Indianapolis that year in 1968 and I just didn't have the time to prepare the Pike's Peak car because I was my own mechanic. So I called Louis and asked him to build me a wham-bammy good engine. I didn't ask him how much it would cost, I just said I needed a real, real good one. And I told him that he needed to come with the engine and babysit it every day that I ran it. And he did all that and we set an incredible record. Louis loved doing that.

I ended up loaning that same engine that Louis had built for me to Mario Andretti, and it gave him his only win at Pike's Peak. That was all fun.

You went to Pike's Peak first in 1955 along with your brothers and all three of you competed. You've spoken about what a focal point the Unser boys were. Did you feel that you had a target on your backs?

No. Honest to goodness, no. In all fairness, I don't think we thought we had any chance of winning the race. There was a little argument about who was going to end up driving what. Jerry ended up driving the Offenhauser that Louis was originally going to drive. My car had a Jaguar engine, but when they took Louis out of his car it made me very angry. So, I gave Louis my car and Daddy and I ended up taking my super modified car and changing the body slightly. We called it 'The Ugly Duckling' and it really was. We had to put in a transmission and a clutch and stuff that had nothing to do with the oval tracks. It was a rush, but we made it.

But the three of us competed that first year and we made a good showing. Louis snapped the brake handle off his car, as we had handles not foot brakes in the cars as we had no room down there in the footwell. Around turn 16 he pulled the handbrake and the frigging thing broke clean off. So he didn't have any brakes for a third of the run at Pike's Peak. But he still finished third. Jerry finished fourth in the Offenhauser and I finished fifth in my super modified. Now, considering it was a family deal and we were all helping each other out, I think it was a pretty good first year, you know?

The next year I got my Jaguar back and I won the race with it. Then the next year after that I changed the Jaguar a little bit and lost the race, but I knew what I'd done wrong and after that I ended up with my own car and that won all the races, except for one when I had a flat front tyre.

How did your appreciation for Pike's Peak change from that first time you visited when you said that it had scared you, to being a competitor?

I always had a lot of respect for Pike's Peak. If you make a mistake, you're looking at going down all the way to Colorado Springs sometimes. That's the first time you're going to hit anything, right at the bottom, you know? So, you have to have a lot of respect for the place and you have to do everything accordingly. You have to deal with it scientifically, learn the road better than the other guys, learn how to make the car work better in different conditions and then it goes on for ever after that. Daddy and I broke many records up there. We changed the whole concept of race cars running the Pike's Peak hillclimb. We didn't do it the same way the others did it. And we did it with no money, basically. Neither one of us had any money.

By the time I had my own car to go up there I had dribblings of money but still very little. Maybe like $1,000 of sponsorship made you a big, big yahoo. One time I got up to as much as $3,000 and we couldn't believe it. Things were going well. That's how I got the money to buy my first airplane which enabled me to go to weekly races in California, because driving out there one way was 18 hours, which I couldn't keep doing. So in 1959 it was what we call a good pay year at Pike's Peak because the purse was quite healthy. We didn't get paid deals in those days. You got paid for what you did, like 40 percent of the gate or something like that. That's the way the money came.

Well, in 1959 I had a little money left over so I went down and bought a little junky airplane so that I could make California in seven hours. It cost me about the same in gas as it would have done in the car anyways!

Jerry was older than you. How much did you look up to him?

Oh, very much. He was the best. He won the National Stock Car Championship in 1957 and he had a spare car that he let me drive at Riverside, California against Troy Ruttman, Sam Hanks and all the big guys. I set it on the pole and damn near won the race. Part of the body came off and cut a tyre, otherwise I had the race totally won. But I had no money for that. I didn't even have the money to buy the tyres. But somehow Jerry figured out a way that I could run his car and it was as good as the car that he ended up running, too. It was a good deal and got me started in Stock Cars because the guys who owned them thought I'd done pretty good.

Who was the best, would you say, out of you brothers?

You can't compare. Jerry basically ran Stock Cars and it looked like he was probably going to remain there and stay in that class of the business. He was really good at it, he had a lot of connections and a lot of people really liking him. He really wasn't into the Indycars, at least it seemed that way to me, as much as he was into the Stock Cars.

I was the opposite. We both changed over and we'd drive either one if it was there to be raced. But Jerry's bread and butter was Stock Cars while my focus was elsewhere.

Why, then, do you think Jerry crossed over to run Indycars?

Because that's Indianapolis. Man, that's the biggest race on earth. That's the biggest single sporting event on this earth that we live on. Nothing is as big as Indianapolis. Anybody who thought he could race wanted to be there. It was the place to go.

How much excitement was there within the family when he landed that first Indianapolis drive in 1958?

Oh wow, yeah. We were all really excited. But you know, Jerry was doomed to some bad times. The first year there was a big crash on the opening lap when Ed Elisian spun, which caused a real bad accident with about 15 cars. Jerry couldn't do anything with all those cars wrecking in front of him and he ended up going over the top of one and went over the wall. Only driver to ever go over the wall at Indy and live. He came out with a really torn up shoulder but totally fixable. But that was Indianapolis.

What you've got to remember about racing drivers is that we will want to race anything, anywhere and no matter what physical condition we are in. Because if you're not racing, you're not a racing driver. Jerry had to keep running after Indy, wherever there was a race. One year after a big accident at Pike's Peak, he had to get that frigging car fixed just like he had to get his shoulder fixed — in a hurry. Because that's how you make your money. That's how you feed your family.

We were all the same way. Sometimes you got your tail busted up a little bit, but you just had to get fixed up as quick as possible.

What did he tell you about Indianapolis, when he came back with his injured shoulder? I mean you guys were brothers. Did he talk about the wreck at all?

Jerry always thought that Indy was where I should have been. Not just Indianapolis, but fully fledged race cars or what we'd call open-wheel. His whole reason for going there, for meeting with people, was that he was hustling for his little brother Bobby. It didn't look like Louis was going to be all that good as a racer, but it did look like I was going to make it. So Jerry went to Indianapolis to race and hustle for me.

That first year he got in that first-lap wreck and there was nothing you could do about that, but it ended his deal right there. As I look back, the cars he was driving were not very good cars. They were roasters without any special gift to them. No mechanic, no nothing to make him go any faster than anyone else. When I went, I had a bit more than that. I had Parnelli Jones helping me. That was the guy who made sure that I did good. But Jerry didn't have that. He was all on his own for two years in a row. And two years in a row he got into bad wrecks, the first year early on in the race, the second year early on in practice.

And that's what ended everything.

He was lying in the hospital that second year in 1959, and he died from his burns. If he'd got those same burns today, this weekend, it'd be a ho-hum deal. I mean he'd still have been burned, but he'd have lived through it easily. He'd have kept on racing. He'd have just had some scars. But that didn't happen in those days.

Unfortunately the technology in racing and in medicine hadn't quite happened yet. But it was right behind it. Jerry was wearing cotton, which would burn faster than you could believe. But everyone did in those days. That's what caused Bill Simpson to go down to the guys at NASA to speak to them about technology and fireproof suits and that's where it all came from. All because of the likes of my brother. But he had to die to get it done. And that's how racing got turned around in safety.

But laying in that bed, the day before he passed on, I didn't think Jerry was going to die. He didn't even look all that bad. He was still talking, still cheerful, and the one thing he brought up was that he'd already found a car for me to take my driving test in and become an Indycar driver. And the next day, he passed on. And that starts the whole story on that.

I couldn't believe that he was going to pass away. I didn't even give it a thought. I spent pretty much all day, every day with him in the hospital for the 17 days after the accident until he was gone. And it was all from blood poisoning which they had no good cure for in those days.

You mentioned earlier that you believed Jerry had gone to Indianapolis for you. To try to get you a seat. Did you ever feel responsible for his death?

No. You see, I had no desire to go to Indianapolis at that stage of my life. All the way into my 20s, actually. If I hadn't met the great Parnelli Jones at Pike's Peak, I'm certain I would never have gone to Indy because I was convinced that I wasn't good enough. Parnelli was the one who told me that I was.

But he never made me think I was going to be a winner or something like that. It happened because we spent so much time together, so many hours just us, as I would teach him the way up the mountain and show him the road. And then Parnelli just told me, flat ass out, that I was more than good enough to be at Indianapolis. I'm the one that didn't think so. I'm the one that turned it down. I'm the one that would have probably never ever gone.

I loved sprint car racing. I loved midget racing. Man, I could get a car to drive by just getting on the telephone. I could figure out where I wanted to race and there'd be a car for me. People liked me in all those races. They thought I went fast. So, dreams of going to Indianapolis just weren't there.

It was all because I met Parnelli at Pike's Peak. Every time he got close to making an offer I would change the subject. But after the race was over and I returned home to Albuquerque, sitting in the same chair and in the same place as I am talking to you now, I received a call from him saying he had lined up a car for me for Indianapolis the next year. He was so powerful, all it took was a phone call.

The car was no good. But that's OK. The team was no good. That's OK also. Because what it did was it took Bobby Unser to Indianapolis to race.

How did Jerry's death affect you?

Getting hurt didn't bother me. Having my brother get hurt bothered me. I didn't know if I was going to want to continue on. And I wasn't a really super good driver yet. I was still kicking the can and trying to figure out if I had a place in this sport.

But everything changed real quick. I came home. Jerry had a beautiful funeral. But for me and for Al and Louis, we didn't know what we wanted. It's a pretty serious thing when your brother gets killed. There was nothing we could do about it, but still, this was 1959 and I was at home and I was a lost fool. I didn't know what the hell to do. But something inside of me said I've got to keep driving a race car. I thought about it a lot.

I had a 1957 Ford, nine-passenger station wagon. I didn't say anything to anyone I knew. I just went to the local surplus store and bought a blow-up mattress, two army wool blankets, threw them in the back of the wagon and headed East. I was going to go back to Indiana and start driving.

I didn't ask anybody. I know my folks were edgy about me going, but it didn't make a difference. Jerry had barely been put to rest.

I got to Tulsa, Oklahoma. I had got in contact with John Locks, who was the guy who ran Firestone Racing in those days for the whole Midwest of the United States. He was like a father to me and really supported my racing. I was going to live with him because I didn't have enough money to rent a place.

I stopped by to visit John Zink, who'd won Indy in 1955 and '56 as a team owner to Pat Flaherty and Bob Sweikert. They were a big team, like a Penske today. I stopped there and he was playing around with a twin-engine go-kart and I just said 'hi' to him because this is a guy who one day, I wanted to drive one of his race cars.

He asked me on to stay and try out his little go-kart, which was tricky to drive because the left foot drove the left engine and the right foot drove the right engine. Well, that was a new thing that nobody had ever tried before, and I gave it a go outside his office and almost put it underneath a car. I missed the car but slammed hard into a building and broke my head open.

I had cracked my skull and had spinal fluid running out of my right ear. And this, just a few days after we had buried my brother. The chances of me dying were given as at least 90 percent. I was guaranteed spinal meningitis by the doctors. I had to wear a patch over one eye as I could not even blink.

Well, that took a whole year to fix. I didn't get meningitis thankfully and I was back to driving race cars again as soon as I could. My Dad tried to stop me, telling me I was doing it too soon, but I would sneak away. It didn't make any difference. I just couldn't stop driving race cars.

I guess in some way that helped me to forget about what had happened to Jerry. The more I raced, the more it became normal again. Louis and Al would come along, Al was winning everything locally, and in the end my father and I actually went to Amarillo in Texas to buy a car because they were picking on Al. We entered me in the same races to back him up. Man, we were better than anyone else. We'd fight those grown-ups and they were no match.

Slowly, Jerry went out of our minds and Al and I got back into racing full-time. Louis had his own company making engines and he became a legend. I took off and things went good for me. Sometimes they went bad. I got hurt lots of times. Everyone did. But the good times outweighed the bad.

The head injury sounds horrific. How long did it take before you got back into a race car again?

I think I knew I had to get back into a race car about six months before I finally got back in. I had been on and off in the military over the years and so as a result I was in the Veterans' hospital quite a bit. Now, I don't want to pull them down but they would never tell me what they were going to do to me. This one time I'd been in for a few weeks when finally they said they were going to pop my head open and operate on my brain. It was the only time I'd seen a doctor in two friggin' weeks. And I've got a guy right next to me in the bed who's trying to die and it's tearing me up. It's not a fun time.

The doctor came to me on the Saturday morning, and in those days you had all the rooms and at the upper end of the hall was where the nurse was. She didn't have an office, she just had a desk in the hall next to a window that she could look outside. The doctor came into my room and he didn't say a word and he took the notes on the end of my bed and I asked him, 'What's the deal, what are we going to do, Doc?' And he said 'I'm gonna operate on your head.'

So he leaves. The guy in the bed next to me has died by now, so I've got a room to myself, and I just got up out of that bed and I walked down to the nurse's desk and I asked to use her phone. She said sure. Then I asked if I could have my clothes. She told me I couldn't. So I grabbed the phone, I called my wife, and I said get up here right away because I'm leaving. She knows not to argue.

The nurse looked at me and I said, 'Honey, in 15 minutes there's going to be a station wagon under your window. If I don't have my clothes by then I'm leaving in what I've got on. And another thing, there ain't nobody big enough in this hospital to whoop me. I'm going home.'

She told me I wasn't going to leave and I wasn't going to have my clothes. And the two of us sweated it out until the car arrived and I just got up and started to leave.

'Wait, wait, wait,' she called after me. And she handed me my clothes.

I dressed leaning up against her desk. To this day, that was the last time I was in the Vets' hospital. And I'm 83 years old now.

I never went back to the hospital. But, there was a doctor in Albuquerque, a man named Dr Klebanoff. He was the highest rated neurosurgeon that we had in town. I had no money to pay him, but he helped me out. He helped me a bunch.

When I got better, the first race I ran was a midget USAC race in Albuquerque, New Mexico. My home town. On the entry list was Parnelli Jones, Roger McCluskey, and all these legends. And I won the race.

And the last guy to come out of the grandstand... was Dr Klebanoff. The guy who had saved my life. And we just cried. It was too much to be real.

And that's what led me to go on to win three Indianapolis 500s. To win the Pike's Peak hillclimb 13 times.

You have days when the good Lord knocks you down. But if you keep getting up, pretty soon something good happens, you know?

Carlos Sainz

'Even if you win, ask yourself, what can you do better? The worst thing you can do is to either keep celebrating or to keep crying. Analyse. Turn the page. And immediately start putting your energy onto the next race.'

Carlos Sainz Cenamor, *El Matador*, is one of the finest rally drivers in history. Through one of the sport's golden eras, he became one of the most revered and respected racers in one of the world's most diverse and intense disciplines.

Racing wasn't always the goal for *El Matador*. Born in Madrid, Spain, in 1962, in his youth he had trials for the Real Madrid football team and was a champion squash player. But in his late teens he caught the racing bug and from that point on there was no looking back. From his tentative début in 1980, he was making waves in the Spanish championship by the middle of the decade. His ascent came fast after that. He was crowned Spanish rally champion in 1987, the year in which Ford gave him his first-ever World Rally start.

In 1990 he won his first rally in the year that he won his first World Rally Championship, driving a Toyota Celica GT4 with his co-driver Luís Moya. They took the honours again in 1992 and remained a force in World Rally for more than a decade more, although never taking championship honours again, proving to be consistent rally winners and podium finishers in one of the category's most competitive periods. They came closest to the title again in 1998, robbed cruelly just metres from the finish.

Retirement seems to be a word alien to the great Spaniard. For the past decade and a half, since he left full-time competition in the WRC, he has missed just one running of the fabled and monstrous Dakar rally. A two-time winner, his latest victory over the gruelling course came in 2018, at the age of 55.

A true great of his sport, and a tremendous man born of humility and grace, Carlos Sainz is one of the most decent, respectable and respected men in his field.

For me, when I think about the lowest moment I think in two different areas. I think on the sporting side and I think on the personal side.

By far, the personal side has been the worst and I had two moments that were so difficult that they really hurt me. If you can imagine how difficult it is to be talking with somebody before a special stage of a rally and then you arrive at the time control, have a little bit of time to wait, get sent on your way, attack, finish the stage and suddenly you hear on the radio that somebody has had an accident and it's not looking very good. Then, 30 minutes later, you get the news that this person you were speaking to not so very long ago, has died.

That has happened twice and for sure this is the lowest moment you can reach. It really hurts.

If I am talking about the sporting side and the toughest time from that viewpoint, then the hardest moment for me was the 1998 RAC Rally when for three days I was cruising, I had the championship in my pocket because all I had to do was finish in the top six and I was easily sitting in fourth. We did the first day, then the second day, then we came into the last day, then five stages to go, then three, then just one stage to go and you think OK, the championship is finished.

And then you have one kilometre to go. Then with 200 metres to go you see the yellow panel that indicates 100 metres before the red panel that marks the arrival at the end of the final stage... and then, bang. The engine blows.

When you look, and you can see the panel. You can see the finish. This was the hardest moment, sportingly, of my career.

Luckily, and I say luckily, at that time I had already won two World Championships. And I've always thought that if, at that moment, I had not already won those championships, it would have been really terrible. But nevertheless, at the end of the day you think, I've won two championships, maybe I should have won three or four more with a little bit of luck, but you have to think to yourself how lucky you have been.

When I was a child I wanted to drive rally. I managed to compete. I managed to win first at the local level, then regional events, then my dream was to race internationally with a factory car. You know, all of these dreams came true. My dream was then to compete in the World Championship and I managed to do that. The first rally I did in the World Championship, the first stage I drove, I made the best time.

At that moment of the greatest disappointment, the film of your life comes in front of you. Because you have to keep it in perspective. You have to say, OK, hold on a second. For sure I was very upset. How is it possible to have such bad luck? But on the other hand, now I put a positive spin on it. I had a very nice career at that time. I had won the World Championship already, I had won many rallies, I had managed to become at that point the first non-Scandinavian to win in Finland, I'd won the RAC. And so I said, no, I will not allow this to drag me down. Whether it is one day, two days, whatever. Because this is a sport and I have been very, very lucky and with many positives.

From a personal perspective I am fine. I didn't have any accidents. My family is perfect. My wife is good, my children are OK. And you say, OK. Let's move on. Let's turn the page. And I always said to Carlos, my son, whether you win or you lose the first thing is to analyse. Even if you win, ask yourself, what can you do better? Sure you've won, but if you want to keep winning you must find what you can do better.

I will practise. I will test. I will prepare physically. Always try to analyse all the race. Even if you win. And then, try to improve. Celebrate, of course. But only for one day. If you keep celebrating too long, the next race you pay.

If you have bad luck, the story is the same. Analyse, again, what happened. Then if you want to cry, cry. But for one day. No more. Immediately turn the page and start working on the next chapter.

I think the worst thing you can do is to either keep celebrating or to keep crying. Analyse. Turn the page. And immediately start putting your energy onto the next race.

It's not an easy thing to do though, especially if that defeat comes not in one race but at the end of an entire season. Looking back to the RAC and that 1998 season, did you always think you'd be champion?

I think we knew before the RAC, even at the beginning of the season, that in the WRC at that time it was very tight. There were many factory teams, many good drivers in that period. Colin McRae was around, Richard Burns was around, Tommi Mäkinen was around, Marcus Grönholm, Didier Auriol, Juha Kankkunen... many, many drivers could win rallies and the championship. We knew that it was going to be a tough season.

I was returning to Toyota for the 1998 season and I was really looking forward to it because I had good memories with them. Ove Andersson, who headed Toyota's programme, was a really special man and I had a very strong relationship with him. I was confident that we could fight for the championship, even if the Corolla was not the best car that I'd ever driven. It was not like the previous period with the Celica. Sure, I managed to win many rallies with the Corolla but I was never 100 percent happy with it, especially on gravel. But we managed to get a good compromise that saw us in a good position when we got to the final round, just two points off the championship lead.

And then we get to the RAC and immediately Mäkinen made a mistake on the first day in the Mickey Mouse stages. He hit some concrete, lost a wheel, and I thought, OK, now all I have to do is finish in the top six to win the championship. I was lying third or fourth but really cruising, you know?

One thing nobody knows is that, in that rally, Marcus Grönholm, who was with Toyota too, retired with a con-rod failure. And then I retired in the last stage with a con-rod failure. My team-mate Didier Auriol retired on the second-to-last day with a clutch problem. But the day after the rally we were supposed to be doing some media things with journalists. I decided after what had happened that I wasn't in a good mood so I left it to Marcus and Didier to drive the journalists around. They had repaired Didier's clutch, but his car broke. With a con-rod failure.

In the end they found out that there had been a problem with that batch of the con rods. All the cars broke. Marcus's car went in the rally, Didier's car went the day after but probably only because the clutch problem meant he was out of the rally early, and mine went 200 metres from the very end. Right at the last moment.

A little bit later, in the road section, you remove the boost as you arrive to the podium. In the road section you don't have boost and you drive carefully. And so if we'd made it we'd never have known. But that's the real story of what happened. They found the batch of con rods in Köln was not correct.

So on that last day did you take any risks at all or was it genuinely a cruise for you? A Sunday afternoon drive in the park?

Absolutely. Absolutely no risk. It wasn't needed. In your mind you just have to bring the car to the end.

Were there any nerves at all?

None. I was happy. I was convinced. It was done for me. I never expected to have an engine failure.

When did you feel it go?

It was quite a bang. Suddenly I heard the engine noise change, a loud clank, a vibration and then the engine note just carried on dropping. We stopped, we opened the bonnet and I saw a hole in the block. Luís Moya my co-driver, I remember, was shouting, 'Try to start it again!' because we could see the finish line.

I said, 'Come on, it's finished. End of story. It's finished.'

When you felt that bang, what was the emotion?

I could not believe it. You know? This is a joke. This is impossible. This cannot be true.

How is this possible? How is this happening? It's too cruel.

Why wait until you can see the finish line? This is too hard. It is too much to take.

I remember walking away and then, that is when I started to think, OK, and I started to look for the positives. I will learn from this. For sure it made me stronger in that way. Because after that, apart from problems with family, nothing on the sporting side apart from accidents could be worse.

At that moment I thought, well now I am prepared for everything.

When I went to Dakar for the first time and I retired, I went because I wanted to be the first Spaniard to win the Dakar in the car category. It was hard, because I was leading by more than half an hour and with two days to go. Again, I had the race in my pocket and just like the RAC it is not over until you cross the line. We made a mistake with the navigation and we fell into a huge hole with the car, a 15-metre cliff. And at that time I thought, well it's no worse than what happened to me at the RAC.

Of course I was very upset, but the next year I came back and I won it.

It made me stronger.

We all remember the emotion of that moment in the RAC.

Well, yes. Luís threw his helmet through the window and everyone recalls that. But I was calm. I closed the bonnet and I walked away. I wanted to be alone for a while before talking to anybody. I knew all my family was only 500 metres away and all the journalists would be waiting there too to talk about the third title. But I wanted just to stay for ten minutes completely alone to just try to think about what had happened and to try to take some positives and think about all my life and how lucky I was. Even if it was so hard, and I must say it was not an instant thing. I was in a bad mood for a few days and from time to time even after a month I remember I was still thinking about it and asking how it could be possible, but I turned the page.

How soon did you get back in a car?

That was the last rally of the season, so maybe two weeks later I would have been back in the car testing for Monte Carlo. It was OK.

The next time you were in a position to fight for a championship, did you allow memories of that loss to enter your mind again?

No. Apart from accidents I was prepared for everything. So I said that whatever could come my way could never be as bad as the RAC. It cannot be worse. You have a world title in your hands and you lose it by 200 metres.

In some ways, because you were so sure that the title was going to be yours, did you ever allow yourself to be so confident again? Or did you have to forget all thoughts of expectation in the future, because the heartache of losing something you thought was a guarantee was too much?

Absolutely. That situation taught me that until you finish, until you cross the line, you can never be 100 percent sure.

You said at the start that you had personal low moments that affected you deeply as well. People that you knew very well. What do you recall of those moments?

One was in Australia, Rodger Freeth. One was on the RAC.

On the RAC, Michael Park, who was the co-driver of Markko Märtin, died. It was just… I don't know how to explain it. You are with somebody. And 20 minutes later they tell you he's died. It's crazy. It's really hard to accept it.

When you are driving you think nothing can happen to you. You know, of course, that motorsport is dangerous but somehow in your head you think that nothing can happen to you. If you don't think that then you probably wouldn't race.

How did you get your head together to go out and drive?

That was the hardest thing. The emotion at the time, the feelings that you have. It was really hard. It is a situation that you don't like and that you never think can happen, a situation you really hate. It's difficult to accept why it has happened to this guy. You start to think about his family. And you think about Markko, how he is feeling, as the driver. To know that ultimately it is your responsibility when something like that happens. It must be so hard.

To have that responsibility, for the guy sitting alongside you, how did you deal with that? To know that if anything happens it isn't just you in that car. There's someone alongside you, an incredibly close friend, that in other forms of racing other drivers don't have.

You spend many, many days with your co-driver. The relationship is very fluid, very strong. You go through a lot of emotions and a lot of moments together. In my case I haven't changed co-driver a lot and so that relationship is very strong.

Your first reaction after an accident, once the car stops, is always to ask, 'Are you OK?' And as soon as you hear 'Yeah, yeah everything fine', then you can breathe. And so far, in my career, I have been lucky and I touch wood, that I have not had big, big problems in those moments except maybe for broken ribs or things like that. But nothing important. I have to thank God for that. It is a big responsibility.

Did you ever question taking that responsibility for someone else's life?

No. I think if you start to enter into that situation, that is when you have to stop, jump out of the car, give the keys to the team and go home. Everyone knows motorsport is dangerous and rallying is extremely dangerous, much more than people think. The speed, at any level, but at World Championship level is so high. The safety is there but so are trees. If you make a small mistake or have a mechanical problem or whatever, you will not have a doctor there in ten seconds like in Formula 1. There the doctor will take time. It's the same in the Dakar. It will take time to have the first doctor close to you. This is something you never want to think about but this is a fact.

You spoke about turning the page and dealing with the good times and bad times the same way. Is that something you always believed or something you had to learn?

Of course you learn with experience, but I think I had it from the very beginning. I like always to improve. So for me it was always important to turn the page, but before you do so, to analyse and to learn. Even if you have won during the weekend I always like to think about what I could have done better.

I believe in talent, but talent without work will never succeed.

Fortunately it wasn't my mistake. I could not have done anything differently. It would have been even worse if I'd made a mistake. But this is a sport. Motorsport isn't like playing tennis where if you're winning 6–3, 6–0 and 5–0 in the final set and then in the last game you break your leg or something like that! Your racquet broke! And you concede the whole match.

But life goes on. And after that I won rallies, I was fighting for championships, I won the Dakar. Life carried on.

It taught me that life can be quite tough sometimes. But most of all it taught me that until you pass the finish line, until you hold it with your hands, you can never be 100 percent sure.

Damon Hill

'You talk about getting out from the shadow, but what shadow? Formula 1 or Graham Hill? Graham Hill wasn't a shadow to me. Graham Hill was a hero. I wasn't trying to bury my dad. I was trying to honour him.'

G raham Hill was the only man in history to complete the fabled Triple Crown of motor racing. Whether one accepts the holder as being the winner of the Indy 500, Le Mans 24 Hours and the Monaco Grand Prix, or whether the Monaco race should be replaced with the Formula 1 World Championship (as Hill himself believed), matters not. He holds the record in either case. In the 1960s there were few sports stars more famous nor more revered than the moustachioed and debonair English World Champion.

His death in an air crash in 1975 rocked the sporting world. But it destroyed his family.

Aged just 15, Damon Graham Devereux Hill had to carry the emotional and financial weight of his family on his shoulders. Working as a labourer and bike courier to make ends meet, he had to grow up fast to support his mother and two sisters. But the lure of the race track would eventually prove too strong. The Hill name returned to racing with Damon first competing in bikes at the comparatively late age of 21. He moved to open-wheel single-seaters where he showed far greater promise, yet despite his famous name he always struggled for financial backing.

His talent began to shine through however. Within a decade he had fought his way to Formula 1, signing as a test driver for Williams aged 31 in 1991 and making his début for the unfancied Brabham team the next year.

He was signed full-time for Williams to race alongside Alain Prost in 1993, winning his first Grands Prix and announcing himself on the world stage. In 1994 he partnered Ayrton Senna until the Brazilian's tragic death at that year's third race, the San Marino Grand Prix. Suddenly he was the Williams team leader in impossibly tough circumstances, carrying the team much as he had his family 20 years before.

His rivalry with Michael Schumacher became the story of mid-1990s Formula 1. Hill narrowly missed out on the 1994 title, won in controversial circumstances by Schumacher in the final race of the season, but made amends in 1996, becoming the first driver to follow in the footsteps of his father to be crowned Formula 1 World Champion.

By 1999 Hill was retired and for some time disappeared from public view. Having spent his life within the bubble of Formula 1, existing in the real world finally allowed him the time and the reflective space to deal with the tragedies and hardships that had been thrust on him and that he now realised he had never fully resolved.

Damon Hill fell into depression, rooted in that tragic evening in 1975 that had robbed the young man of the father he adored and idolised. His path through therapy to understanding brought about a rare level of introspection that resulted in *Watching The Wheels*, one of the finest and most unexpected sports autobiographies of recent years.

My dad was a pretty macho person in that he didn't often show his emotions. In the face of real danger, he was quite stoic. And stoicism, and I suppose American gung-ho, macho culture, was ingrained in us. It's still there. You can see it all the time, you know? In sports branding of no limits, no fear, you might also put in there no feelings as well. I mean we're real people and I don't think it's deliberate, but it was there all the time. If you watch the film *Zulu* or something like that, it's about stoicism, it's about stiff upper lip and building up courage in the face of overwhelming odds. And so my dad was someone who very much portrayed that Britishness of 'big boys don't cry'.

You can understand how that is heroic in many ways, to be able to carry on when all your friends are dying around you and somehow still have the strength to put danger and that side of it behind you. It is a strength, it is a power and requires an enormous amount of discipline but it doesn't mean that you have to do it. I mean if your nation is in mortal danger from invasion then maybe that's the time for it, but when you're playing a sport, you know you wonder whether it's necessary. And that's the interesting bit.

Formula 1 is imbued with the idea that this is a matter of life and death, that there's nothing more important. The people that are competing in it are supposed to take it so seriously that they will do anything to win and there's nothing else that's important. Their relationships go on the back burner. Everything in their life does. And that was very much the culture at Williams. Frank Williams is stoic. He's put everything aside in his life to have the most successful Formula 1 team and he's proven his point. Through 100 percent dedication he's produced a winning team out of sheer willpower.

But there's real damage along the way. Somewhere, something has to give. Because it's actually not that important. What is really important in our lives? That's the crux of it. We need to recognise, and humans come to realise this at some point in their lives, that the most important thing is not usually their job. Their job is nice, but it's not everything.

If you're Picasso and you're making paintings, well that's your job and maybe that's everything to him. I don't know. But, look at Picasso's relationships and tell me what you think. When we become obsessed to the point where nothing else matters then you have to ask yourself whether that's sane or not, you know?

We've all done it. I've done it. When I was racing I was on this mission and it was really the most important thing in my life to get there. What I was going to do when I got there, I never actually thought about. I'd never gone beyond that. But the challenge was very important to me. It was a way of showing your true colours and there is some truth to be found in that. Maybe it's a rite of passage thing, maybe as guys we need to show we can do all those things. We can be fearless and we can be skilful and we can be competitive and we can triumph over adversity and all those things. Maybe it's necessary.

But we're kind of fabricating it in order to prove ourselves and, actually, you ultimately wonder whether they really are the key elements of what it is to be a successful person. Those achievements do matter. They do express something about you but they're very specialised. You only need them in a certain case or certain situations. You don't need them throughout your life. I just don't think anybody could take that amount of stress for their entire life.

You grew up as the son of one of the biggest celebrities and sports stars in Britain. Yet you came to racing very late. Did you always have a desire to race or did you come to it through a search for affirmation?

No. I loved racing. I would say that's absolutely undeniable. I love speed. I love the sensation of going fast. I love competition. I love going around race tracks whether it's on a bike or in a car. I like skiing. I just love the feeling of motion. I think one of the best quotes I've ever heard from a motor racing person is from Stirling Moss when he said that 'speed is tranquillity'. That's the only way to explain it to someone who's never experienced what we have. You can look for tranquillity sitting under a tree. You can try meditation or walking or something like that. But people that are wired like us, when you're going really fast there's a kind of quietness that you get. What I just said about nothing else really mattering, there's a kind of release from life through just focusing on one single task.

Maybe that's why we get so absorbed in it. We want to get back to that place. Being in a racing car and going around at times is very boring, it's very repetitive. You're just trying to do it again and again, you try and do it faster and faster and faster, as much as possible.

But it's ultimately very calming in some ways.

I was racing because I absolutely loved it, but at the back of my mind there was always the question of, well, how good am I?

If my dad was two times World Champion, well then how good am I compared to that? It's got to be in there somewhere. Although the other part of you is saying you can't really compare. I mean was Fangio better than Senna? We don't know and we'll never know. So in the same way I couldn't really compare myself to my dad.

But I tell you what, I wouldn't have been able to put myself through the same risk that he did. I've had a couple of team-mates killed. There have been lots of people who've been bike racing or car racing that I've seen die and it's a very unpleasant experience. It takes its toll after a bit. So God knows how dad got through that.

You experienced an awful lot in what was a comparatively short Formula 1 career of seven years.

It's not even as long as The Beatles' career which was only about eight years!

True, but like them you did so much in that time from début to becoming team leader in those awful circumstances in 1994, champion in '96 and retired by '99.

Career planning was never really part of my career at all. It just happened. I mean how could I have planned for there to be a seat at Williams? It just happened. The doors just opened and then suddenly you're team-mates with Ayrton Senna and you're thinking that this is a good crack, you know, because I was unemployed about five years before then.

But that's not to say I wasn't focused on maximising every chance I got. I wanted to see how good I was. Alain Prost may not have been at his best when we were team-mates but occasionally I was quicker than him. Could I ever have been quicker than Senna? I would have loved to have found out. I mean, probably not because when he was fired up he was unbelievably quick. But, you know, what a benchmark. And anyway, fate stepped in and threw me into the deep end again.

Everyone had to go through that process of questioning what the hell they were doing. Why were we playing this game where people got killed? And to his credit, and you can criticise him for a lot of things, but [FIA President] Max Mosley did force through safety measures. And I'm probably still here because of that. A lot of drivers are probably still here because of those things.

You talked earlier about stoicism and stiff upper lip. Did you feel you had to have that with Williams in 1994, to take that team-leading responsibility on your shoulders?

Part of me wanted to. I wanted to be important. I wanted to be relevant and show I could be entrusted with that job. I never felt like I got that across 100 percent. Something about my demeanour or whatever it was, I never really communicated that very well to Frank and I always felt they never quite thought I was up to scratch. That's the way that Formula 1 operates and I think that culture came from the top.

If you ever did a deal with Bernie Ecclestone he'd always make it abundantly clear that it was you who needed him and not the other way around. In a way, drivers are always faced with that problem in Formula 1 teams, despite whatever I felt I was doing, and that I was giving everything I had for the team. Yeah, I wanted to win. I wanted to do the very best I could. It was like an obligation we had to Ayrton as well. To do the very best we could. And in some kind of slightly skewed romantic way, we thought we were honouring him if you like by taking the battle to the evil Benetton team who seemed to be prepared to do anything to win. We kind of painted ourselves and saw ourselves as the good guys up against the bandits. That was the feeling at the time, certainly.

On reflection, over the years, you look back and they were just doing what they did. They weren't the bad guys at all and we weren't the good guys, but we played within certain rules and I think that was part of the stoicism of the Williams culture too. If Frank said you can win but we're going to have to beat you with birch tree branches, you have to walk over hot coals, you go OK!

You've told me before that you really struggled between 1995 and '96. Having had a year and a half after Senna's death and having put everything into building the team back up, and with '95 being such a defeat at the hands of Benetton, how did you get it all together for '96?

The whole '94 thing was tainted with this tragedy that happened with Roland Ratzenberger and Ayrton. I just thought it was complicated and it turned out in a controversial way so let's start again in 1995. Let's see how I can do. I'm going to start off the year as potentially the challenger to Michael Schumacher so let's see how I can do from the beginning to the end of a season. And I threw myself into it with everything I had. But we were outsmarted by Benetton. To be honest, tactically we were way behind them. We were made to look ridiculous. Some of them were my mistakes and some of them were just bad luck as well.

So how did you reset over the winter?

I think I took a lot on myself and I was also slightly naive in playing the game against Michael in the press and so forth. I turned it into a bit of a laugh and it actually backfired in my face because the press sometimes doesn't have a sense of humour. And, of course, they're after making things controversial. So, it's all great to do well but when you're not doing well you become the first in the line when it comes to getting slapped with a wet fish. I didn't take that defeat in '95 very well. I didn't have the confidence in myself and so the roof caved in emotionally and it all came down on top of me. But once it had, once we got beaten and the Japanese Grand Prix at Suzuka was done I thought, thank God! That's done. It doesn't matter any more.

And I can remember getting out of the car and we'd had the most shocking, awful weekend so we were thoroughly humiliated. David Coulthard, who was my team-mate that year, had a bad race, I had a bad race and we just got back to the changing room and there was Frank and Patrick Head. I don't know what they thought of me but I mean, it was catastrophe. I can say now that I honestly know what it means when people use the expression that they didn't know whether to laugh or cry. It's so awful, that actually it's funny but you want to cry at the same time.

It was such a low point. That was a proper low point. And then, I suppose, something in me said there's nothing I can do about that. It's done. You just go into the next race, which was the season finale in Adelaide, and I won with what I think is still the biggest winning margin in a Grand Prix. Two laps!

And then, of course, everyone's thinking, well, why didn't you just do that earlier? So you have this relationship with fate where you sometimes have to ask what is going on. A lot of this stuff is out of your control.

So I got a bit of luck at the end of the season, I got the race win and then I went and saw Mary Spillane. I'd seen a piece on TV with Mary, who was a political adviser, and she had started coming to some races with me in '95. Actually, it was a good example of how everything I did went wrong that year. Mary had come in to advise me on how to cope with the press, but then this mate of mine dropped the news that Damon's got this media adviser and so the press made a big story out of it. Well, gee, thanks.

But I went to see Mary after the season, and what she did was to give me a few key tips and put me on the right track. She just taught me to separate everything and to say, OK, that's not important, don't get involved in that. Focus on this instead. I'd never had anything like that. I'd gone from being someone who was just in the background struggling to get into Formula 1, to suddenly being in Formula 1 and being on the front line of being Britain's next great hope for winning a Grand Prix and a World Championship. I'd read the papers, I thought I knew how it worked, but once you become the focal point of all that power then you just feel like the cat and the mouse. And you're the mouse.

So, she just gave me some simple rules and I stuck to them and it just made life a whole lot easier. And she actually was really crucial in helping me cope with the pressures of being in the media spotlight. I wrote to her after I wrote my book and I thanked her because I was going to title it, 'Save it for the book', because that's what she said to me. I'd sit there and say this is a problem, that's a problem, and she'd just say, 'Save it for the book.' I thought that was great. That was one of the best bits of advice. You have to get from

A to B without getting destroyed by digging yourself in.

It put a spotlight on the fact that this is a game being played and it's a media game. They have to make a story. You have to be really careful with what ammunition you give them. You have to give them a story, but you have to give them a positive story. You have an opportunity to actually say what you want them to write and if you give them ambiguous messages or distracting messages or you try to be funny, when it doesn't work then you're playing with fire.

You were loved by the British people. I remember in 1996 you were on your way to winning the World Championship and then three-quarters of the way through the season you get the news that you're not going to be retained by Williams for the next year. I recall the press seemed to be very much in your corner over that. It certainly seemed like it to me, but I was only 15.

Well *Autosport* certainly wasn't. It was their front cover story! It really is a case that you learn you're sacked when you read it in the paper. I didn't know if it was a made-up story, but it was true.

What did you do?

I was furious!

And in the middle of your run for the championship, too.

I asked Williams and they said it wasn't true. But it was. So… thanks guys. You know?

Did that take the shine off the title?

Oh yeah. Completely. I mean, for me, I just thought OK I'm sick of this. I thought the rules were like this: we will let you do your best and if you're good at your job and you deliver then you're going to keep the job. I thought the only thing I can do is just get the championship. Forget all the rest of it. It's beyond my control. Following the championship, I can stake my claim. So to be told that even winning the championship is not good enough really soured my faith in Formula 1 as a sport.

After that I just thought, OK, there is something not right with this system.

You persevered for another three years but at the end of 1999 I remember the line was you said you were mentally fatigued. How tired were you at the end of those two years with Jordan?

Again, it was a relentless battle off the track with the business end of things and I found it very hard. I just found it disheartening and demoralising. I was so sick of it. Even when you're with the team you're having the carpet pulled from under you the whole time. I mean, the whole time. You know, I've been through it. I did my best. I was a test driver, I got promoted and I'm ever so grateful to Williams for everything they did but they dropped me at the moment of my greatest triumph, or in fact just before. And then I went to these other teams where they were constantly trying to undermine me the whole time and I just thought I'm sick of this. I am so sick of this. I'm going to get out. I've had enough.

I enjoyed the driving but I was 39. I'd done enough laps, so I got out at the right time. I mean I would have liked to have got out earlier, but I couldn't because of contractual negotiations.

And then you kind of disappeared for a while.

Ah, no. I didn't disappear. I just didn't go back to Formula 1.

You weren't around in terms of public consciousness, then, shall we say? What happened in those years afterwards? Did you enjoy not racing?

Yeah. I wanted to completely reset myself because actually one of the big motivations for wanting to succeed, quite apart from loving racing and wanting to win, was the emotional baggage from when my dad died. My dad was a very successful person and then everything was lost when he died. My mum lost a lot of the social life she had and the opportunities she had and I just said, well, if my dad could do it then I can do it for my family and for her as well. Which I did. And so a lot of it was about recovering something that I felt was taken from us.

It was like I had completed some sort of cycle but what I didn't realise was there was a whole lot of emotional stuff which hadn't been dealt with. I'd been paddling my canoe upstream for so long that I'd never really dealt with what I'd paddled through. When you get to the end, you get to that place where you can just meander and think for a minute, when you're not constantly on a mission. A lot of things catch up with you. And so, I had to deal with all of that. I went through quite a serious period of confusion, I would say.

I just wanted, simply, to protect my family. I wanted to be able to give them the life I didn't get from my dad. To be able to be there with them. But always in the back of my mind I was like, will I live longer than my dad? My dad died when he was 46 and I stopped racing when I was 39 going on 40. So there's this thing telling me I've just got to live longer than he did. I had this kind of ogre lurking in the back of my mind. But I didn't want the same thing to happen again and that was also part of why I stopped racing because I just didn't want to put my family through what I went through.

You talk about completing that circle. Was it your circle to complete or was it your dad's circle? Was it then that you could step out and find where your circle starts?

You see, the thing is there was no obligation for me to do that. It was purely my own creation, my own idea. But you do. Young people take responsibility for the world and as you grow you realise there's actually kind of an ego in that because it sort of implies that you are that important to the world. Eventually you realise it's not my responsibility. We all have our own responsibilities, but they're limited. And so, there was a lot of catching up to do and also realising what I put myself through, along with being grateful to myself and recognising that I had taken on an enormous challenge. And that I had succeeded, actually, because I'd come out ahead. I was still in one piece and I could be there for my family.

That notion of completing circles, in 1994 when you won the British Grand Prix, Jim Bamber did a cartoon in Autosport *of you stepping out of your father's enormous shadow. Did you feel that was something you needed to do?*

You know, these are people's ideas that they have. I was always myself. But you can't escape other people's expectations and other people's imagined realities. There's nothing you can do about that. You can't change that. You can say it as many times as you like but ultimately it's in people's heads and they see it that way.

You know, what if actually I wasn't out there racing for everyone else? It's seen that you're racing for Great Britain. I wasn't. I was doing it for myself. Me first. My family first, actually. And I understand you really want me to do well and I understand that it would be great and I would love for us all to share that. But I am not doing it for Team GB.

You are presented in a certain way and so you are having to deal the whole time with society's expectations.

And is that why it was so hard afterwards?

I just felt the whole thing, or at least a lot of it, was phoney. I didn't want anything phoney. I wanted a real life. But then you try and form relationships outside of the sport when you've become a famous person. When you're presented as that, all the time it is reflected back at you. So then you are faced with trying to have a normal conversation with anybody about anything without it becoming about Formula 1. And that is really difficult. So, you can feel isolated.

Now, I sound like I'm complaining and I'm not at all. I've been through all of this, I've written my book and I've explained what I've been through. But Formula 1 has blessed my life and it's blighted my life. There is yin and yang involved. It's a very powerful, potent force. There's nowhere you can go in the world that doesn't mention Formula 1. And I was born into that so in my very earliest photographs I'm surrounded by Formula 1 drivers at my christening and my whole life has been foreshadowed.

You talk about getting out from the shadow, but what shadow? Formula 1 or Graham Hill? Graham Hill wasn't a shadow to me. Graham Hill was a hero. I wasn't trying to bury my dad. I was trying to honour him. You know? And this is the problem people have. They see it completely the wrong way around.

Why did I carry the same crash helmet? Because I was proud of him. Not because I wanted to beat him. Fuck that. I wanted to add to his legacy.

I joke with Jackie Stewart that he's got three World Championships, but the Hills have got three as well. We might have had to do it as father and son, but we still got three World Championships.

Having had this bubble of Formula 1 frame your life, how hard was it getting used to the real world?

Well, one of the things that happened, I suppose, was that my son Josh wanted to be a racing driver. So when he turned around and said, 'Dad I want to be a racing driver', at age 16, 10 years behind the curve, it was a bit of a moment. You think you've escaped and then suddenly you're sucked back into the whirlpool. Obviously I'd do anything for my kids, but there has to be 100 percent commitment for something like this. So we went through all the tests and the trials and I could tell he just wanted to know how good he was, and he was good. He had talent. But ultimately he made the right decision, I think. He just said it's not the thing for him.

I feel good in that he's found what he likes in life. And also that, in a way, he's broken away from a Formula 1 culture that can be overwhelming. It's not for everybody.

In following that path with him, though, I ended up going to races and I started to literally go back to my very beginnings, my roots as a racing driver myself and in a way it gave me a perspective on me. I could watch him and I could see how people might have seen me. I watched his development and got a job with Sky because I thought if he's going to go all the way I need to relearn all the stuff I'd missed out on in Formula 1 after I retired, so that I'm prepared to help him because, clearly, my dad wasn't there to help me.

It was another strong emotional revisiting, but it was interesting coming back to Formula 1 because I was standing there watching these guys go through the motions and I'm thinking, you can't see what's going on. You guys, in Formula 1, you're in the eye of the storm. You can't see out. I was watching myself watching them and through that I was able to watch myself in that situation through older eyes. I've learned a lot. It's been interesting as I've gone through the whole spectrum, from someone aspiring to Formula 1 to going to the races as a fan, I've been involved in the racing, I've won a championship and I've come out the other end and now I've gone back.

And now I'm looking down, if you like, from my more elderly standpoint and I'm looking back at these guys coming up and going through this loop. They will go through all the same things when they stop racing. It's going to be really difficult for a lot of them. Because they are going to have to come to terms with the person that they are when they are a Grand Prix driver and the fact that they will want to be that person all the time. But they can't be.

Do you have to relearn who you are once the racing ends?

I think it might affect some people more than others. There's an adjustment, definitely. Because people adjust to you differently, too. You can't demand the same attention that you had as a driver. You are no longer relevant to the story. You're a past driver, an ex-driver. You're someone who's not actually doing it now. And you may have a lot of experience and you might have a lot to say about it, but if you're not actually doing it, is anyone interested?

Is there a big feeling of rejection or is it just a sort of realignment of what your reality is?

It's a big change to go from one thing to the next very quickly. So... playing golf is good. You can carry on playing until you're 70. You've got the seniors tour and you can still whack a ball. The idea of a seniors tour for racing is just ridiculous though because it is about being young and about committing 100 percent.

Jean-Claude Killy, the great French skier, won his Olympic gold medals and never went skiing again. Never even went for a recreational ski. He said, the thing is, you can't go back and do it less than you were able to do it. It is a kind of heartbreak when you realise you can't get back to being that good again. I got to my limit and I occasionally had days of inspiration, but I could never do it consistently. And that was that. You know?

Of all the things I'd say that gave me the greatest satisfaction it was that actually I reached my maximum potential in a racing car and I could say that my max potential was at least as good and maybe slightly better sometimes than some of the best guys in racing. I can be proud of that. I couldn't do it as many times as they could or for as long, but then I didn't get into racing until I was 33. I lost a lot of time, maybe because of what happened to my dad. So all the best years, I don't know.

That's my perspective on my experience.

I'm not dead. I'm not broken. You know, I survived it. And I can be proud of that. Not that I've been lucky, but you get to be thankful for everything after a bit. You're thankful for your own story. It's just different. It's not the fairytale story, it's a different story.

And it wouldn't have happened if I hadn't kept trying. Whatever you put yourself through, you've only got yourself to blame really.

Dario Franchitti

'I had no passion for it. It had completely gone. I was just doing a job. I wanted to enjoy it, but... I was scared of it. I was scared of getting in the car. But I didn't know what else to do.'

F our Indycar championships, three Indy 500 wins, 31 race victories and over 90 podiums. Statistically, George Dario Marino Franchitti is one of the all-time greatest drivers in the history of American open-wheel competition. But the scale of his achievements and his standing in his sport extend far beyond simple numbers. At a time when the Indycar paddock became a place of unity and brotherhood, Dario became its *de facto* figurehead. Its leader. And at its darkest moments, its empathetic, grounded and steadfast rock.

Born in West Lothian, Scotland, in 1973, Franchitti, like many of his compatriots, owed much in his early career to the guidance of touring car ace David Leslie. Franchitti won Scottish and British karting championships before progressing quickly through entry-level open-wheel series to arrive in British Formula 3 in 1994. But unfortunately for him, the timing coincided with the most dominant display ever seen in the Formula 1 feeder as Jan Magnussen rewrote the history books, outgunning the records set by Ayrton Senna over a decade before.

The Scot's attentions moved to the German and International Touring Car championships for 1995, as part of the Mercedes AMG operation under Norbert Haug. But in 1997 his big break came with Hogan Racing in America's CART (Champ Car) Series. So impressed was the American open-wheel community with the Scot's immediate impact that he was signed to race for Team Green in 1998, thus beginning his streak at the very top of his sport.

Franchitti flirted with other spheres of racing. In Formula 1 he tested for the

Jaguar team and turned down an offer to become McLaren's test driver. He proved successful in sportscars, winning the 24 Hours of Daytona in 2008, but made an ill-fated switch to NASCAR that year. However, Indycar (the successor series to CART) was where he discovered his richest vein of form. He was Indycar champion in 2007, 2009, 2010 and 2011, and Indy 500 winner in 2007, 2010 and 2012.

But his time at the top of motor racing was book-ended by tragedy as the deaths of his friends Greg Moore in 1999 and Dan Wheldon in 2011 shook his sport to its core. The Scot felt the pain most keenly of all. Accidents, too, blighted him both physically and mentally, the truest extent of their effects not being fully realised until many years later, after a career-ending crash in 2013.

It is only now, with the passage of time, that he can look back, reflect and fully appreciate the hand that he was dealt and the bravery with which he played it.

I thought about three different things. First there was Formula 3 and getting my arse kicked by Jan Magnussen. I won the first race and he won the next 15! That taught me a lot. Then later in my career, making the move to NASCAR, massively out of my depth, that was challenging. But neither were life-changing.

So, for me, I think the one thing, the one time, the one situation that really hit me the hardest was at the end of 1999, into 2000. That was the point where I grew up very quickly. Up to then it's all been fun. There are no consequences. You just get to drive fast cars, travel the world, have a great time and get paid good money for it.

And then Greg died. And it was just devastating. He was my best mate. I remember I went back to Beverly Hills and I just sat in the room in floods of tears. Just absolutely crushed.

I went to his funeral and I was in a daze. I was really lucky because my boss at the time, Barry Green, is a good man. I said, 'Alright Barry, I've got no interest in driving the car. I don't want to be near a car.' And he said, 'Fine. That's fine mate. You come find me and you come back when you're ready.'

So all through the winter my team-mate Paul Tracy did all the testing and I finally got back in the car at spring training at Homestead and at the end of what I think was the first day the right rear spindle broke as I turned into Turn 3 on the oval. The car went round, across the grass on the inside then went up and hit the wall. As did my head. I've got the helmet at home and there's concrete still in it where it hit the wall. So I've hit the wall and I've got a broken pelvis and a massive head injury, although I didn't realise at the time it was as severe as it was.

And that sets the scene for what happened next.

When Greg died I had to ask the question of whether I wanted to drive a racing car again. But I thought, yeah, I think so. So I did it and then the next time I'm in the car this happens. But I was back in the car three weeks later, broken pelvis and all, which I really would not recommend! Having the car dropped off the jacks when your pelvis is in three pieces is really not enjoyable.

And then the next two years were just shit: dealing with the head injury and really not enjoying driving racing cars because I couldn't concentrate because of the head injury, my balance was screwed up and it was just a really shit time. It was no fun. I would have given up but I didn't know what else to do. I had no passion for it. It had completely gone. I was just doing a job. I wanted to enjoy it, but... I was scared of it. I was scared of getting in the car. But I didn't know what else to do.

There were times when I could go out in the car and throw a lap together. I broke the lap record at Road America in the August, but I just found no joy in it.

My trainer, who I worked with at Mercedes, Tony Mathis, he put me back together again when I had that accident and helped me with rehab, and then his son Tino came over to the US to get me back to full fitness and they said, 'Right, we're going out running at nine o'clock in the morning', and I was like, 'Yeah... no.' He showed up for two months and I didn't do anything. I wasn't training. I was done.

But I kept thinking, and I think what finally got me past it was the thought that maybe if I can get through this it will get better.

When you first came to the States, what made you and Greg such firm friends?

Norbert Haug and I used to sit together after the DTM races on a Sunday and have a beer and we used to watch the Indycar races. I just remember thinking, who is this guy? Because the first race he did at Homestead, I can't remember what had happened but he was a few laps down and he just smoked the field. He was brilliant. It was just unbelievable. And it really was a case of, who is this kid? And this guy gets out of the car with his little round glasses and you're shocked. That was him?

So when I went to Homestead for my first Indycar test he was there and I walked up and introduced myself. And we just hit it off. It was 1997 that we started to become mates, touring the world and hanging out. I didn't go home for six months. We just travelled around the world, chased women, drove racing cars.

What made him so good?

He was fearless, of course. But he had an ability to drive a car, a feel for the car. Those cars, at the time, you couldn't get away with driving them with a lot of yaw. If they snapped once and you didn't catch it, the second snap was going to hurt. But he had this ability to run the thing sideways. You look back now, you watch the footage of him racing, how he drove those cars and having driven them myself I still can't fully understand how he did what he did. I couldn't do what he did. It was incredible. He had a gift. He was a really good driver on road courses and street courses too, but his ability on an oval was above everybody.

And he was a great guy. He was just a cool dude. The reason all the Indycar drivers hang out together today and have this brotherhood is because of him. He brought it together, organised the parties. He was the catalyst. He showed that you didn't have to hate the guy outside of the car to beat him inside the car.

It does seem from the outside looking in that there was this amazing clique of you guys in the late '90s. You raced each other so hard but you were friends off the track.

Yeah. I remember that his dad, Ric, who I still speak to all the time actually, he was over in Scotland last year, top man, but he was worried. He said, 'You guys are all mates but you're supposed to be out there racing each other.'

Well, we were at Fontana in practice in 1998 and I was rocking up the straight and Greg came towing up behind me and I could see him out of Turn 2 come alongside me and he just chopped down right in front of me. And that made me laugh. I thought, well, OK, if that doesn't show Ric that there's on track and off track then I don't know what does.

But there was a big group of us, Tony Kanaan, Max Papis, there was a whole group of us that just became friends.

Does that make the racing more enjoyable? That you can go out there and you can push properly hard and take it right at the edge with somebody that you know and that you respect, in the knowledge that you're not going to do anything stupid with each other?

I enjoyed it because to me it was almost like going to the go-kart track with your mates. It was bragging rights afterwards like, I kicked your ass today or more often than not it was the others saying that. You had that enjoyment. It was a much nicer place to go racing. On the track the competition was just as fierce if not more so than Formula 1 or somewhere else because the dangers were higher as well. And I think maybe that danger is some of the reason that we all hung out because we realised that with what we were doing there had to be a level of respect. Because if not people could get hurt.

In terms of the wider picture of global motorsport at the time, the notion of safety was very high in everyone's mind. Indycar was then and is today still viewed as being a very dangerous sport. Was that something you guys felt?

At Fontana those cars would do over 250 miles per hour. Anytime you are doing those speeds, with no run-off and a concrete wall, you're aware of the danger. And the series did everything it could, but the danger was inherent in that style of racing. You go back to looking at those circuits where there was grass on the inside of the track and you ask today why something so simple would be missed. But the people were doing their best to make it safe.

But it was a dangerous thing. It still is.

Greg's accident. How did you first become aware of the severity of it?

I didn't know until the end of the race. Juan Pablo Montoya and I were fighting for the championship and I'd come into the weekend with a slim lead in the points. At my last pit stop there was a mistake with the right rear wheel and I lost a lap and we ended up on the same points, with him champion on count-back.

I didn't know any of this. I knew the fight was going on. Obviously I didn't know what the result was at the end. All I remember, and it's very vague, but it's the radio being a bit muted afterwards. And I was wondering what that was all about.

I came into the pits, got out of the car and my dad pulled me to one side and we walked along and he said, 'Son, I need to tell you something.' That was it.

What did you do, in that immediate moment?

I don't really remember. I remember walking back with my dad and one of the mechanics, Jack, who was a great pal of Greg's. We walked back to the truck.

Did they make you do any post-race media?

Nobody cared about the result. The team were fantastic. Again, it was Barry and all those guys. They just said, 'You do what you want.' But nobody cared about the championship. I think Adrian Fernandez won the race. I only know that because I saw a photograph in the book they made about Greg. But I couldn't have cared less about what happened that day as far as the championship and all that.

I just wanted to get out of there.

I got caught speeding that night on the way home, on the 10, driving back to Beverly Hills. Ashley [Judd, Dario's then-girlfriend and first wife] and I were in the car and I got pulled over and I just looked at the cop and said, 'Please, just give me a break. I've had a terrible day.' And he looked at me, and he did. He let me go.

Did you talk at all on that journey, or was it just silence?

I think it was silence. Shock. Just absolute shock.

You guys are always aware that the danger is there. But when it is suddenly this real, and so much worse than an injury, were you already asking questions about the future or was it too much of a haze?

I wanted nothing to do with driving racing cars or anything at that point. Straight away I thought, fuck this. Why are we doing this? Bollocks to it, basically. Forget it. I was very angry.

Out of the paddock, into the car and that's it…

Yep.

What did you do in the days afterwards?

Honestly? I don't remember. I think we might have stayed in LA and then gone to the funeral. I remember jumping on a plane to the funeral up in Vancouver and again just being in almost like a daze. The only way I can explain it is, you know when a bit of glass is dirty? Like when you're sitting on a train with dirty windows and everything comes at you through this slightly soft, dirty focus? It was like that. Everything was slightly opaque. It just didn't seem real.

Then, did we go to Scotland? Probably.

I was talking to Mario Andretti and he said that he couldn't bring himself to go to funerals of friends because it brought home the realities too much. Was there ever that fear for you, that this was really the reality of the sport you love and the life you lead?

It was more important for me to be there. You know, whatever effect that would have on me driving a race car didn't come into it. But, again, at that point if I never drove a race car again then I didn't really give a shit. I couldn't have cared less.

It was different when Dan's accident happened because we went to his funeral and his memorial service and then a couple of days later Tony Kanaan and I were back in the cars again at the Speedway testing the DW12. That was a very different reaction because it almost felt that we had a duty to Dan as he'd done all the testing with that car. They were trying to make the sport safer, so having lost him like that, of course you put yourself forward to make sure that all his work comes good in the end.

You're a decade older at that point, too. But back in 1999, as a young guy, how long did that feeling of not wanting to race last for? Because you guys dedicate your lives to getting in a car and driving fast. So to suddenly have this feeling of 'I don't want to be anywhere near a racing car', did you lose a sense of identity? If everything you'd dedicated your life to was suddenly something you didn't want to do...

So there's two things going on here. There's pre-Homestead accident and post-.

Pre-Homestead they really had to push to even get me to come and test the car. I wasn't dragged but I really wasn't very willing. And then afterwards, with a head injury, well I wasn't functioning clearly.

So who was it that managed to cajole you back into the car? Who was it that said, come on man, you need to get back on the bike?

It was probably Barry. And he wouldn't have forced me but I'm sure there was a little bit of the, 'We either do this or we are going to have to get someone else.' Understandably.

And then after that day the confusion sets in with a head injury that size because you don't think clearly and you get into emotional situations that you can't fully compute. But I couldn't tell you where my head was at when I went back to Homestead to do that test because the hit was so big that I've lost that memory.

Did that redouble your thoughts of, 'Well, fuck this, I'm done', in that the first time you got back into the car you had such a huge accident?

I don't know if it did because I got back in the car three weeks after the hit and I convinced Indycar's Dr Terry Trammell that I was alright. We did a test at Nazareth, the worst place to test a car in the winter time, and I remember I had to stand and do this bizarre pose that showed that my pelvis had healed. Of course it hadn't. But I held it together and just said, 'Yeah, yeah, I'm fine.'

So I went to Homestead and I did the race and I was terrible. But I was in there swinging. From that point on I was trying my best when I was in the car, I really was. I gave it everything I had... which wasn't very much at the time and I hate to say this but I really didn't want to be there. I just didn't know what else to do.

I was pretty low and I couldn't think clearly to get my way out of it because of what I'd done to my brain. There were small rays of sunshine but generally those 2000, 2001 seasons were just horrible. Just terrible, you know? Everything about them.

Did you know at the time how bad the head injury was?

No. I didn't know until probably after my last big accident when I started to understand what had gone on. It's like, you look at yourself at the time and you ask if you've forgotten how to drive. Well, no. But you know that you're no longer able to concentrate properly. You physically can't concentrate, your balance is shot, your thought process is all messed up.

If you imagine before, your brain and your actions had a direct route. Well, now whatever your brain is thinking has to pass through some old rusting cables and it messes it up.

And then, out of nowhere, I was offered a test with the Jaguar Formula 1 team.

Again, had I been thinking clearly, I probably would have never done that but I thought, yeah, I want to try that. So I showed up with a head injury and some other injuries going on in my back where I'd damaged the discs so I couldn't train my neck, which is really not what you want when you're testing a Formula 1 car and trying to show people what you can do. So, yeah, that didn't help.

Were you getting help at the time, either medical or psychological? I think it's fair to say that America's always been far more up on its counselling than the UK. There's still that machoism of men not seeking help that exists, whereas Stateside it seems that it's more accepted to seek help and guidance. Were you seeing anyone to help you deal with either losing Greg or your sudden shift in emotions and almost apathy towards racing?

I think they were really two separate things. What I was going through in 2000 and 2001 was more about the accident than about Greg. Greg's death took the passion away. It stole the enjoyment of racing from me. That sounds shit because obviously it was a far bigger deal. Personally, it was all much more than that. I'd lost my best friend.

But as far as just driving a racing car it was more about the head injury when I got behind the wheel. The difference between doing a good job and doing a great job, I always felt, came down to desire. You know? How much do you want to win? How much do you want to put into it? And at that time, the answer with hindsight was, well, not a lot. I couldn't do it.

As you said, you didn't know until much later that there was something physically wrong upstairs. Without that knowledge, did you start to think that the results weren't coming and you couldn't concentrate because you'd lost the passion? That one was the result of the other?

I didn't know what was going on. It just didn't make any sense to me.

For the first two seasons I'd been quicker than Paul Tracy, which isn't an easy thing to do. And then all of a sudden Paul is up front and I'm languishing at the back. And I didn't know why. So I tried harder and nothing would happen, so I'd try less and then I'd just give up. Balls to it, you know?

I've always taken racing really seriously and it hurts when it doesn't go well. And really, I'll think about it for weeks afterwards. But at that time, it just didn't bother me any more. I just hung my head and accepted it and walked away every weekend.

You talked about the closeness that you as a group of drivers shared. Did the other guys notice a change in you? Not just from a competitive perspective but from a personal one? Did they try and help you figure things out?

We all kind of helped each other deal with Greg's accident, but nobody understood what was happening with me after my own accident. I think they all just saw my results and thought I was having a slump. 'You'll be fine.' 'He'll be back.' That kind of stuff. But everybody is focused on their own job, and rightly so.

There were definitely some questions being asked though. Again, I go back to Barry Green and the people in the team and you have to say, wow, they were really supportive. There was never any question of whether they were going to hire me again, it was just OK we're doing another deal. How much do you want? They never had a doubt in me or a question in my abilities. If there was, Barry hid it really well.

How about those closest to you? Ashley, your dad, your brother? Did they notice a change in you?

This is interesting because my brother, Marino, and I discussed it afterwards, after I'd retired. I said to him that I thought my personality had completely changed after my 2000 accident. And he said that he hadn't noticed it. And I just said that in here, in my head, it's a lot different. It's a lot more serious. Whether that was Greg's accident, understanding more about life or whether it was my accident I don't know, but I had changed a lot. But he said he didn't really notice. And I'm closest to my brother. Of anybody.

As far as Ashley? I think she bore the brunt of the frustration. Perhaps what really took its toll on her was the ability that my mood had to swing between the enormous frustration I was feeling, to really not giving a shit. I'd get angry, but getting angry wasn't working. But then at the same time I'm dealing with this head injury I didn't know I had, and so nothing was wired up properly and my reactions could be completely out of context. For her to deal with that must have been pretty hard.

On the positive side you develop a coping mechanism. You start thinking about how you go about life. I was quite a cerebral driver and I gave a lot of thought to what I was doing. I was never one of those guys like Scott Dixon who could be sitting on the phone, you know, doing some kind of deal with someone and just say, 'Right, got to go mate', click, phone off, in the car, whomp. Straight on it. I couldn't do that. I had to be really focused. So I learned a lot about the mental side from that. And I learned a lot, I think, about determination and to just dig in. And I think, at some point, that part of me gave me the confidence to think, well, it's going to get better. If I can just get through this, it'll start being fun again.

And when did it?

In 2002. We won some races. The cars were really good fun to drive and I had started to put some distance between Greg's accident and going racing. Although I didn't know it, my head injury had gone a long way towards healing itself and so I started to feel a wee bit more like myself in the car. Not fully. Not fully, but, you know, getting back to it.

Then we went and did the deal to go to the IRL which, I think in hindsight we may like to call a pragmatic deal. And I had to go and learn something new. And I struggled. I quickly discovered after the accident that I was really struggling to learn something new. Again, I was getting back to my old self in a CART, but when I threw myself into something new whether it was an Indycar or a Formula 1 car, I wasn't as adaptable as I'd once been. And it was like that for a while.

So I thought, oh crikey, this is going to be a big learning curve. I'd driven the Indy 500 in 2002 and enjoyed the race. I didn't enjoy driving the car mind you. And then I broke my back riding a motorbike, testing my new boss Michael Andretti's patience. I was out for a year, just as I'd started to build momentum again to get back on track. Christ.

What carries you through all that? Because it's so easy for any of us to get into a place where we hit borderline depressive states if things aren't going right. Especially if, just as things start to get good again, we get knocked back. How did you, or indeed do you, manage to stop yourself from getting into a low place?

I think at that point I was worried about my job. Barry had sold the team to Michael Andretti, I'd broken my back, which I'd like to point out wasn't my fault as the bike I was on essentially shit itself, sprayed a bunch of oil onto the back tyre and off I went, but it was not an ideal situation. They would have been well within their rights to send me down the road.

And so I had two big concerns. The first was getting let go by the team and the second was what would happen with my back. Dr Trammell's telling me I'd need to have an operation if I ever wanted to drive a racing car again. I said, 'Are you sure?' And he said, 'Well you know, we'll give you 10 weeks to let it heal but if it doesn't heal properly then we are going to have to operate.'

So I suddenly hit this moment of thinking, well, do I want to keep driving racing cars? And that's when it really sunk in. Yes. Yes, I do. And that's when I really started to get my passion back for this thing.

So, and this will show you the mind of a racing driver I guess, the 10 weeks came and went and Dr Trammell says to me, 'Well, it's as good as it's going to get.' So me, being a racing driver, takes that as being great, OK, we're good to go. So I phoned Michael Andretti and told him we were good for Pike's Peak that weekend, Pike's Peak not being the famous hillclimb you might be thinking of, but a one-mile oval. And I get in the car and despite everything in my back still squelching and crunching, and despite doing no training for three months because I physically couldn't, I did the race and finished fourth.

So the next morning I was back in Indy, pre-flighting my helicopter and I'm hanging off the main rotor hub when the phone rings and it's Julian Jacobi, my manager.

'Dario...'

'Oh hey Julian!'

'What are you doing?'

'Oh I'm pre-flighting my helicopter.'

'No,' he said. 'What are you doing?'

'What do you mean, Julian?'

'I've just had your very irate wife on the phone, who's had an irate Dr Trammell on the phone, who wants to know what the hell you're doing.'

'What do you mean, Julian?'

'Trammell told you under no circumstances to go near a racing car and you did a race this weekend.'

And so that's when that whole thing started again. I had to get the operation done and I was out of the car for a year. That kind of reset me.

Did you feel like a new man after that? To have the time away from racing, to rebuild your body and to actually get back to a place where you wanted to be in the car?

Do you know what? It probably did. The thing was I got back in the car and my team-mates were Tony Kanaan, Dan Wheldon and Bryan Herta, so it was a fun place to go back to. Again, it wasn't easy. I had to learn the cars, adapt and all that stuff, but I started to feel at that point that I was getting my passion for driving a racing car back and I was starting to enjoy it and thinking, thank God I didn't throw the towel in three years ago.

So, to take it kind of full circle I guess. Towards the end of your career you had to live through those same two things again. To have to deal with what happened in Vegas and Dan Wheldon's death, first of all. You're a decade older, but was there anything from what had happened before with Greg that helped you through what happened with Dan? Was it harder because it had happened to you before? Or, and it can't have been easy in any way, but in an odd way was it somewhat easier because you'd experienced it before?

There was still that feeling of total devastation. Dan and I were good pals. But if I'm honest, the feeling really was one of, what a waste. Because he had two young boys, he was married to Susie, he had a great family life and it was only getting better. He'd had a fucking tough time professionally and he'd come through it so well, he'd won Indy and he'd signed the deal with Andretti and it was just such a waste.

And what we did, all my mates from Scotland who were good mates with Dan, they were all in Vegas, and we all just went out and got shitfaced. And bit by bit, most of the Indycar paddock ended up in this one bar. There were three of us to start with and by the end there were 200-plus people and we just had a little wake. But I never hit that point that I had with Greg where I didn't want to get in the car again. It was a different point in my life. I was able to deal with it better and I felt an obligation to get back in the car quickly.

Did the fact that you guys all got back in again to complete those laps help at all? That you had to get back on the bike straight away? Because I remember the footage of you getting strapped back in, in floods of tears, and it was harrowing watching it.

No. No, no, no. It didn't help me. At all.

How did you drive those laps?

I don't know. I couldn't see.

Do you know, this will maybe sound cheesy, but the way you got through that was your mates. You know, we were talking each other through it, myself, Dixon, Marco Andretti, Tony. I don't think I can remember a time when there was a starker feeling of this being real life. We played a game of racing cars but it had very real consequences. At the time I was married but I didn't have family and my mindset had changed. I would put myself through whatever I had to, to win. I'd become much more aggressive. And I wanted to get back in the car. It wasn't going to change what had happened to Dan or how I felt about it. It was just a different mindset. As you said, a decade on.

And then obviously the accident that brought an end to it all for you. Did you know, now with the hindsight of the other head injury you'd had, that this was really serious?

I really don't remember. I lost five or so weeks of my memory.

I do remember lying in hospital thinking this is different. I'd had an accident at Goodwood as well which was one of the most obvious ones they cited as being a contributor to the severity of my head injury, but there were a lot they didn't know about either. But it felt different. And this may make some sense, it may not, but the reaction of the doctors was different. Trammell, Steve Olvey, before we'd have been wondering how quickly they could scoop me up and get me back in a car. And I was still in that place, but they were different, they clearly knew more than I did in the early stages of recovery. And that was that.

At that point I was just happy to be alive. My mindset was that I was alive, and a lot of my mates hadn't been so fortunate. So when they told me it was over, I pretty much just accepted it. I'd had a good run.

Occasionally I miss it a little bit. But I'm in my mid-40s, so I'd be tailing off anyway.

How much do you think, then, that those hard years after Greg and the head injury you sustained, framed the shape of the character you think you've become?

I think that period taught me the resilience to get through the shit and the tough times in and out of the car, and in life. And when the success came... well winning one championship is difficult. But to win two more back to back, then finally a fourth, each one becomes even more difficult because there's a danger that you become relaxed. I didn't want to let it go because I knew what 2000 had felt like. I was still hungry for the next one and the next one and every race afterwards. And I think that's how it helped me.

I realised that I enjoyed driving racing cars. But I loved winning.

And to have lost the love, to have been willing to walk away from it all... when that championship came, did it mean all the more?

It was bittersweet. When I won the championship in Chicago they stopped me on the back straight while they set up the stage for the championship celebration on the main straight in front of the grandstands. I remember sitting there in the car and I lost my shit. I just completely fell apart thinking about all that had happened, all my family had endured, all I'd gone through and then thinking about my pal Greg. Thinking about my mate. And the safety crew showed up and I'm in floods of tears and I'm like, 'Oh hey, alright boys!' Because in Indycar, the safety crew are the same at every race. These are the guys that had actually pulled me out of crashes. It was all too much. They understood.

You miss your mates all the time. But those kinds of situations make it all the more poignant.

Derek Bell

'I did everything I could… You give your all. All the time. And I think in many ways, as racers, this is something that helps us. Our careers can help us through moments we would otherwise have found difficult.'

Derek Bell's name is synonymous with success in sportscars and endurance racing. In a career spanning five decades, this affable English gentleman won Le Mans five times, the Daytona 24 Hours three times, the World Sportscar Championship twice and, so it is said, took so many victories in sportscars that he struggles to recall them all.

But Bell never set out to be an endurance racer. Growing up within earshot of the Goodwood race track in southern England, it was open-wheel single-seaters and Formula 1 that held the greatest allure to the aspiring racer. And it was to Formula 1 that he ascended. Quickly.

With some of the biggest teams in racing clamouring for his signature, it was for the greatest name of all that he duly agreed terms. And so it was that, quite incredibly, within four years of his first competitive motor race, Derek Bell made his Formula 1 Grand Prix début for Enzo Ferrari. At the Italian Grand Prix.

Warnings from peers that *Il Commendatore* had ruined as many careers as he had launched were soon realised, however, the termination of his relationship with the Scuderia forming the first in a series of gut punches that shattered his dreams of racing in Formula 1 and looked set to derail his career completely.

Yet these early days and disappointments fashioned the nature of his character and led him to try new opportunities and take new chances. Ultimately it was to lead him to a path on which he created not only his name but his legend as one of the all-time greats, and one of the Princes of Le Mans.

People don't like to dwell on the hard things, they tend to get straight into talking about their successes. People don't realise that every single driver you've ever seen in your life has had good times and bad. The stories are endless. Everybody has a story.

So how and why did you want to get into racing?

Well, I have always lived in Pagham, which is on the south coast in England and is actually so close to Goodwood that from my garden I can see the grandstands for the horse track across the downs. From the age of nine I was always out on the farm, driving tractors. We never really went on holidays as we spent our time harvesting and all the rest of it, so I would be out on the farm hoeing sugar beet or picking potatoes and all the while I could hear the cars going around Goodwood, and in those days you had Formula 1 cars testing there. You could hear every gear change.

So I grew up with the sound of racing cars, and to get close to it I joined the Bognor Regis Motor Club and through that I started marshalling at Goodwood. I was actually marshalling the day Stirling Moss had his big crash. I was two corners earlier. I was at Madgwick and he crashed down at Fordwater. That was unbelievable, because he was my hero and always will be.

I used to fantasise about racing when I was ploughing or cultivating or whatever it was and I'd hear those cars. I used to dream of one day driving at Goodwood, never mind go on to race at other tracks and become quite proficient. That was actually how it all started.

You were successful from the off and your rate of progression was incredible. From your racing début in a Lotus Seven in 1964 you were racing Formula 3 in '65 and Formula 2 in '67. Did it come easily to you?

I'd applied to the Cooper racing school when I was 17 but they'd written back and said that you needed to hold a driving licence for a year before you could come along and learn, which is ironic given the age they all start at now. But they were bloody good because, when the school was disbanded a year later, they wrote back to me and returned the five pounds deposit I had given them when I'd originally applied.

It would have been 1960 or '61 that I was at the Royal Agricultural College in

Cirencester, learning how to be a farmer. Of course, you end up with like-minded people and my group of friends were all racing enthusiasts and so me and my friend decided to go to the Jim Russell racing school which was all the way over in Norfolk. That's a good 180 miles from home, but we'd seen the advertisement in *Autosport* magazine and so we went all the way to Norfolk once every month or six weeks and I did my 10 quid. I was earning 20 quid a week back then, but 10 pounds would give you tuition on a particular corner and then you put it all together and paid a pound a lap to go around the whole course.

You'd gradually increase your revs. So you'd be allowed to do 10 laps at 4,500rpm, then 10 laps at 5,000, 10 laps at 5,500 and so on upwards, but of course I couldn't afford to do it all at the same time. So I'd go all that way, stay at a pub, do my 10 or 20 quid and then bugger off home before going back to do it all over again.

In the end I got up to about 8,000rpm in their Formula Junior car, a Lotus 18, and Jim Russell lined the eight of us up and asked who'd been driving this car, and pointed at the one I'd been driving. I was struck with an awful feeling of, 'Oh shit, that was me', because I'd only ever heard him give people a bollocking. Anyway I put my hand up and admitted that it was me, and in front of everyone he just waxed lyrical about my future.

Well, I didn't have a clue. I didn't know whether I'd been driving well or not, I just drove the way I could. But Jim stood there and said that he guaranteed I would be in a factory team within a year.

So I knew then that I had to go and buy a car to prove my ability. I couldn't just walk into Cooper or somewhere like that and ask them to put me in a car. And that was it. I came home and my old man, my stepfather, the Colonel, the dear man, he just asked me how it had all gone. Well, I was like a dog with two dicks and I told him what had been said and he told me that if I could prove to him that I had the ability then he would help me, and that was that.

Two years later a chap by the name of John Penfold came to sell us some farm machinery and we got talking and decided to build a Lotus Seven together. He was very good with budgets and suchlike. I was just a driver. We started building it in 1963 and finished it the night before the race, my first race, at Goodwood in 1964. Which I won. In the pouring rain.

I've still got the leather-bound travel clock that I won for taking victory in that race, inscribed to Derek Bell, winner, Goodwood, 66.48mph, 13th March 1964. It's unbelievable when you think about it. I'm looking at it right now. It's sitting alongside my Le Mans trophies. Looks a little bit overwhelmed. But we all start somewhere.

Was Formula 1 the goal for you?

Absolutely. For me it was the ultimate. Those days of Formula 3, Formula 2 and Formula 1 were just bloody wonderful. It was a natural progression. Now you've got so many different championships that you wouldn't know how to advise a kid on the best way forward. In our day it was much more straightforward. I guess there were fewer kids around in those days, much less publicity and fewer teams, so it was much quieter working behind the scenes before anybody really found out you were doing it. Plus, no TV really.

And back in those days the championships were far more interchangeable. Today you do a season of Formula 3 or Formula 2 and do little else. Certainly when you get to Formula 1, that is your sole racing focus. But back then you'd all do a bit of everything. You'd have Formula 1 drivers doing Formula 2 races, Formula 3 drivers getting the nod for a Formula 2 race or even Formula 1. All sorts.

Oh yes. It was absolutely remarkable. My first international Formula 2 race was at Barcelona in 1968 and I didn't qualify. The next race was at Hockenheim, which of course was the race where Jim Clark was killed. Today people can't believe that these Formula 1 drivers would be happy to come back and race against us in Formula 2, but they were. Actually, Jim wasn't at all happy that day because he could have been at the BOAC 1000 at Brands Hatch, but that was part of his deal with Lotus.

I mean, in my third Formula 2 race, at Thruxton, I was on the podium next to Jochen Rindt and Piers Courage. It's amazing when you think about it because there I am in Formula 2 and you just think, hell, I'm on the podium with two of the greatest drivers in the world. You got in amongst these guys and it was such a wonderful way to see someone's ability and how they handled themselves on track. There wasn't the bitterness that exists now. We revered these drivers and so respected the fact that they came down to potentially get the chance of being shafted by us. It was a hell of a risk for them, but they just loved racing.

You talked about 1968 and starting in Formula 2, but of course you made your Formula 1 début that year too, and for Ferrari at Monza, no less. The pressure must have been tremendous.

It is so strange. I guess it is because I'm getting older but sometimes it seems a bit surreal. I have a fabulous photograph of Enzo and I talking at the back of the garages at Monza, and it just seems so amazing to think that I knew him. He'd pick me up at the hotel and we'd go out for dinner. I never saw the evil side of him that people spoke about. To me he was a gentleman, but oddly enough someone who was at that time also holding me back. Even qualifying for my second race at the United States Grand Prix he wouldn't let me go out and do that many laps.

After the Italian Grand Prix I came across to do the US Grand Prix at Watkins Glen. It was my first ever foray to America, and I remember staying at the Glen Motor Court hotel up on the hill. We'd been flown in by helicopter because there were 80,000 wild American fans trying to use the only road to the track, but that was part of the amazing experience of racing in Formula 1.

But then you get told you were going to get two laps, no timed laps, just a couple of laps, to go, bed in pads and discs and nothing else. Come in and out of the pitlane, keep out of Chris Amon's way and learn the track. My only job was to go out and not make any mistakes so they could report back to *Il Commendatore* that I'd had a great race and was learning. They were using me as a test driver. I subsequently found out that they were trialling lots of different materials in the engines they were putting in my car, which it now seems is why they kept blowing up. But it was an experience and I wouldn't have missed it for the world.

Ken Tyrrell, Jackie Stewart, David Yorke, John Wyer… they all said Ferrari will destroy your career. But, to me, it's the greatest thing I ever did. To drive for the greatest name in racing is unbelievable.

This is a team that gave you not only your Formula 1 début but also a start at Le Mans two years later.

That's right! It's amazing that it happened to me, really. My first professional race for Ferrari was at Monza in the Lotteria Formula 2 and I got pole position somehow. And from there they put me in my first Formula 1 test. And at the same time I was testing with John Cooper as he was interested in putting me in his Formula 1 team, so I was commuting back and forward between Italy and England before I'd agreed to drive for Ferrari. But Cooper was onto me anyway at that point and tried to apply some pressure. Major Owens said, 'We're offering you Formula 1 and Ferrari is only offering you Formula 2', and I said, 'Sure, but have you seen your Formula 1 car?'

In the end I'm so glad I made that decision.

Also the deal wasn't fabulous. Cooper had generously offered me five pounds payment. They believed that because my dream was to race in Formula 1, I'd take anything. But I went back to Ferrari and we did the deal on a handshake. I didn't actually sign anything until after that first Formula 2 race, where I was on pole. The race itself saw a monumental accident involving four or five of us, including three factory Ferraris and my personal Brabham that Peter Westbury was driving. It was caused by me but I'd actually been hit up the arse and so I know it wasn't actually my fault.

I was thinking, hell, I should have actually signed before the race and that would have been it. But about a week afterwards I received a telex telling me to come to Maranello and sign a contract, so I jumped on the next plane and rushed down there like a scalded cat. Apparently, *Il Commendatore* had been so impressed with my pole position that there waiting for me was a $1,000 bonus. They put the contract in front of me and I signed it faster than you could imagine.

My first sportscar race was in 1970 in a private Ferrari 512S at Spa and after doing well against the factory drivers I got a call from Ferrari to go to Le Mans with them in that year and share with Ronnie Peterson, who was a good friend. In fact, I was told I had to race for the factory team or the team that I would have driven for wouldn't get any parts. So I had to get on with it. That was it. And it was an amazing experience even though we didn't finish.

So, I have to ask, from starting in racing in 1964 to making your Formula 1 début with Ferrari in '68, did you ever allow yourself a moment to think that you'd got it made? This is the dream. I'm going to be World Champion.

It's funny you should say that. It's the way perhaps that one should think. But I never overestimated my ability. I was driving along one day back then and

I reached down and I pinched my backside as hard as I could, to remind myself for the rest of my life of that moment. I was in a Fiat 124 rental car on the way to Modena. It was a realisation that I was driving for the greatest name in motor racing. I had to tell myself, point it out to myself. I couldn't quite believe it. And I can admit that today. I had to wake myself up to the realisation of what was happening.

My first Formula 1 race was the Gold Cup at Oulton Park, and my first championship Grand Prix was the Italian, sitting on the third row of that grid next to Jackie Stewart and Denny Hulme, in front of that incredible crowd at the theatre of speed.

Chris Amon was on the front row, John Surtees was on the pole, but I was ahead of guys like Jochen Rindt, Pedro Rodríguez, Dan Gurney and Jack Brabham. My biggest thing, though, was that I was so pissed off at being a hundredth of a second slower than Jackie. In reality I should have been delighted that I was anywhere near him. But I wanted to be on the front row. I wasn't conceited or unpleasant about it. I just couldn't believe that I couldn't go quicker. It wasn't that I thought I deserved to be. It's that I hadn't been able to drive faster.

On reflection, they were all a couple of years into their Formula 1 experience. I should have been moderately content with that. But I wasn't. That's the truth of it.

How did your career progression, then, take you from a Formula 1 seat with the greatest name in motorsport to a future of only sporadic races in the sport and it all essentially coming to an end a few years later?

Back in 1968 after Jim Clark had died I had Colin Chapman ask me to test the Lotus Indycar at Silverstone, Cooper had me on line for Formula 1, John Wyer wanted me to drive the Ford GT40 for him at Le Mans — and so I suppose when I reflect, although I never thought at the time that I was hot to trot, I suppose I was the young guy that was going places.

I'd like to think that Ferrari saw that and were moulding me for the future and that's why they kept a hold over me.

I never thought I was all that good. My wife calls me a 'Doubting Thomas'. But when you drive in Formula 3 and Formula 2 and you've got Ronnie Peterson and Piers Courage, Jonathan Williams and Jochen Rindt and all these guys, you just think you're a run-of-the-mill Formula 3 driver. Sure, in my last season in '67 I won eight races, the most of anyone in Europe, but I don't think any of us thought we were that special.

So when I went to Ferrari it was a real surprise. When I had the call, it was beyond my wildest dreams.

After the Formula 1 season was over that year I went to do the Tasman Series, racing Ferrari Dinos with Chris Amon in January 1969. It was an amazing championship, seven races on seven weekends with some great drivers: Jochen Rindt and Graham Hill for Lotus, Piers in the Brabham, Frank Gardner and a bevy of drivers from New Zealand and Australia. Chris and I won what was then called the Australian Grand Prix at Lakeside on Enzo's 50th birthday, so I was driving moderately well.

And people will say, well, yes, but look at the likes of Senna who came in as a rookie and blew the doors off everyone and so did Lewis Hamilton, but that's why I knew I was never like one of those guys, like a Jochen Rindt or a Ronnie Peterson, because they were another world to me and just being close enough to watch them was fantastic. The papers in Europe called Jochen and I the King and the Dauphin because I'd always finish behind him. Well, everyone finished behind Jochen. But I never in my own mind considered I was that good. But I was learning I suppose.

Why did it all come undone? Honestly, when I went to Ferrari I wasn't ready for it. But when is the right time? As a young guy, what do you do? Do you say 'no' to Enzo Ferrari? How can you? But in hindsight, it was too soon in my career. And I often thought about that while I was there. But I'd never have had that chance again.

As it turned out, things were about to take a turn that none of us expected.

We came back from the Tasman Series and Clay Regazzoni and I, who were due to be racing for Ferrari in Formula 2 that year, were on the back row of the grid for the first Formula 2 race of the season. Which didn't make any sense to me.

Chris and I had done well in the Tasman Series with the 2.4-litre Dino engine but Formula 2 was 1,600cc. Well, Ferrari had dominated the Formula 2 Temporada Series that winter in the car and with the engine we'd be driving in Formula 2 and against the same cars that we were going up against that weekend at Thruxton. So the fact that Regga and I were so slow has never made any sense to me. Something wasn't right.

My contract was to race in Formula 2 for 1969. And suddenly, Ferrari pulled out as a factory team.

That was it. That was the end of my career with Ferrari in single-seaters. Although they did release me to race for McLaren at the British Grand Prix that summer, which was good of them.

So there I was, a young guy with no real results.

I phoned John Wyer and David Yorke again when the Ferrari thing ended and told them I was available to race anything. Their answer was that on the basis of the start of 1969 they had no real idea of my current ability. So, piss off, basically. I was tremendously disappointed in that kind of response to be honest. You don't just lose your ability like that. Sure you can lose some confidence, but not your ability.

Having to leave Ferrari like that, honestly, was incredibly tough. The way it ended and the ensuing year was one of the hardest moments of my career. I hadn't yet really proved myself in Formula 1 and losing Ferrari's patronage was a big hit.

I'd won a few races in Formula 2 over the years, and the wonderful Tom Wheatcroft turned around and offered to help me. So I went to him and he financed the 1970 season for me, when I had what I'd describe as being some bloody good races in Formula 2 and Formula 1. We came sixth in the US Grand Prix in a one-off with Surtees and I often wonder what might have happened that day if I'd been running a new engine rather than the three-year-old Cosworth I had in the back.

I was so happy with that result.

Things never really got going again for you in Formula 1, but I know that it came close in 1972.

In the end, my last real go at Formula 1 was with Tecno. The history of that is an interesting one. David Yorke had been running John Wyer's team in sportscars and they were interested in going to Formula 1 because one of their big sponsors, Martini, wanted to go there too. So David said to Martini, well, if I go to Formula 1 then Derek Bell is going to be one of my drivers. He believed in me.

The whole thing was supposed to be based on Martini going to Brabham and teaming me up with Carlos Reutemann. I always used to beat Carlos. I don't remember him ever beating me in a proper race, so I knew that I could beat him in Formula 1. And the thought of racing for Brabham was so exciting. You knew that every time you got into a Brabham you had a chance of winning, whether it was in Formula 3, Formula 2 or Formula 1, and there I was about to join the works Brabham team in 1972 for a full season of Formula 1.

But out of the blue, David Yorke called me and said, 'You won't believe it lad, Tecno have gone along to Martini and said that they can build a Formula 1 car that can beat Ferrari, wouldn't you like to beat Ferrari?' And the Martini brothers thought that sounded wonderful. An Italian team, with Italian backing, beating the works Ferraris? Of course, they loved the sound of that. So off we went to Tecno.

The car should have been ready in October or November of 1971 but we only tested it for the first time just before Christmas at a freezing Pirelli test track with ice on the road and in fog. We couldn't properly test it because the guard rail was the same level as your head as the track was used to test trucks, and if you'd slid on the ice you'd have taken your head off. So the car wasn't really run until midday, but then it ran like a dream, engine-wise. The issue was that we hadn't put any speed on it because it was just too dangerous.

Well, Yorkie came to me afterwards and said that at least it ran well. And I said, sure, but we've not run it at Monza, we haven't run it at a proper track, you just don't know. And that was the last we saw of the car until June. It was that late.

I drove it at the French Grand Prix and the thing just gradually broke in half. The bolts were breaking where the engine was attached to the rear suspension. David Yorke came to me on the morning of the race and just said, 'Derek, son, you're not going to be racing today. That fucking thing is far too dangerous.' So I didn't. And that was the story of me and Tecno.

The biggest disappointment with that was that 1972 should have been the year I was at Brabham. The Martini deal should have seen us at Brabham. Not Tecno. And that would have been a completely different story. I mean, Reutemann put the Brabham on pole in the first race of the season. It would have been brilliant.

So I had two downs pretty close together. Ferrari was a big one, but then we went back to Formula 2, built ourselves back up again and finally found ourselves at a place where we were going back to Formula 1 with a big sponsor and into a proper team like Brabham, only for it all to turn upside down again.

And then Brabham got the Martini deal in 1973. With Martini saying that you were their man and then moving on to Brabham without you the very next year, that must have hurt.

It was horrible. But you know what it's like. You're only as good as your last performance, as they say.

After the results had gone my way in 1970, I'd had a call from John Wyer and we'd ended up having a good year with the Porsche 917 in 1971, winning my first race with Jo Siffert in the Buenos Aires 1,000kms. I was going to go back to Surtees after that sixth place, but Rolf Stommelen came along with 30 grand and I just didn't have the money to compete with that. So that was 1971 out of the picture for Formula 1 full-time. That TS7 car was basically a Formula 2 car. It was stunning and so quick. With a proper engine it could have been dynamic.

I did the Argentine Grand Prix for Frank Williams in a March with that same old cooking engine I'd run in that US Grand Prix in the Surtees. I was running second until the camshaft went, so that was the last time I ran that engine.

Surtees said he could give me Formula 5000, but in those days driving Formula 5000 was frowned upon. It would have been better to return to Formula 2. Maybe I should have bitten the bullet and gone back and started again but I wasn't prepared to do that.

But then you look at 1972 and with the mess at Tecno I was just driving the odd thing here and there. I drove a Ferrari Daytona at Le Mans, I was literally going around hawking for drives. Sportscar racing was in a mess and there weren't enough drives in Formula 1 to go round.

Having done so well in Formula 2, but only getting those sporadic chances in Formula 1, did you start to fall out of love with it?

I became very low. It didn't do much for my confidence. However, by the time we got to 1973–74, I was the development driver for John Wyer driving the Ford Mirage, a Formula 1 engined sportscar. We'd won the Spa 1,000kms. I came fourth at Le Mans in '74 with Mike Hailwood, and I would win it in 1975 with Jacky Ickx, but comparatively I was getting old now. I was 36 by then, and people always went for younger drivers. But 1970–72 was when it all had to happen for me in Formula 1. You never stayed at the top in Formula 1 for long in that era. And if you did there was a chance you'd end up in a box.

My one dream would have been to have had that Brabham drive. But here's the thing. If I'd got that drive, if I'd raced Formula 1 in 1972, would I have gone on to have the career that I did? Would I have carried on racing for another 25 years? Would I have had the most wonderful time racing with the most fabulous drivers all over the world? Probably not. But it was my dream. And that's why it hurt.

But it's about now that you started to find your feet in all sorts of other categories, but above all sportscar racing.

Oh yes. I won a couple of races in that Mirage which culminated with winning Le Mans with Jacky Ickx in 1975. I raced the works Alfa Romeo T33s that year as well, driving with Henri Pescarolo, and we won three races against the works Renault team. I put my Alfa on pole at Watkins Glen in 1975 ahead of Mario Andretti, so in my own mind I was driving well.

In 1973 I won the TT at Silverstone in an Alpina-run BMW coupé, the first time I ever sat in a saloon car. That suddenly boosts your morale. Then I got some works BMW drives the following year.

Then I won the Gold Cup at Oulton Park in a Penske in a non-championship Formula 1 race. That was just glorious. I always loved driving Formula 1. It was the ultimate, a car built to race without compromise. They were cars you could drive the hell out of.

So although I could complain about the '70s not being such a good era, it was incredibly interesting because I got to drive so many different cars in so many championships.

And when you put it all together I was still pretty good if not better than I was before.

When did you leave the Formula 1 dream behind?

I drove that Penske in 1977, but I think really the dream started to end in 1973 or '74. I was failing to qualify, throwing the car into the bank at one of the corners at Brands just trying to get one of 35 places on the grid. Jochen Mass

146

said to me, 'When we are nearly killing ourselves just to qualify, what the hell are we doing?'

But you did it because you thought the miracle might happen. Jo Siffert once said to me, 'Any chance you get to drive Formula 1, take it. You never know what might happen. Lady luck might be on your shoulder. You might get in the car when it is just right for that day and that's it.'

That's why many of us shuffled from team to team because that might have been the day when it all came together.

But certainly, I think by 1974 I knew my future lay elsewhere. I was driving the Mirage a lot by then, so one weekend I would be driving a sportscar and winning or placing on the podium in one of the 500-kilometre races, which were flat out, competitive races, and then the next weekend I'd do a Grand Prix and be dismal. It was only driving the sportscars that kept my morale up.

You've mentioned so many names who died racing. In an era when so many bit the bullet, and when you were busting your ass to qualify in 35th place, did you have a moment of clarity when you realised you just couldn't do it to yourself any more?

Yes I did. But it was more a moment of saying, you're doing bloody well in sportscars. Stick with that. You're showing people that you're just as good in a sportscar as anybody that's beating you on an Formula 1 weekend. So do you really need it?

But I had a great time through the rest of the '70s. I raced a lot and I won a lot. I'd gone to Renault and driven the Alpine at Le Mans twice with Jean-Pierre Jabouille and Jean-Pierre Jarier, I'd raced the Mirage with David Hobbs and had a wonderful time. But the opportunities started to dry up, and with that so did the money.

In 1979 I took the decision to quit racing. At the age of 38 I realised it was about time that I went and got a proper job.

But then, by chance, Steve O'Rourke, who'd become Pink Floyd's manager in the late '60s, asked if I wanted to drive with him at EMKA Racing. He salvaged me, thank God. And as a result of that, Porsche asked me back into the fold for Le Mans and, alongside Jacky Ickx again, we won it in 1981. And from that, everything flowed. Four more Le Mans wins including that one, three Daytona 24s and two World Sportscar Championships. Just when I thought it was all over.

Do you think that, because you'd had those two disappointments so early in your career, first Ferrari and then Brabham, you had a strength or an inner calm to just take whatever life threw at you?

Oh absolutely. Certainly an inner calm. Your life comes in chapters and when I look at my career, those first five years were pretty manic. You go from my début in 1964, as you say, and by the end of '69 I've been in and out of Ferrari's Formula 1 team. I'd done so much in that short time, but having experienced things doesn't make you experienced. Yes I'd been through a lot, but I was in no way ready for the big, big world of motor racing and what it can do to you. I don't think I was in any way mature enough. I'm sure I wasn't ready to be at Ferrari, but a few years later, by the mid-'70s, I know that I was. By the time I was racing for Surtees and dropping back into Formula 2, I was really ready for Formula 1. But I was already being spat out because I was into my 30s.

Did that help you deal with your career after that point? To know how to deal with things and not react in a certain way?

I think I'm a fairly calm person. Things don't wind me up, certainly not any more. I just get on and take life on the chin and carry on. Those early years possibly created that part of me. You have to be realistic. I used to bump into Jenson Button on several occasions over the years of his career, and he used to get so low, really depressed. And I'd say to him, 'Jenson, you're still the same bloody driver that you always were. It's just that you're demoralised by what's going on around you and within the team. It happens to everyone.'

But you see it a lot. It amazes me these days that we see on the TV, the teams get on the radio in Formula 1 and say, 'OK, can you do five quick laps now', and as a driver you think, 'Fuck it, I'm already going flat out! What's wrong with you?'

We didn't have all that. Well, we didn't have radios, so nobody could talk to us. But I think there is so much pressure on racing drivers these days that they can get very demoralised and feel terribly inadequate. I don't remember ever thinking I'd not given it everything. I did everything I could. And I think that's the same with all racers. You give your all. All the time.

And I think in many ways, as racers, this is something that helps us. Our careers and the lessons we learn can sometimes help us, and certainly helped me, through moments we would otherwise have found difficult.

And without those early disappointments, who's to say what would have become of Derek Bell?

You wouldn't be talking to me now, probably! Would I even have been alive?

Tragically you have to ask that. So many great drivers from that era are no longer with us. And I think that may be why there is such a special rapport between the racers of that era, the likes of Mario Andretti and Jackie Stewart and, bless his heart, the late John Surtees, because there was this sort of honour among thieves, a great respect that somehow they had dodged the bullet. It makes a much better person of you, and I think that seeing what went on around us humbled us and made us all appreciate that we somehow made it through.

And the danger is still there. Goodness, that delightful kid Dan Wheldon got killed in Indycar. We were doing an event at Laguna Seca and I was standing there with my wife Misti and son Sebastian, and she was crying and he looked so shocked when the news came through. And I thought, shit, I can't get back into a car again and race because I can't put them through that. One day it will happen to me if I keep putting myself in harm's way.

But I'll tell you, even with that being said, I'd drive every weekend if I could. It's awful, isn't it? But I'm a racer.

Emanuele Pirro

'For me racing cars was more than a dream. More than a mission... There was no Plan B. I really was ready to make a deal with the devil and say if you let me race I can give you my life at the age of 30. I don't care.'

Bewilderingly, Emanuele Pirro is a racer sometimes overlooked in the pantheon of the all-time greats. And yet with two championship titles in Italian Touring Car, one in Super Touring Car and two in the American Le Mans Series, plus a staggering six class and five overall wins at the Le Mans 24 Hours, his raw results are matched by few other drivers in history.

Born in Rome in 1962, racing for Pirro was always a distant dream. He didn't come from wealth and opportunity and so he took every chance when it came to him. It was this outlook, combined with an overwhelming desire to simply race anything that he could, that framed the direction of his career, and ultimately took him to Formula 1 as part of the all-conquering McLaren team of the late 1980s as team-mate to Ayrton Senna and Alain Prost.

Despite reaching the pinnacle of single-seater competition, Formula 1 results did not come Pirro's way. But his decision to run touring cars alongside his Formula 1 chances opened the doors that led to the greatest successes of his life. And, eventually, to Le Mans.

Emanuele Pirro would write his name in bold letters at La Sarthe, his five overall victories placing him third in the all-time list alongside Frank Biela and Derek Bell and behind only Jacky Ickx and Tom Kristensen.

Today, Pirro sits as a steward for the FIA, his years of experience and calm manner ranking him as one of the most considered and respected judges in his field. Such is the nature of this quiet and humble Italian, however, that he'd never dare alert you to his astonishing achievements if you weren't already aware.

There were two areas which affected me throughout my career. One concerned the future and the path of my career and the other concerned accidents. If I have to look back and answer the question of which was the moment that concerned me most in my career, then I think it is more related to the risk of not continuing my career rather than the accidents I had.

It's funny but I've been a lot more concerned in these situations, especially one in the early days of my career, because every day of racing was a bonus and the future was absolutely a question mark, and so I would like to start talking about this.

Just so you understand, for me racing cars was more than a dream. More than a mission. It was really by far the most important and probably the only thing I was wishing for in my life. There was no Plan B. I really was ready to make a deal with the devil and say if you let me race I can give you my life at the age of 30. I don't care. I wanted to race so much. But, of course, because I come from a normal family if I wanted to do it, I had to do it by myself. And I had no idea how I would do it.

So karting was the beginning. And in fact when I started to race in karting it wasn't with the goal of creating it into a future career, it was just because I discovered these little machines which were not too dissimilar to a car that you can drive and race and this for me was an incredible discovery. So I started to race karts just because I loved driving.

There was never a plan beyond just racing karts because anything more was like dreaming to go to the moon, you know? For me it was so out of reach. I had no idea how anyone could build up a career. And also, I had no idea of my potential abilities. I've always been very critical about myself and very objective about my ability. Throughout my whole career, I could never establish the level of my skill, let's say, and whether what I achieved was above or below what I deserved and what I should have achieved.

My results in karting proved that I wasn't too bad. And so, year by year, from 1973 to 1979, I could race karts without paying. Things were looking quite good.

The big question mark was how to switch from karts to cars. Fortunately in the years before I turned 18, which was the age you could start racing cars, there were quite a few drivers who were good in karts that had started to race cars and prove to be as good. And this was guys like Riccardo Patrese, Elio de Angelis, Andrea de Cesaris and Eddie Cheever, all of who came from, let's say, the neighbourhood of my country. So I got an offer to drive single-seaters when I turned 18 from a team which would only charge me 50 percent of the cost and in return I would get 50 percent of the potential prize money. And with this, I could find sponsorship.

So I started and I won the championship, and this was the first time when this picture of becoming a racing driver started to take a little shape. I would say that before this day, I was dreaming of becoming a professional racing driver, but I hadn't even dared to really dream it too much. Certainly not to believe it. Then after this first year and winning this Formula Fiat Abarth championship, you know when you are hoping but you don't dare to hope too much because you are afraid of being disappointed? If you start hoping it means you start believing. If you start believing and if it doesn't happen then you are afraid to be really disappointed. So I never had hope or belief before that. Then after winning the championship I thought maybe there is a slight, slight chance.

And here comes the point.

I found a little budget to do the European Formula 3 Championship with a small team that was fairly inexpensive and basically didn't make any money, because they believed in me and we started this adventure which was all paid by the little sponsorship money that we could generate. But then the results were not so good for us for the first half of the championship. I was driving a private Martini and I was around 10th position, basically a good second to a second and a half away from the works Martinis which were my benchmark. And I knew very well that if you don't stay at the top of each championship you do in the ladder then you will not make the next step. It's like the Peter Principle, you know? You rise only to your level of incompetence. In other words you perform competently at each level you progress, until you reach a level at which you cannot perform and are no longer competent.

I was trying really, really hard but basically every race, yes every circuit was new, yes we didn't do any testing, yes the team was private and the others were in a works team, yes, yes, yes. But still, the results were not good, until one moment where we had an engine problem in Zandvoort, three-quarters of the way through the season, and so we could not race.

The outfit which was supplying engines for basically the whole field did not have a replacement so after free practice we thought, OK, we have to go home. But then we found an engine from another tuner which was supposed to be really not so good but better than nothing. We put the engine in and from that moment my career had a big change because I qualified in fourth. So basically I gained that second, second and a half, that was missing and from that moment in the last three or four races I was always in the top two or three. I had one pole position, I won one race and this earned me a sponsorship proposal from Marlboro, which was a very big deal in Formula 3 back then.

There were a couple of teams sponsored by Marlboro in Formula 3, one was Euroracing and the other one was Martini. And if you were sponsored by Marlboro, you were not asked to bring a budget. You'd be hired and even paid to race. So this Euroracing team, which was the champion in the last two years, asked me if I wanted to drive. And this was the first time in my career where I thought I can really make it. I don't have to look for sponsorship, I can really make it.

I signed a contract for the 1982 season but this was a contract to be a second driver to Oscar Larrauri who was, of course, the championship contender. So we finished 1–2 and everything went according to plan. At the end of that season the deal was that we would continue and that I will become the lead driver in 1983. But during the winter I read in the news that Euroracing was going to run the Formula 1 Alfa Romeo works team. But Euroracing was my team. So I called them and I said, 'What's up?'

They said, 'Oh yeah we are going to do a Formula 1 team. The works Alfa Romeo. And, yeah, here we are.'

And what about Formula 3? For me, I had an agreement to continue and to be the lead driver and to try to win the championship.

'Oh, sorry. We have to close it because we can't do Formula 3. And by the way I'm really busy I don't have time to talk to you.'

So basically he hangs the telephone up and from one day to another from having, I don't want to say the future in my pocket, but from feeling like I can make it and I have a contract and I don't have to bring money and I am with Philip Morris [Marlboro] and so on and so forth, in one telephone call everything collapsed and I had nothing.

And this was, in terms of my career, the biggest shock that I had. Maybe it doesn't sound so bad, but for somebody with huge hopes and little certitude it was heartbreaking. I never had any skill to look for sponsors, to look for opportunities, so I did not really have any tools to rescue myself.

During the winter from a place where everything appeared to be fine and organised, everything collapsed. And if I look back in my career it has been the biggest shock I could have, because from starting to believe that I could make it, and making it to me in those days didn't mean to become a great champion just to keep racing, to keep being a racing driver for the rest of my life, suddenly it looked like it was all over. And that had a big impact.

Fortunately things turned out to be not so bad because Philip Morris kept helping me a little bit and somebody else helped me a little bit so I continued racing but that was, I don't know, like a big mountain falling over my head. And I thought everything was gone.

But also I learned that to get the best out of me I had to touch the bottom. So when things sorted themselves out after a while and I had a season organised again, I found myself being even stronger. I learned that when things look really bad, when I feel hopeless and I see no future and I really feel empty and shredded... when this time is over somehow I find myself to be even stronger.

I still remember where I was, with which telephone I was talking, the time of day that it was, because it was such a shock to receive this telephone call, also in such a bad way because they told me in such an indelicate way that my season was over and they were too busy to explain why. You know even now that I look back so many years later I remember exactly where I was standing and what I did. I started to cry. It was a massive shock for me.

And you were only 20 years old. From expecting nothing to having all those years of succeeding in karts and getting the chances to move on, did you think that was it? That it was all over?

Yes. Because by then I had very few connections in motorsport. I had sponsorship in Formula 3 and in Formula Fiat Abarth which was basically a couple of people who gave me a few thousand bucks for, I don't know, I don't want to say charity but I don't really know what they saw in me or why they wanted to help. So I had no idea how to make it and my family had no resources. So really I thought that was it.

And in fact this shock was behind every decision I would come to make. A couple of years later when I was in Formula 3000, I was a Philip Morris driver and they were sponsoring my career which was excellent, but every year was a new challenge. I wasn't walking on the red carpet, let's say. And because

I was so afraid to lose the chances that presented themselves, there was an opportunity to drive a BMW in the European Touring Car Championship halfway through the season through Roberto Ravaglia and Gerhard Berger, who were my friends in Formula 3. Roberto had already switched the year before to become a full-time, permanent, professional touring car driver and Gerhard was doing it part-time. In those days touring car racing was not really something you would set as a target as a junior driver, but I was so afraid to lose my opportunity in single-seaters where every year is a completely new challenge, new game, new story, new book, a new thing to get organised, that I wanted to have a Plan B in case my single-seater career didn't work.

So I accepted to do this race. I found the cars enjoyable to drive and a good way of racing and since then throughout my whole single-seater career I raced touring cars. To say I did so as a Plan B is not really fair, but on spare weekends, to make sure that I had a potential career in case the single-seaters didn't work out I raced tin-tops. I knew that to race single-seaters every year was very difficult from both a results and a sponsorship perspective. And so racing in touring cars was a really lucky and ultimately smart decision because when I finished my single-seater career in my last season with Scuderia Italia in 1991, I was already an established touring car driver and I had probably the best part of my career still ahead of me.

And everything that followed would not have happened if I hadn't invested time and energy in racing touring cars alongside my single-seater career.

You said that racing had always been your dream. Was that a love of Formula 1 that had driven you? Were single-seaters always the driving ambition?

Probably yes, because I didn't really know about touring cars. My dream was to race Formula 1, but just because Formula 1 was the most popular thing. Later in my career I switched the dream to just racing.

I still race historic cars and I still enjoy them very much. In those days I was dreaming to become a Formula 1 driver because I only knew Formula 1, but looking back now it is clear that my motivation was just to be a racing driver.

As a kid, what was it about Formula 1? What created that life goal? Was it just the impression of speed, the excitement? What was it that drove you to want to be a racing driver?

For me, it was the driving and the competition, since the early days of my life. I started to ride motorbikes when I was six years old, even to drive cars on the country roads when I was eight or something like that, and then go-karts when I discovered they existed. For me, driving a piece of machinery is what excited me the most initially, and then that developed into racing this piece of machinery.

As I said, I was dreaming about Formula 1 because it was the most popular thing in those days. But then the driving and the racing and the competing is what fascinated me. So the joy came in challenging myself first before challenging the others and always in trying to do the best I can do. This is something, I think, that is part of my DNA. Everything I do, for me it has to be a challenge, I like to be on the edge and I like to do things in the best possible way. If there is a risk involved it's even more exciting. Plus, the enjoyment of driving. So if you put this all into an equation then the answer is car racing.

Driving has always been a wonderful thing. For me it meant freedom. It meant challenge. It meant skill. It meant pushing the envelope and racing allowed this to all fit together.

For instance, Le Mans is something I didn't really know about in those days until I started to look at it and understand it. And for me it's been one of the most exciting things I did because it's not only speed and competition, it's also squeezing out every drop of energy you have. But in the early days of my career I didn't really know so much about it.

What seems really interesting for me are the doubts that you had in your career. First of all the doubts in yourself. You said that you were never sure of your own talent or whether you deserved to be there. And so when you lost that drive in Formula 3 was the immediate reaction of yours a positive one to say, 'I'm going to fight for this', or did that situation put you down because you'd never really been sure if you should have been there in the first place?

There was no doubt for me because it came after a good season in Formula 3 and I did well and I was happy with my performance being a second driver. Maybe rather than doubting myself it would be better to describe it as always questioning myself. And this questioning myself was a way to try to improve and become better.

But also, you know, I always hated excuses. In our sport it's really difficult to assess your ability, your merit, because for as much as it is a single man's sport, it's really a team sport. So when things go wrong it's probably not only because of you not delivering well enough and when things go right it's probably not only thanks to you delivering a lot. Every driver, during their career, has ups and downs. It's not a straight line. If you have to make an average and assess your ability, I always questioned whether what I'm doing is what I deserved or not. Not in a negative way, but I always questioned am I better than this, am I worse than this and where do I stand in comparison to this and that? Really, I never had a clear answer.

Like my Formula 1 years which were not particularly special. What was the reason for that? Should I have done something different? Why was I more successful in other categories? And these were not necessarily easier categories, because we know how competitive touring cars are and how competitive sportscars are.

So I always tried to assess myself and I never really had a clear answer. But I only tried to do this because I'm a very analytical person and because I really wanted the answer. And I don't know. But at the end of the day I believe that in the long term everyone gets more or less what he deserves.

You said at the start that accidents had also shaped your career.

Yes. As I told you, I was prepared to make a deal with the devil. And I'm serious. I thought about it when I was a kid, and I'm not kidding you, I would have signed a deal that at 30, 32 I could terminate my life in exchange for a racing career. I thought, because as a kid we all do, that at 30, 32 years old, well life is almost over anyway.

Did you ever do that? Did you ever go to that extreme, of either praying to God or of making some pact even in your mind with the devil?

No. I just thought that if I had the opportunity I would do it. But I'm a very pragmatic, realistic person and I knew that this sort of thing does not exist. But I knew I was ready to do absolutely anything to have the chance. And so for me, dying in a car race was not a big concern. If they told me you can race but you will die in a race car, I would have done it 100 percent, you know?

And also I liked the fact that in racing your destiny was in your hands. Your life was in your hands.

Because when we talk about late '70s and early '80s when racing was far more dangerous than now, and even looking a little bit further back it was extremely dangerous, so the risk of dying was big. You were thinking about these things. Now, I don't think a racing driver is afraid of dying in a race car.

As I said, I liked the fact that your destiny was in your hands. Basically, I always believed in a meritocracy. So the better you are the more you should achieve. If you screw it up, it is fair to be punished, to lose something. And this was a pretty straightforward equation in my mind until I experienced two big accidents in 1981 in my first Formula 3 year. One was a crash I was involved in, and one I witnessed.

That year everything was forming in my character, in my head, in my life. Everything was taking shape. I drove Le Mans in 1981 with the works Lancia team because this was the prize for winning the Formula Fiat Abarth championship the year before. They took me to Daytona, to Le Mans and to Kyalami with Martini Lancia. And Daytona was a wonderful experience. In February we won the race and it was really, really great.

Then we went to Le Mans and it was a nightmare of an experience because everything was too much for me. I wasn't ready for something that big. In my first stint in the race, after I did one full-speed lap, there was a big accident. Really big. It was on the straight and at a time before they had put the chicanes in so the speeds down there were incredible. And what I saw was a horror scene. There was debris spread around for hundreds of metres and then there was a wreck of what was left of the car. The driver was still inside. Dead. It was Jean-Louis Lafosse. And so behind the safety car you were passing through the accident scene several times and it was something very, very difficult to see.

Then they cleared the track and we did one quick lap and again there was another crash with the WM Peugeot of Thierry Boutsen, again on the Mulsanne straight, again debris flying everywhere. It was a really horrible thing and there were people lying on the ground and then there were ambulances on the track. A marshal was killed and a few others were injured. It was horrible. So in that first stint I saw two people killed, and I passed by them several times.

But the point I wanted to make is that neither of these accidents happened because of a driver error. I always thought, I'm happy to pay if I make a mistake and even pay a very big price if I make a big mistake. This is part of the game and I accept it. But I did not take into account that you can lose your life with zero personal responsibility. This was quite, quite shocking for me.

A month later I was doing a race in Misano with Formula 3 and my brakes failed. The pedal went completely down, I went straight in the corner and I smashed through the catch fences, the last one getting stuck on my helmet before the car hit the wall. The car went easily under the catch fences until the last one which hooked my helmet. And fortunately the car then hit the wall and stopped but I found myself suddenly being strangled because the helmet was pulled back. If you imagine the catch fencing is really long so it acts like a huge elastic band, like a bungee cord, because you're pulling it and it wants to return to its original position.

And so when the car stopped, the fencing tried to spring back, pulled my helmet with it and the chin strap of my helmet cut into my throat and started to strangle me. It was brutal. I was trying to fight, trying to get free, but I couldn't do it. I was losing consciousness and in that moment I was absolutely convinced that I was going to die. This was free practice. No people. No rescue crews. But somehow the strap slipped open and the helmet flew away and I found myself out of breath without the helmet, with some scratches but still alive.

That was a very shocking moment because in my mind I was dead. OK, I had some injuries which I still have because my throat has been all bent and damaged, but I survived. And you know, it's like dying and coming back to life in a way because to me the light went off already and had the helmet not come off, I would not be here. And even today I don't know how or why the helmet came off.

But, again, this accident happened because of a mechanical failure. So in a short period of time, first I saw that somebody else could die without having made the mistake, and then I experienced it myself and this completely changed my perspective of motorsport. I learned that this is not only dangerous if you do something wrong, but this is dangerous... period. This was a time when... well it would be wrong to say I questioned my career because I really never did, but it made me look at motorsport with a different eye and respect it in a different way.

How did you view your career after the accidents? Again, you were still so young, just coming out of your teenage years and into your early 20s.

My motivation and my desire and my will was so strong. It's just that before I thought that providing I don't do anything wrong, I'm not going to get hurt. From that moment on, I thought, you can get hurt. I never believed in luck, quite frankly. I thought your destiny is not only in your hands but it's also in somebody else's. And so I knew that every time I left for a race, maybe I would not come back. But it did not affect me because my desire to drive was so strong that all there was in my mind was to keep racing. I never ever thought of changing. Not even for one split second. It just changed my perception.

You ended up at McLaren in 1988 in one of the all-time great Formula 1 teams. What did you learn in that year from the likes of Ayrton Senna and Alain Prost? Just being a part of that?

A lot.

When I was asked by Ron Dennis to do this role of test driver, which in those days was quite a new job and the potential consequences were not so clear, he said, 'I will ask you to sign a driver's contract with an option on our side, just in case, but,' he said, 'I believe it's very unlikely you will serve this contract because you'll have to be better than Prost and Senna' — who as we know were two of the greatest drivers in the world.

So it would be unlikely that I would be taking one of these places. However, he said, 'If I were you I would do this job because you will probably learn a lot from them', and quite frankly I did not quite believe what he had said. To me, at that time, I thought that the ability of a racing driver was something that was like a gift. You had what you had, and you could not have any more or any less. It was something you were born with. And I was very wrong. And this was really important for my future career and life, because by being in contact with Senna and Prost I saw that they were doing things better than me in areas where actually I could do it as well. They had a commitment and a dedication, an attention to detail and they were never completely happy. They had an attitude and way to motivate the others and an intensity. And in all those areas what they did was better than me.

To be a good racing driver is not only to produce a quick lap time. There is a cocktail of skills that you have to have, but to be a successful racing driver it's also about making sure that the people around you, man and machine, are always in the best shape possible. This can be achieved by working really hard, by giving the example to the people around you because even your team and your engineers will deliver a better quality of work if they see that you are trying really, really hard. They will give you everything they have.

So, for instance, motivating people around you and trying to get them to deliver better quality work is something that I didn't think about before. I just thought, OK, my job is to sit in the car and drive as fast as I can. And for the rest it's not in my hands. But Senna and Prost were doing more than this. They were pushing. They were pushing themselves and pushing everybody around them to a level that I thought was impossible. So by looking at them I definitely became a better driver and a better person, in every way.

When you look at the champion and superficially think, OK, he was born with a gift from God, this is wrong and this is true in every sportsman. Unfortunately the message is not spread in a correct way because great champions could be more of an example to juniors if the world or the media was able to explain better how hard they work to achieve their success.

When you see, for instance in football, Cristiano Ronaldo. I've been told that he's the one who trains the most, that he is the first one at a training session, the last one to leave the training session. So when you see people like him a lot of people think, OK, he is an incredible player, but that's because his parents or God or whatever, gave him this incredible talent, this gift. It's in his DNA.

It's the wrong message. And somehow if juniors have the possibility to really see how hard successful people work to get there, it would be really worth it and a good lesson. But you know it's boring probably to tell this kind of thing. It doesn't make so good a story. But it's the truth.

And this is really what I saw. Physical preparation, mental preparation, never being completely happy with the technical debrief, especially Senna... all of these things make a difference. If you want to make a car lighter, you don't have to look for a 50-kilo piece of metal to remove. You have to remove grams here and there. To make the 50 kilos it's a lot of little things together. The same is true in every aspect of a team. You have to work on the small aspects to create the big change. So to me it was an important lesson.

Fortunately I have this characteristic where I don't think I am better than anyone. I look at other people and I try to see what they do better than me and try to see why. I'm not saying if he is beating me it's because he has a better car, I always strived to see what people were doing better than me and I think I was able to capture quite a bit of this message from that time at McLaren.

Obviously the Formula 1 dream didn't pan out as you would have hoped but what it led to was not just touring cars but then an amazing Le Mans career. Do you think it was the early disappointments in Formula 3 and the fact that you had bounced back from that moment of disappointment that gave you the strength of mind to keep pushing and to keep racing no matter what?

Not really, because when I was a kid my dream was to be a racing driver. My really crazy dream was to win a World Championship and to retire and do something else in life. So I saw motor racing as one part of my life. Later on through the years I enjoyed it to the extent that the dream became to never stop. And this is thanks to all the different styles of racing that I did, especially touring cars. I had so much pleasure in driving touring cars.

Formula 1 was a period in my career that I remember with, well not with bitterness but not really with incredible enjoyment, so racing touring cars beside the Formula 1 was more enjoyable. And I enjoyed the success. For me to continue driving in Formula 1 was not my top priority.

By the end of 1991 I was quite happy with my Formula 1 performances. We had a pretty good car at Scuderia Italia, I was team-mate with JJ Lehto who was a good guy, a good racer, we were pretty equal and I was happy. But then when the team decided to keep him and they had to get rid of one driver because they were going to use the Ferrari engines the following year and Ferrari wanted to put one of their drivers in the car, obviously I had to be dropped.

But for me it was not a drama. Formula 1 was a part of my career, not my career.

And yet in those days I didn't believe that I could have such a rewarding and enjoyable career after this 1991 Formula 1 season, which was supposed to be my last one.

You said — and I have to go back to it — that you would have done a deal with the devil just to race and live until you were 30 and yet it was at 30 that your career really got started!

The lesson I learned was that, you know, you never sign the deal unless you are 100 percent sure, because it would have been a bad deal for me!

To think that your first victory at Le Mans came when you were almost 40 and then you had this amazing run of nine years in a row when you were on the podium, you won the race five times, and you became one of the greatest drivers in the history of Le Mans!

And all in a race that I hated! I never quite finished the story of 1981, actually. I gave my car to my team-mate Beppe Gabbiani after my first stint and he goes out and when he's about to finish his stint I'm waiting in the pitlane with a helmet on for him to come and give me the car. But he doesn't come back and he's not coming, he's not coming. What happened? In those days we had no radio, no television. So you didn't really know what was going on. And then the news reaches our pit that car 67, which was ours, had a big crash on the straight. Which was true. And the driver was killed.

Probably people assumed in the wake of the two tragedies that happened the hour before, I don't know, but it is true Beppe collided with another car on the straight and he went over the barrier and the car was destroyed, but he was unhurt. Still, they told me he was dead.

And I said, 'No, this is too much. I will never come back to this race, even to this place, ever again.' When Beppe came back he was also shocked about the accident because he had a big crash and so we said to each other, 'Let us leave this horrible place.' And we drove back to Paris with my little Volkswagen Polo and I remember looking in the mirror after I exited the Le Mans village and looking at the city signpost and saying, 'This is the last time I come to this horrible place.'

And I could never have imagined that not only the results but the feeling, the satisfaction, how much at home I felt in this race and the very strong bond I developed with the fans, with the people, just enjoying the place very much afterwards, that it would ever come from Le Mans.

I guess the real story in life is never say never.

Is that the lesson?

The lesson is never to take anything for granted and that nothing is 100 percent sure, you know? Whatever you think, whatever happens, nothing is 100 percent fixed.

When I was a kid I told you, I had my dream and the dream was to race, to become World Champion and then to retire and do something else. Well, this was a wrong dream. The real dream was to race for so long at the good level and enjoy every single day of all of it up to today.

In a way I guess a dream you never had to wake up from.

Yes. Correct. Every day is wonderful.

Emerson Fittipaldi

'When I lost consciousness, I thought my life was coming to an end... I had no oxygen, I could not breathe, and I felt myself drifting away. But then I saw, in my mind, my children... And I knew in that moment that I was still alive.'

E merson Fittipaldi, or 'Emmo' as he is lovingly known, was at the time of his first title in 1972 the youngest Formula 1 World Champion in history. He went on to become a legend of open-wheel racing, competing for a decade in Formula 1 and winning two championships before switching his attention to the United States and Champ Car, where he became champion in 1989 and also won the Indy 500 that year and again in 1993, all in one of the sport's most competitive eras. He raced on until he was 49, taking his last race victory at the age of 48, at the Nazareth Indy 225 in 1995.

Emmo's love for racing came from his father Wilson, a famous Brazilian journalist and commentator who helped organise the first Mil Milhas endurance race in São Paulo, having been bewitched by the wonder of Italy's famous Mille Miglia. The young Emerson was brought up in a racing household, but didn't start competing himself until he began racing motorcycles at the age of 14 at the Interlagos race track.

From there, his ascent was rapid. He transferred to cars and a year after winning the Brazilian Formula Vee title he moved to England for the 1969 season and won the British Formula 3 crown. The following year, in the midst of a competitive Formula 2 season as a works Lotus driver, he made his Formula 1 début for the team.

But entering the sport at one of its most dangerous times, Emmo quickly learned that the sport he loved could be viciously cruel. A man of God, the Brazilian has drawn on his faith to pull him through the hardest times, moments that cut into this racing giant as deeply today as they did over 40 years ago.

When I arrived in England, in 1969, it was my dream to be a Grand Prix driver. I had never been to Europe before. The whole history of Formula 1 was something I had watched on television in Brazil, since I was a very small boy and a fan of Juan Manuel Fangio, buying magazines and following him. I had a dream when I arrived in England and I was very lucky.

I won the British Formula 3 Championship driving a Lotus. Then Colin Chapman asked me to drive Formula 1 for him at the beginning of 1970. It was difficult to say 'no' to that opportunity but I went to Colin's office in Norfolk and my legs were shaking.

I said, 'Mr Chapman...'

He said, 'No, no, call me Colin.'

So, I said, 'OK, Colin, I'm not ready for Formula 1. I cannot accept your offer. Give me six months of Formula 2.'

He said, 'OK.'

From arriving in February 1969, I was driving in Formula 2 in 1970. And incredibly I was on the grid for my first Formula 1 race at the British Grand Prix at Brands Hatch the same year. For me it was a fantastic dream.

And then... and I get very emotional... I'm sorry.

But, you see, one of my heroes was Jochen Rindt. I went to Monza. We had breakfast together. He said, 'Next year I want you to replace me because I don't want to drive Formula 2 any more.' He had a team with Bernie Ecclestone and Roy Winkelmann and he said, 'Don't worry about the contracts, Bernie will organise everything.' And I said it would be my honour to replace you, to drive for you.

Three hours later he was killed.

To me, living with that was horrible. It was the toughest time for me. To live in that period and to lose as many friends as we lost. I asked myself, why did I choose this sport? Is it correct to continue?

We lost Jo Siffert at Brands Hatch in 1971. I was running five seconds behind him. He turned the BRM upside down and I stopped to help him. As I arrived, the car blew up.

When I won the World Championship in '72 I asked whether I wanted to continue in this sport. It was not a correct sport. Something was wrong. I told my father and my brother that I was retiring. They said, 'Really? At 25 years old?' And I said yes. I am World Champion, what else do I want in life? And then my father gave me very good advice. He said, 'You like the sport so much, you're going to miss it and you're going to come back.' And he was right.

But then, God has always been very good to me. I won the race after Jochen died and there was a big celebration and a commemoration. This sport can take you from tragedy to victory very quickly.

How did you weigh that up? To have something you loved so much but something that was so dangerous and could take your friends so quickly?

It's like I switched off. When I walked into the paddock on Thursday or Friday I said I am here to commit, to enjoy my sport and give 110 percent of myself. But when I left home on the Thursday I was always wondering if I was going to be coming home on Sunday or not.

I think the work that has been done in motor racing over these years has been fantastic. You see the crashes now, I have my little boy and even my grandchildren are now racing, and I know they are much safer driving a race car than driving on the Marginal, the highway in São Paulo. You know? And that's thanks to all the efforts for so many years in this sport. Technology and safety is much better now.

Were you embraced when you came into racing? As you said, you made it to Formula 1 very quickly after arriving in England. Did the other drivers bring you in?

I was lucky to get Colin Chapman as my mentor. Immediately he called me to drive for him and it was a big surprise. And then to be in Monza and to be the third driver at Lotus was amazing. There was Jochen, John Miles and me.

After Jochen died, Colin called me when I was at home in Switzerland and told me I was going to be the number one because John had retired. I said, number one? I've only done three Grands Prix! That was how quickly I was accepted in Formula 1.

It was a very different time to today. Particularly, I think, between the drivers. Certainly it seems as though you hung around as friends outside the race weekends more than the guys today.

Outside of the Grand Prix car, we were very good friends. We joked, we played together, we had much more camaraderie. We were very close to each other. In our subconscious we all knew the risk was there and perhaps that is why we were much more together. We knew that anybody could be gone at any time.

You said you lived in Switzerland. Did a lot of the drivers live out there?

Jochen was there, Jackie Stewart was there. I lived there for 12 years, just outside Lausanne, near Crissier. I loved it there. Jo Bonnier was there too. He was very Swedish, very cool, a lot of wisdom, and he was always working on the Grand Prix Drivers' Association. He worked so hard and did a fantastic job for the safety in the sport. He was a very wise guy.

Really thank God for Jo and Jackie because you have a much safer sport because of people like them.

Lotus, of course, had only just dealt with losing Jim Clark when you arrived on the scene in 1969. His death in 1968 shocked everyone. Was there ever a feeling that if it could happen to him, it could happen to anyone?

Jim Clark's death had a very big impact. There are people that get killed and you said it's not correct. Jim Clark? For racing fans all over the world it wasn't right that he should be killed. Ayrton Senna in 1994 was not correct. You think these guys are immortal. Jim Clark was immortal. Just like Ayrton. He cannot die in a race car. Guys like that should never get killed.

And the same, many would say, was true of Jochen. When was the first time you met him?

I started the season in Formula 2 in April 1970 at Hockenheim and it was then that I started talking to Jochen. He liked me and I loved talking to him. We raced for three or four months together in Formula 2 before I jumped up to Formula 1 in July. He was always giving me advice. Always very good to me.

I went to watch the Monaco Grand Prix and I saw Jochen driving the Lotus 49, when Jack Brabham went off at the last corner and Jochen won. I was at Tabac corner and the way Jochen was driving the 49 sideways was so impressive. I said, 'Fuck! This guy is amazing.'

Obviously, Colin had already told Jochen he was going to sign me for Formula 1. I think that's why Jochen was always very close to me in the Formula 2 days.

But he became more than a friend to me. He was a mentor and an adviser. When I started driving Formula 2, the first few months were very difficult for me. The first time at the Nürburgring I had never raced there. Colin Chapman gave me a Lotus Seven and I spent the whole week there. Jochen qualified second, I think Derek Bell was next and I was just behind him. On my first time at the Nürburgring.

When the race started, on the first downhill I got the jump and I was right behind Jochen. I said, great! I will follow him and I'm going to do exactly what he is going to do. The old Nürburgring was very difficult, you really had to know it. So I came by at the end of the first lap right on Jochen's gearbox, and I thought this is great! I looked so good, I'm doing great and I'm right with him. And then, when we started the second lap, Jochen put his hand up, waved to me and just disappeared. He was gone. And then, honestly, I was in a boat with no compass.

Derek passed me and shot off and in the end I finished fourth. Afterwards I said to Jochen, that really was not fair! You left me all alone. And he laughed.

It must have hurt to lose him.

It was the first impact that I had, of the reality of this sport. To me, being a racing driver, especially a Formula 1 driver, was a dream. And then you have your dream starting to be realised, and suddenly you are shaken awake. This is the reality.

With both Jim Clark and Jochen Rindt killed at the wheel of a Lotus, did you ever worry getting into one?

I knew they were fragile. But I had a lot of confidence in Colin. He was a genius, an aeronautical engineer. Everything was light, minimal weight. But anything could happen. And after I won my first World Championship in 1972 in Monza, Colin came to me, looked to me, and said, 'Emerson I don't want to get any closer to you than I already am. I'm afraid that one day I will lose you too.'

I had a few mechanical failures. I broke a front wheel at Zandvoort when I was Ronnie Peterson's team-mate. I once broke my rear wing. But I wouldn't say that in my years at Lotus I had more mechanical failures than anyone at any other team.

And what I learned with Colin and Peter Warr at Lotus was fantastic. Colin was a genius. He would know what to do. He'd listen, go back to the garage, change something and immediately the car would be much better. His intuition is what let him get the car right.

You spoke earlier of Jo Siffert's death at Brands Hatch in 1971. Was that harder to take because you were there and there was a chance you might have done something to help?

It was horrible. My visor melted from the heat when the car blew. The marshals were screaming, they couldn't do anything. But that was, by then, already the reality.

And then François Cevert was killed at Watkins Glen in 1973. I stopped the car, just like I did for Jo, to go and try and help. What I saw was horrible. But that was part of our racing world.

I think perhaps today we take it for granted that you guys accepted this as part of your world, but it must have had a tremendous psychological impact on all of you. Did you every receive any treatment? Did you ever go to talk to anybody or have any kind of counselling?

I'm a believer in God and a man of faith. I talked to God.

After François I didn't want to talk to anyone and so I went to the car park for one hour because there was nobody there. Just me. Colin came to me and I said, 'I'm sorry, Colin, but I need to be alone.' I spent that time praying and asking God, should I go back? Should I continue with this sport?

At the same time I heard my father in my head, telling me how much I loved the sport and how much I would miss it.

Did you ever question your faith or God, that he would allow these things to happen?

No. I knew it was part of the risk. I have a lot of faith.

What gave you the strength to go on? Was it the words of your father when you thought about retiring? Was it your own faith and beliefs?

My own belief and my commitment to do what I love in life, which was to drive race cars as fast as I could. And to always enjoy myself.

Did you ever doubt that what you were doing was the right thing?

No. I was 100 percent sure. It was my dream. I was committed for any cost, any price. My love and my passion is what pushed me. But mentally I had to switch off. When I arrived in the paddock I was there to drive as hard as I could. And I was enjoying myself. I wasn't worrying about anything. And that's what is great about the sport, when you push yourself to be the best you can be and to do the best you can do with your life.

When did you reach the point of knowing that enough was enough?

Michigan in 1996. I was racing in Champ Car for Penske and on the Saturday after qualifying I told Roger Penske that I was going to retire. There were only two races to go, but I knew that my time had come.

Roger said, 'As a friend I'm happy that you're going to retire. But as your team boss I'm going to miss you.'

And the very next day, in the race, I had the biggest accident of my career.

Did you think that was it?

I thought I was dying, yes. My lung collapsed and I had no oxygen, I could not breathe. I said to myself, that's it.

But my faith pulled me through.

In the end they had to operate on my neck. I had broken six or seven vertebrae and was a few millimetres away from being a quadriplegic. After seven hours of surgery I came out, and my father and brother were there and asked the doctors if there was any chance for Emerson to drive again. They said, 'Yes, but let us go back and reinforce his neck.' My father said, 'I know my son and he will want to get back in the cockpit.'

You know, he was right.

I have much more titanium in my neck than bone these days.

When you were in the car in Michigan, to have gone through the most dangerous period in Formula 1 history, but to have lived to being almost 50, still racing. To suddenly have the thought that in this moment you are going to die... was there panic, sadness, or did you just accept it?

When I lost consciousness, I thought my life was coming to an end. I thought I was dying. I had no oxygen, I could not breathe, and I felt myself drifting away.

But then I saw, in my mind, my children. I could see them all. And then I heard noise. A lot of noise. And I realised at that moment it was the other cars driving past. And I knew in that moment that I was still alive.

But I was suffering. My lung had collapsed, my body was bleeding internally.

The rescue team arrived and took me from the car. I arrived in the medical centre and the doctor said, 'Emerson, I have no time for anaesthetic.' He put a tube in me and blood went everywhere, but I was able to breathe again. They saved my life.

If they hadn't done that, another 30 seconds or minute, I would have been dead.

At the end of it, then, what do you think was the biggest thing you learned from those moments?

I think it is the love that you have that motivates you. It is what carries you through the ups and the downs. When you lose, you always look to the next challenge. You come back better and stronger. That's the way to always be.

Felipe Massa

'You always have some hope. You know, you always have a target and you always need to have hope and you always need to believe. Nothing is impossible. You need to believe that things will change, things will get better.'

While the history books will never record Felipe Massa as a Formula 1 World Champion, to many he is deemed worthy of the accolade he held for a matter of seconds and ultimately missed by a single point in 2008. That he should have come so close in an era of the sport marked by the domination of the likes of Michael Schumacher, Fernando Alonso, Lewis Hamilton and Sebastian Vettel, shows the extent of the task that lay before him, and makes his career statistics — and in particular that 2008 season — all the more impressive.

Massa began karting at the age of eight, and a decade later was making waves in his native Brazil. Moving to Europe at 19, his ascent to Formula 1 was rapid and he reached the pinnacle of open-wheel racing just two years later, in 2002. Four years later he became an important part of the all-conquering Ferrari Formula 1 team, and one of Michael Schumacher's favourite and most highly regarded team-mates.

Massa's finest season came in 2008. After a troubled start to the year, he mounted a stunning challenge to Formula 1's new crown prince Lewis Hamilton. The title fell to the final race, in Massa's native Brazil and home town of São Paulo. The *Paulista* triumphed to the roar of the adoring crowd, believing, as did the rest of the world, that he had done enough to be crowned champion. But when Hamilton made up a position on the final corner of the final lap, Massa was denied what would turn out to be his one chance of a World Championship.

And yet it was his reaction to such heartache that marked him out that day. He stood on a podium that should have seen him crowned champion against the backdrop of his greatest triumph with tears streaming down his face, his clenched fist beating his chest, saluting his fans and screaming in disbelief. It was a moment of rawest sporting agony. And it made him a hero.

Yet this was not to be the hardest moment of his career. Eight months after his title defeat, Massa lay in an induced coma in Budapest's ÁEK hospital with what were described as life-threatening injuries, following a crash in qualifying for the Hungarian Grand Prix. A spring had broken on the BrawnGP car of his countryman Rubens Barrichello, bounced down the track and struck Massa's helmet hard enough to cause major injury to his skull.

He recovered, he returned to the cockpit and he stood on the podium again. But a year to the day after his accident, he had the cruel knife of sporting politics thrust into him.

These were his hardest moments. The ones from which he learned the most.

I had two moments that were quite difficult for my career. The first was my accident at the Hungarian Grand Prix in 2009. I really thought it could have been finished for my career, for such a big accident that everybody saw. It took a little bit of time for me to be 100 percent cured after what had happened to me. I think it was quite tricky and really a very difficult moment. You always believe you will be the same in the car, that you can drive the car again, that you can be what you were before. But you don't realise that there are so many things that you need to start from zero.

The waiting was hard. I had two operations, one straight away after the accident and another one after some time. It was not an easy operation either.

I think I was quite confident that this is what I love to do and I was feeling positive that I will be OK back in the car. And I was actually. But definitely I passed very close to it being over, and I think you learn a lot after difficult moments like that. So I think that was the first one.

The second one was 2010 when I lost the opportunity to win the race in Germany. And I think that was... well, you feel like shit, to be honest. People taking away the victory from you when you're doing an amazing job, when you have a great opportunity to win the race, especially coming the same day as my accident, you know, the 25th of July. One year after. I think maybe that day was one of the saddest and toughest days of my career.

So let's start in 2009 and the accident. I remember the afternoon in Hungary very clearly. We hadn't seen anything of the crash on the screen. We just saw red flags around the track, and then your Ferrari in the barriers and you not moving. Do you remember anything?

No. I don't remember anything. The only thing I remember is maybe the lap before. I remember I was finishing my lap and Rubens Barrichello had disturbed me a lot on the last sector. I lost maybe a few tenths of a second that could have put me in a better position to go through to Q3. I mean, I got through to Q3 anyway with my lap time, although obviously I never actually got to take part.

I remember I was disappointed to lose the time behind Rubens. That's the only thing I remember. The lap when his spring hit me was my in lap to the pits. For Rubens it was his flying qualifying lap so he was pushing and I was slowing down, so when I had the spring hit me I was not pushing to the maximum. I was slowing down and getting ready to pit, but I don't remember anything. For sure I didn't see the spring, but I don't remember anything.

What's the last thing you remember?

Just that. Crossing the line, being disappointed that Rubens disrupted my lap time. Then nothing.

What's the first thing you remember?

I don't remember waking up. I remember maybe more towards the end, already at the hospital. They gave me a lot of strong medicine to keep me in a coma, and I think I had so many drugs that you need some time to really be conscious again. I remember being in hospital with my family. I remember my wife, a lot. I remember my parents and my brother. But also, I remember when I had to do an interview for Ferrari and I had to speak in two or three languages… well that was a little bit complicated but I managed to do it. Michael [Schumacher] was there but I have no memory of that. [Ferrari President] Luca di Montezemolo and [Ferrari Team Manager] Jean Todt were there too, but I don't have a great memory of that either.

Do you remember those things because people told you about them?

I don't know. Maybe. Maybe. My wife and family I remember 100 percent. And also that interview. I don't know if everything else is because people told me, or if I really actually remember it.

Were you scared?

No.

Did you know why you were there?

No. But then my family started to tell me slowly, but for me it was too slowly and I just said, 'Tell me! Tell me what's happened!' And then when they told me and showed me the footage I said, 'Fucking hell. This is unbelievable that it happened to me.' They were trying to tell me slowly.

Actually talking about it now, I remember my engineer Rob Smedley was there in the hospital too. He came and I was talking to him because we had three weeks until the next Grand Prix and I was telling him I would be OK to race. And he just looked at me and said, 'No, I don't think so.' I said, 'Yeah for sure, my face is a little bit blue and a little bit big, for sure I will be OK.' And then he was a little bit quiet because he didn't know what to say.

When did you know how bad it was?

I think when I saw it for the first time, I truly understood what had happened to me. You are blue, bruised, swollen, but you don't know exactly what has happened. So then when I saw the footage of the crash, I started to ask the doctors more because I wanted to understand what's happened. When I saw it, I understood it had been a big accident. You ask to see your X-rays. I learned that I needed to have a plate attached to my skull because all of the bone around my eye and forehead was broken.

So the first operation was to remove the pieces of bone that had broken in my skull, but it left a big hole and just the brain. You had to replace it with something, so at that moment I knew that the operation would not be small. Plus, when I was talking to the doctors they said they hoped they could do the operation by opening up the same cuts they had used the first time. Because if you need to increase the cuts then you have to open the whole head and that would have been a big, big, big operation. Luckily everything happened in the right way.

Did you ever ask the question of whether you'd be able to race again?

For sure. I asked myself the question many times. For my family, not so much. But for myself? Yes. A lot.

Was it something you asked the doctors? I mean, when they said they were going to put a plate in your head...

Oh sure. I asked them and they were always professional. They said they didn't know if I could race again this year. Maybe next year will be OK. But they never said 100 percent.

I had a very good relationship with the doctors. In fact one of the doctors around me, Dino Altmann, he was my personal doctor and the one who found the right people to do the operation. He is still my doctor today. Any medicine I need to take I call him. When I had my accident, he was the person my wife called. He helped me, all of us, massively.

In terms of your recovery, how long did it take and did you ever rush yourself?

To be honest I wanted to rush myself to get back to the car but the car that year was terrible. It was really not competitive. Which ended up being a positive. It was a very difficult year for Ferrari so that actually helped me because it wasn't that I was losing a lot. So this actually gave me some patience.

I think I could have returned for the final two races of the season and even the doctors said I would have been OK. The problem would have been if I'd had another accident. You can race, sure. But if you have an accident then it can be really difficult. If you have another impact on your head then it can be tricky.

187

So what was the first thing you did?

I went to the simulator first, then we did a test at Fiorano for Ferrari and everything went OK. My doctor was there too just to make sure everything was fine. In December I did a test with Valentino Rossi at Barcelona. He did two days with Ferrari, and I did the day after in the same car he was driving.

Did you feel immediately back at home? And did the fact you couldn't remember the accident work as a positive for you?

Yeah, I think so. Nobody likes to have bad things inside their brain. For sure, not remembering is a real positive. And when I got back in, it all felt the same. To be honest you have so many things to think about when you are in the cockpit that you don't have time to worry about anything else. Then when you add the competitive element to your brain, too, all you want is to show the best that you can do. I think that inside the car nothing changed.

What it changed in me is that before a big accident you never think these things will happen to you. You see a big accident and you think, wow, that looks bad, but never me. Not me. You always think inside yourself, inside your brain, OK somebody can have a big accident. You know it is possible. But you never believe it will happen to you and I think maybe when it happens to you, you pass through a very difficult situation and the result is that you give a lot more respect to life.

Look at Michael. One day he is skiing and then you click your finger, something happens and like that, everything changes. For what? For maybe no reason. So when these things happen you realise that you need to say 'thank you' every day. It's about appreciating life.

So 2010 starts. You have Fernando Alonso as a team-mate. He wins his first race with Ferrari, which is also your first race back after your accident. Were you just happy to be back racing?

I was happy to be back racing, of course. But I definitely wasn't happy with the result because I started ahead of him in the race. He passed me at the first corner so he did a great job with that, but I had a great pace and then I had to save fuel and also Sebastian Vettel had a problem with his car. So, Fernando won, I was second, and it was a positive start to the season for Ferrari. It was positive for me too because it was my first race back, but when you look back you think how amazing it would have been if I had won that first race. I was close to achieving that, but anyway… Fernando showed his talent and the driver that he is.

It was always really good with him in terms of our relationship but for sure I never liked the way he works. Outside of the car he is always nice to you, but Fernando has two personalities. He has two faces. Sometimes you don't understand why he has to be like that, you know? Sometimes the impression he gives you is not what he is actually doing. He has one face as a driver and one face outside. And he has a lot of power. Politically. To beat him you need not just to be on your day. With the power he has you need everything.

You were the Ferrari driver. You were the long-term driver at the team. How was he able to achieve that much political power so quickly at the team?

To be honest I never had that kind of power at Ferrari, at least never that strong. I think that the team followed him 100 percent and Ferrari always had the philosophy to follow one driver. You look back to Michael who was there for such a long time and Ferrari was his team. After maybe one year, Ferrari was 100 percent Fernando's team as well.

Was that written into the contract?

No. Never. It's just the power. He could do that with his power.

So if you can see that, and you can see it happening, is there anything you can do to stop it? Or do you feel powerless?

Yes, you do feel powerless. Because sometimes, actually many times, you can show the team what you need to do and they don't even listen because they have only one target. So then you lose your motivation.

And all this at a time when you are trying to recover from the accident…

Exactly. Maybe the only thing that Ferrari was not thinking is that to win a Constructors' Championship, you need two cars. To do it with one car is impossible. But they were doing everything 100 percent for Fernando. For sure, Fernando almost won the championship two times and he did that by his talent because we did not have the car to win the championship. But for sure, the amount of points that we could have achieved we did not achieve because of this way of working.

So tell me about Germany. Because it became such a famous moment not just for you, not just for Fernando, but for Ferrari and for Formula 1.

I think we started well and I got into the lead and I had good pace, very similar pace to Fernando the whole race, and because of that he wasn't able to pass me. So then suddenly the team, as you saw and heard, made the order to switch positions. And really, that thing just destroys you 100 percent. You know? You ask yourself, what am I doing here? And then you cannot do your job in the right way. Plus, it's not really the second part of the year where only one driver is in the fight for the championship. Everything was still completely open.

Looking back, sure it was sad for me. But it was sad for the whole world to be honest.

And of course team orders were still illegal at that time so they had to use that awful message of 'Fernando is faster than you'. But he wasn't.

No. In that race he wasn't. He had similar pace, but he wasn't faster.

So put us in the seat. You are leading a Grand Prix, and you get that message. At that moment, what do you want to do? Does your foot waver from the throttle for even a moment? Does your heart skip a beat?

To be honest you think so many things. You think about your career, you start to think about your education, what you've learned in life. You're a professional, you work for a company and so you need to act professionally and that's the way I am. I think you need to show the people who you are as a person and what your heart is telling you to do. It's sad, but you need to do it.

How did you feel after the race, having to do the podium?

I think it was the most terrible feeling. I felt terrible on the podium, it was a terrible feeling in the press conference, terrible feeling to see the face of Fernando when he didn't know what to say, terrible to see the face of the Team Principal Stefano Domenicali, who didn't know what to say. To me it was clear what had happened, but they did not know what to say. And they never explained. My boss, sure, he did. 'I'm sorry, this was the decision of the team.' And that's OK. That's normal and understandable. But the faces that I saw, the faces that everyone saw after that race, it was just sad.

And during that press conference, the media was so angry. I remember how everyone came out in support of you after the race. It was the one-year anniversary of your accident, which seemed to add extra emotion. How did you keep your composure in that press conference and not just agree with them all?

I think I tried not to speak too much because you don't gain anything by fighting there and then. You just have to wait, let it finish. It's better that way.

Was it over between you and Ferrari then?

Oh yeah. For sure. But you always have some hope. Maybe if you start the season well, then maybe for whatever reason things change or maybe your team-mate is unlucky in two or three races and doesn't score points, then their focus might switch back to you. You know, you always have a target and you always need to have hope and you always need to believe. Nothing is impossible. You need to believe. Unfortunately that didn't happen, but you need to believe that things will change, things will get better.

If 2008 had been different and you'd been crowned a Ferrari World Champion, do you think they'd have treated you differently?

No. I don't think that would have changed anything. I think it would still be the same. Fernando had that much power. You remember, Fernando and Kimi had been racing for different teams. And Ferrari had a lot of trouble to put Kimi to the side to put Fernando into the team because he was always fighting with Kimi the year before. They had a lot of problems. That's why they decided to put Fernando in the car. They wanted another World Champion. No. It wouldn't have changed anything.

So when you look back on those two moments, how much strength did they give you? The crash, coming back from it and being able to then get past, one year later, something so soul-crushing. How did you have that strength?

I did my job. I was professional with the team. It was really sad for me and really, really bad and I think even the team they felt the same. A Formula 1 team has a target and they always need to follow what is best for the team. There are times when what is best for the team is not best for the driver. This is the game and I understand it and have always been professional. The team has a direction that must be followed whether it is successful or not. And that goes for every member of the team

That's the way it is.

Sometimes people, especially fans, believe that Formula 1 is like a unique sport where one driver races against another. But it's not true. The two drivers are racing for the same company, with 900 people working for the company, a lot of money invested, so they are employees too and have to be professional and follow the plan. It's not exactly like some people believe.

You said earlier that after the crash, you learned to appreciate life. Did that help in Germany and in the days afterwards? That even after something so disappointing, you have things to be happy about?

I think that what helped me with the accident and everything afterwards is my family, my wife, my son. I have so many good people around me and they are what helps you the most in these situations. Family is the most important thing. Life is an education and having good people around you makes it all worthwhile. What you are is what you learn.

Jackie Stewart

'It was as if God had said, "You've had everything, you've done everything, you've got everything"… and it was as if he'd turned around and clicked his fingers at that moment and said, "But don't you dare take anything for granted."'

S ir John Young Stewart is one of the all-time motor racing greats. A three-time Formula 1 World Champion, Jackie Stewart's career statistics make for quite incredible reading. In his 99 starts he finished on the podium in over 40 percent of the races he ran. His win ratio sat just shy of one in three. He was the master of his craft and the king of Formula 1 in the late 1960s and early '70s.

Born in Milton, Dunbartonshire, Scotland, in 1939, he had dyslexia — undiagnosed at that time — and was forced to leave school at 16, when he went to work in his father's garage as a mechanic. A friend of the family lent him the first car he raced and with it he duly won four races in his first year of competition in 1961. He was quickly snapped up by the Ecurie Ecosse team and proved immediately successful driving their sportscars.

Ken Tyrrell signed Stewart to race in Formula 3 in 1964 and he won all but two races to be crowned champion in his first full season. Later that year he rose to Formula 2 with Lotus and even made his Formula 1 début for the team in South Africa in the non-championship end-of-season Rand Grand Prix, for which he qualified on pole.

In 1965 he joined Formula 1 full-time with BRM and finished third in the World Championship. Eventually he rejoined Tyrrell, taking the team's Matra-Ford to World Championship glory in 1969. In 1971 he raced Tyrrell's own car to a second title and repeated the feat again in 1973, all the while competing around the world in disciplines as varied as the Le Mans 24 Hours, European Touring Car Championship, Can-Am and the Indy 500.

But while Stewart is known and revered as one of the great racing drivers of his age, he is perhaps equally respected for the tireless work and campaigning that he undertook to advance driver safety. After an accident in the 1966 Belgian Grand Prix had left him trapped in his car with fuel leaking all around him and no safety crews to extract him from his perilous situation, he took it upon himself to lead what, at times, was a lonely and much-derided campaign. He pushed for the modernisation of circuits, the fitting of barriers and run-off, the advancement of medical facilities and trained, well-equipped marshals. When it was called for, he led driver boycotts.

His work and the foundations he established have, over the nearly five decades since his retirement, saved the lives of countless drivers the world over. Yet for all of his labour and all of his achievements in the realm of racing safety, the cruellest twist unfurled on what was to be his final ever racing weekend.

I n April 1973 I decided that I would retire from Formula 1 at the end of the season. I was quite comfortable and happy to do so, partly because the last race of the season, the US Grand Prix at Watkins Glen, would have been my 100th race. By the time it came around in October I had already secured my last World Championship at Monza in September. And so, arriving in America, nobody knew. Ken Tyrrell knew, Walter Hayes the great man of the Ford Motor Company knew, John Wardell of Ford Motor Company knew as well. But nobody else. My family didn't know. Helen, my wife, didn't know. Neither did my parents. But I was very sure I had made the right decision.

On the Saturday of what would have been my 100th and final Grand Prix, my team-mate François Cevert was killed in front of us drivers.

The accident occurred at a very quick part of the race track. The amount of debris on the circuit was enormous. The Tyrrell was a very strong colour and there was blue everywhere. I thought, my God, what a huge accident. The yellow flags were out, all the cars had to stop because the debris was so extreme on the track.

Every driver had obviously got out of their car and had gone to see if they could help, and I was the last to arrive. Chris Amon was driving for the team that weekend as Ken had added a third Tyrrell-Ford for the final races in Canada and America. I saw him walking away from the wreckage and I thought, my God, it's Chris that's crashed. As I drove slowly by the scene I asked him, from the cockpit, if everything was OK. And he just shook his head and walked on.

So I got out of my car and went over to where the rest of the car was. It was a terrible sight and François was equally in terrible shape. It was obvious that he was already dead.

So from, if you like, the euphoria of winning the World Championship, the euphoria of knowing that I was never going to race again, suddenly the last race of my career ended in the worst possible way.

It was the worst sight I've ever seen in my life. The severity of the accident, physically, on François was terrible. We all saw it, and everyone who did was shocked by the enormity of it.

I went back into the car. I felt terrible leaving François there. My friend. But there was nothing anyone could do. I drove back to the pits to tell Ken Tyrrell.

I said, 'Ken, François is dead.'

'But how do you know?' Ken just couldn't understand.

'Ken,' I said, 'I promise you, he's not alive.'

'You can't be sure,' he said. And he went off to try and find the doctors.

But it was beyond obvious. There was nothing anyone could have done.

François didn't make mistakes. He was a clean driver and a very good driver and in fact he was going to be the number one driver at the team after I retired. Ken and I had already agreed that. But, of course, he didn't know that I was going to retire.

We had just spent ten days together, Helen, he and I, resting up, because he'd had a little accident in Canada and had hurt his foot and his ankle. We stayed in a lovely hotel in Bermuda all together. We had such a great relationship.

He had been asked by Ferrari if he would join the team and I told him not to. François couldn't understand why. He knew that as long as I was at Tyrrell I was always going to be number one. And I said, 'Yes, but it's a strong team and a safe team. You have to stay.' I knew that in a matter of months he would be leading the team. But he never knew that.

The mechanics, of course, were terribly upset. They thought it must have been a mechanical fault because he was such a clean driver. But I was absolutely certain in my mind that it wasn't.

The part of the track where he crashed was a right turn immediately followed by a left, with an undulation on the road. The Tyrrell was a short-wheelbase car and was overly reactionable and although fast could sometimes be difficult to drive. I had worked out that if I knocked it into fourth gear, rather than third gear, the car became more docile and not as nervous in that section. I am sure François was in third gear. When he hit the bump, the car slewed because of its short wheelbase. He obviously took his foot off the gas pedal, the car hit the barrier on the right and then shot off to the left, going straight through that left side barrier head on.

But the mechanics thought it must have been their fault. I told them I was pretty sure it wasn't. I had felt the way the car was through that corner in third gear and I'd had a moment myself, so because I'd popped it into fourth gear to soften the issue, I found it much easier and faster.

It was the worst possible experience for the team. On everybody. His death was announced and practice was halted because there was such a lot of work that needed to be done to replace the barriers.

As soon as the track was ready, I went out again, more for the sake of the mechanics than anyone else's, because for them to think that it could have been one of their faults or that there'd been a mechanical breakage or whatever, was too much. I had total confidence in them and the car. So I did that, but I then made the decision that I wouldn't drive in the race.

We'd had three 1–2 finishes that year and, ironically, Ken had said that morning, 'I know it's your last Grand Prix, but it'd be a really nice thing if you were to move over and let François through.' And I just said, 'Ken, it's my last Grand Prix, my 100th Grand Prix… to win my last race would be a great thing to go out on.'

He said, 'I know, but you'd be the bigger man by not doing that.'

We agreed to wait until after qualifying and obviously that decision was never made.

Helen had already left the track because she was so upset. I made my way across to the Glen Motor Inn, the little hotel closest to the track, and my exact words to her were, 'I'm no longer a racing driver.'

My motor racing career has a lot of high points and a lot of bad points because so many people were killed during that period. Jochen Rindt was killed, Jim Clark, François, Piers Courage… and in those days they never stopped the race. You kept racing. When Piers got killed, Jochen and I were racing for the lead. Jochen won the race, I was second, but Piers was one of

Jochen's and my best friends. You know who it is, because in his case his helmet came off. So we knew how bad it was. We could see. But the race never stopped. And we never stopped until the chequered flag.

When Roger Williamson died at Zandvoort [in 1973], it was the same thing. I won the race. When Jo Schlesser's car was on fire and we were driving through the flames [at Rouen in 1968], they never stopped the race. It was just the culture of the time.

We lost four drivers in four consecutive months on the same weekend in 1968. Every one of them on the same weekend. We were racing in the fifth weekend at the Nürburgring. I won the race and I won it by over four minutes in the rain, and the very first question I asked when I got out of the car was, 'Is everybody OK?', because at the Nürburgring you'd never know. They'd go through hedges and trees and bushes and you'd never see they'd gone off the road.

So even with all the high moments and great moments in my career, these events were horrendous. The current generation wouldn't understand any of that sort of stuff. The only way I can relate to it, thinking back, is that it must have been like World War II and the Spitfires and Hurricanes leaving the south coast of England to stop the German Luftwaffe getting to London. They were losing their colleagues on a regular basis. And so were we.

You talk about driving past those accidents and carrying on. Ayrton Senna once talked about the accident that happened with Martin Donnelly in Jerez, when the car disintegrated, and he was left lying on the track. He said he had to go out and drive faster than he ever had through that corner, to put it out of his mind. Did you feel that you had to keep your foot down and keep racing to put it out of your mind? To go harder than ever to push it out?

I never saw it like that.

I wasn't racing then, but I remember that accident at Jerez. You have to understand that racing drivers are weird animals. When the visor goes down, the lights go out.

When Jochen got killed at Monza, he was one of my very best friends too. I was crying when I went into the car because I was with him when he died. Ken had said to me, 'Listen, you've got to go out', and I burst into tears in the car.

But I went out and I did the quickest lap I'd ever done at Monza at that time. I was second fastest to Regazzoni in the Ferrari. But I got out of the car and I burst into tears again.

While you're in the car, you're detached in a way. When you're in any type of racing car, you are so consumed by every element of it that you have no capacity left for emotion.

After François was killed, did you ever get the ability to put yourself back into that situation? Where you could just switch off the emotion and get into that place of calm tranquillity that only comes behind the wheel of a racing car? And if not, how did you deal with the emotion of it all?

No. I never did again.

But it was happening so often that we were used to death. I must have gone to more funerals than any person I know.

If Helen and I were at home, now, and we saw the movie of that accident, we'd still be in tears and still be affected by it today. It doesn't go away. It was such a deep experience. But that applies to Jochen, Piers, Jimmy and everybody that we knew and lost. Helen and I once counted 57 people that had lost their lives in racing, not just in Formula 1. It was the Swinging Sixties, of course, and we joke nowadays that in those days motor racing was dangerous and sex was safe.

Racing drivers in those days had an ability, whether it was Graham Hill or Jack Brabham or Chris Amon, to switch off. We were a different animal because we were living with it so regularly. You could say you were being emotionless, but that's not true. We just dealt with it in different ways.

On one hand, I went to so many funerals, meeting mothers and fathers, brothers and sisters, children of these people who died, while on the other hand François never went to a single funeral. Never. He would not go. He just didn't want to. Yet Dan Gurney flew from California to go to Jimmy's funeral. That's how it was. We all dealt with it in different ways.

It must have hurt tremendously that at the moment of your retirement and celebration of your career, your protégé and someone so close to you was taken, particularly as you had dedicated so much of your life to the pursuit of improving safety in the sport.

No question. It hurt tremendously. But my quest for safety had become by far the most unpopular thing that I was faced with. I don't think there's a single corner of any race track in the world called Stewart corner. The organisers, the governing body and the track owners were so angry that somebody who happened to be the World Champion was saying that we were not going to race at the Nürburgring or Spa, two of the greatest and most demanding race tracks in the world. If somebody asked me what the best lap I ever drove was, it would be the Nürburgring. Spa wasn't far behind it.

But the organisers wouldn't do anything. They wouldn't do one thing. I was Chairman and President of the Grand Prix Drivers' Association (GPDA), and different drivers were chosen to do track inspections. Jim Clark was killed at Hockenheim the day that I was doing the inspection at Jarama, where the Spanish Grand Prix was held at that time. Jochen did the Nürburgring track inspection because he spoke German, but they wouldn't do one single thing on that 23-kilometre track of 160 or so corners. Not one thing. They said if they made one change then we'd want another and another, so they said no to everything. So, we had no choice. We banned the Nürburgring.

Now, can you imagine how unpopular that was? Jackie Stewart was not by any means welcome to any track in the world, because they were always worried about what we'd come up with next. We cancelled Spa, which was the second most respected track in the world. They said they'd run the Belgian race at Zolder instead, but when we went there the track surface was breaking up. We told them they had to resurface during the night and they did it. In those days we had such power, because of the deaths that were happening. The Grand Prix Drivers' Association was a very powerful group, not like today.

In retirement did you redouble your efforts on safety?

No. I didn't think it was my job after I retired. I thought it should be the people who were driving the cars. I thought they were the best authorities, so I never continued that. The governing body wouldn't have wanted me to either.

It's why I make the point about corner names. I think there is a grandstand named after me in Melbourne. But my safety work had made me very unpopular. For 44 years I was the winningest driver in the United Kingdom, but there's no Stewart corner at Brands Hatch or Silverstone or Oulton Park or even Snetterton. I was the man who was up front, demanding things that were costing money which wasn't available at the time. I understand that. But we couldn't have gone on racing as we were. The insurance companies would have stopped it eventually. We didn't have any facilities to avoid another catastrophe like we'd had even as far back as Le Mans in 1955, where 83 fans were killed.

Thank God, the current generation don't have to face the kind of things that we faced. The mood on a starting grid today is totally different than the mood on a starting grid in the '60s and early '70s. So many people were losing their lives that there was a different attitude. Nowadays it is fairly relaxed.

So after Watkins Glen, you're no longer a racing driver, you're no longer a part of the GPDA and you've lost your best friend, not to mention the scores of friends you'd lost before François. Did you have a period of reflection?

No, I don't think so. I felt as if I'd done everything I could. Eventually Sid Watkins and Max Mosley together continued that work to where we see it today. I think the sport today is fantastic, and it is so safe that, oddly, it is almost too safe. The drivers are permitted to make mistakes today that they could not have made in past years. They're a lot more flippant today than they were in those days. They can go off the track and there's run-off areas and if they go far enough and hit something it is a deformable structure. The cockpit and the survival cell is an incredible thing. The Head and Neck Safety device is brilliant. It is a whole different world.

But the camaraderie and the relationships we had back then were fantastic. We holidayed together, we travelled together, the whole atmosphere was totally different.

And your relationship with François was obviously at the very heart of that. Do you remember the first time you met him?

Yes, I do. He went to the Elf racing school down at Paul Ricard in France. Ken and I were the judges and we saw some great young talents down there, the likes of Jean-Pierre Beltoise, Johnny Servoz-Gavin, Jean-Pierre Jabouille and of course François. What Elf did down there was incredible, because at one point there were seven French Grand Prix drivers on the grid. That little school developed the drivers so well.

Then I watched François progress through Formula 3 and Formula 2. Ken and I went to Crystal Palace to watch him race Formula 2 and he was so impressive we picked him up right there to come and join Tyrrell in Formula 1.

You became his mentor. What did you see in him as a racer and as a person?

To begin with he struggled, but between Ken being a great mentor and François and I getting along very well, he developed very quickly. I needed a good team-mate, so I gave him everything I ever knew. There were no secrets between us, no resistance. He became better and better and he certainly would have gone on to win the World Championship. He was that good.

And he was a terrifically good-looking guy. He did a lot of damage, if you know what I mean. He 'walked out' Brigitte Bardot for goodness sake, she chose him. He was tall, dark and handsome, great physique and above all just a really great guy.

Was there ever any jealousy between you two?

None at all. I certainly never had to him, and I don't think he ever did to me. He stayed with us at home a lot, he knew my boys, we travelled together. No, no. He was a top, top guy.

And what kind of a racer was he?

Very clean. But there was only the odd driver who would be less than very correct. In those days if you ran into each other, you just couldn't do it. The number of collisions you see today and the liberties that people take, it's just bizarre. Because nobody gets hurt. In those days it wasn't just getting hurt. Fire would get you in a moment because in those days the fire protection and the fuel tanks were very poor. Your seat was part of the fuel tank. You wouldn't dream of driving into anyone. If there was an accident it was usually a big one. There was not much protection in the car, there was a lot of fire, it was a much more dangerous business.

How close was François getting to you in that final season?

Oh, he was quick. The last time at the Nürburgring, I won it and he was second. At one point he was very close to me. I still had some legs as I knew the track pretty well, but he would have been the absolutely perfect number one for Tyrrell the next season. I think he would have won the World Championship within one or two years. He was as good as I was. Lots of people said he might have been even quicker. I don't know as I never had to push it that hard as I was always pretty canny in those days.

We never had any team orders or anything like that. Ken was never a man like that. The only time it ever came up was in that last Grand Prix when he asked if I'd let François win and I said I'd need to think about it. That was the only time.

Having been to so many funerals before, was it worse having to go to one for François?

His mum and dad were already friends, as were his brothers. But it was something we had got so used to doing.

When I think back, Jimmy Clark's funeral was one of the toughest. Helen didn't come. He was to be Godfather to our youngest son. All of the funerals were awful because there's always parents, there's always family. In Jimmy's case he wasn't married and had no children. It was just amazing, how strong the Clark family were. I'll never forget seeing Dan Gurney in tears in front of Jimmy's mum and dad, and they weren't. They were a strong Scottish couple, and there was big Dan, as strong as a horse, in pieces. It was just a bad, bad period.

And yet it was still glamorous and colourful and exciting and a fantastic world to be living in. Maybe because of how dangerous it was. Maybe because of the death and destruction that we saw up close and personal.

There are very few of us still around. Jacky Ickx and I are good friends now. Chris Amon died from cancer. Jack Brabham has passed away. Graham Hill is no longer with us. Dan Gurney has only recently left us.

Losing Jochen in 1970 was a bad one for me. Losing Jimmy in 1968 was a bad one. And here we were in 1973 and losing François like that was just crushing.

But somehow our mentality as drivers, guys like myself and Mario Andretti, I'm sure he would say the same thing. The relationship and the spirit was fantastic, the friendships were so close. We were proper friends. You know? Real, genuine friends. It was a close community. And maybe because death was so relevant, we were tighter and closer because of that.

Denny Hulme, for example, was a tough nut. His daddy had won the Victoria Cross. The two of us did Can-Am together. I went across the Atlantic 86 times that year. He and I would travel together, always in economy. He'd have *Autosport* magazine and *Playboy*. His jacket stayed done up the whole flight. Anyway, we always tried to get home the same night the race ended, and the fastest way to get out is not what you'd think. It's not a police escort. It's an ambulance. With the siren on an ambulance, everyone moves. We'd worked that out. And so every time we needed to get out of the track, we'd get an ambulance driver to take us. But there'd be a rush to get into the front seat, because nobody wanted to sit in the back. You just didn't want to ever be back there. The spectre of injury and death was very real. We took it very seriously.

So was it your friends that helped you get through that time? And, I guess, through it all, the one constant, your wife, Helen?

Helen went through the whole thing. I married her when I was a clay pigeon shooter. She was fantastic. She never once asked me to stop racing, even after all the deaths. In those days the wives were as close to each other as we were. They had a circle called the Dog House Club where they'd all go and have cups of tea when we were with the engineers. We'd always make sure they had a room at the track where they could set up this club, Bette Hill, Helen and all the wives all together. So when one of the drivers was killed, all the other wives had to look after each other. Helen had to look after Nina when Jochen was killed, Sally when Piers was killed… and she looked after me, too.

But to have to go and pack the bags of somebody who had just been killed, because their wife couldn't stand to go back to the hotel room, well Helen had to do that so many times. She went with so many of the wives to the hospital, helping them all in their moment of absolute grief, while I was still driving around in circles. She was so strong.

Do you think the death of François affected you so much because of the unfulfilled potential?

I don't think so. It was just the worst thing that could have happened at that time. It was as if God had said, 'You've had everything, you've done everything, you've got everything, you've won your World Championships and you have all the money in the world and everything you want', and it was as if he'd turned around and clicked his fingers at that moment and said, 'But don't you dare take anything for granted.' François' death was the worst thing that could have happened.

Do you still think about him?

Oh, sure.
    He's sitting on the left-hand side of the fireplace.
    I think about him all the time.

Sir Jackie Stewart is the founder of Race Against Dementia, a charity established to fight against the as-yet incurable disease that has captured his beloved wife, Lady Helen; it is an illness that will affect one in three of us. For more information, please visit www.raceagainstdementia.com.

Jeff Gordon

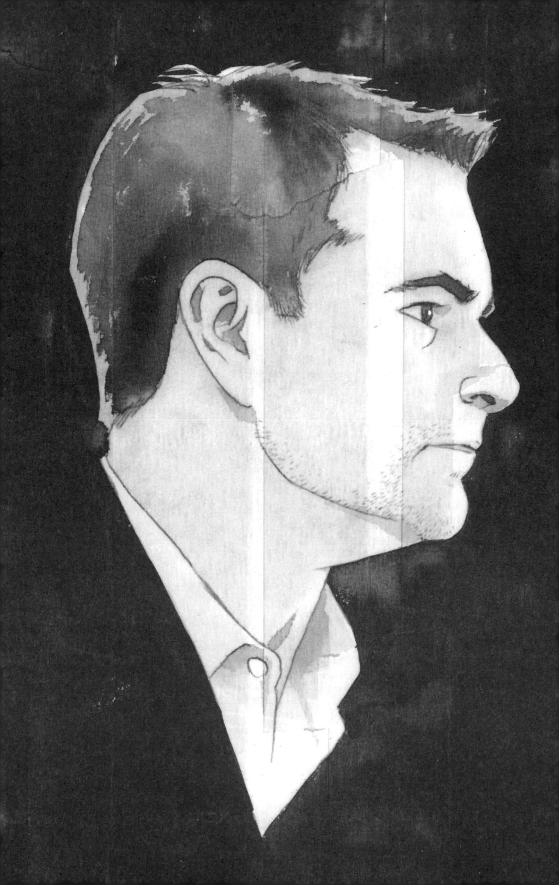

'I had regrets at the time and I knew it wasn't right, but there was
so much distracting me that I thought I'm going to continue down
this path. I hate that about myself. I hate that I did that.'

effery Michael Gordon is recognised around the world as one of the
greatest NASCAR drivers of all time. Entering the top level of stock car
racing in 1993, he quickly established himself as the young pretender to
the throne. His rapid ascent and his rivalry with the mighty Dale Earnhardt
formed the cornerstone of NASCAR's tremendous popularity through the
1990s, establishing it as one of the most watched forms of motor racing in the
world into the new millennium. He won the Winston Cup four times in seven
years in a career that saw him amass almost 900 NASCAR starts and take
home just shy of 100 race wins.

Gordon had it all — talent, speed, good looks. He was a marketing dream
and his rainbow-coloured number 24 Dupont livery became one of the most
recognisable schemes and Gordon himself one of the most successful and
marketable brands in world sport.

Born in California in 1971, Gordon was six months old when his parents
divorced. He was raised by his mother and stepfather, who doted on their
young family and moved mountains to afford the clearly talented youngster
every chance to achieve his dreams. But as Jeff's racing life took off, and as
external influences captured his focus, his relationship with his family suffered.

Jeff Gordon was about to become one of the biggest sporting stars in
the world and one of the most distinguished and revered NASCAR drivers
in history.

But looking back today, the moments of his life that should fill him with the
greatest pride have instead become memories of his deepest regret.

My stepfather, John Bickford, is the one who got me into racing. I was young when I made it to the highest level but it was always the ultimate goal. We worked since I was five and a half years old and my parents had been there supporting me throughout, running my business and helping me align myself with other teams and sponsors and all those things, making the ultimate sacrifice so that I made it to Cup.

But I saw myself wanting to separate myself from them because I wanted to be my own man. I was married at a young age and I wanted to not necessarily think that my mom does this for me and my dad does this for me. So I started to slowly separate that relationship, hoping that it would become a family relationship, not a business relationship. And the way I went about it was one of the worst things that I've ever done. I tried to do it suddenly. I had to be aggressive with it, and my parents were devastated.

I got married in 1994 and I split things off with my parents in '95, the year I won my first Cup Series championship. They should have been there and they were never a part of it. I can't get it back. They should have been there to experience that because they built it. They made it happen. I may have been the one on the stage representing their hard work and sacrifice, but they should have been there, too.

Luckily things eventually worked out for the best because I got them back involved, I got divorced and went through that stage of my life. The divorce was not the most devastating thing. It was tough, but not the worst thing that's happened. I mean, financially it was rough, but not emotionally or mentally.

But that thing with my parents, that was the lowest, toughest thing that I went through and it lasted for seven years.

So take me back to the start, your stepfather being a big influence in your life. Was it something you wanted to do or was it something you were pushed into?

Well, I didn't know anything about racing. I lived in a neighbourhood with a big hill and all the kids in my neighbourhood were a bit older than me and they rode whatever they could down that hill, whether it was a big wheel, a bicycle or a skateboard. So I wanted to be like those kids and I learned to ride a bike at a very young age and started going up and down that hill before going on to race BMX bicycles. My stepfather is very driven and motivated and can build a lot of confidence in you. Immediately it was OK, Jeff is riding his bike so let's take him to the BMX track and make him a bicycle racer. And I started racing BMX. Obviously, my little body wasn't really set for it, but really I would have kept doing it if not for my mom seeing some kids get hurt and deciding she didn't really like it.

Now, my stepdad designed products for people to drive passenger cars without their feet, but on the side was a sometime race-car builder and crew chief. The next thing I know he brings two quarter midget cars home, one for me and one for my sister who is four years older than me. My mom was like, 'I don't understand what's going on here. I thought the bicycle was dangerous and you bring them something with an engine?' And yet he convinced her that it was safe, so that was how I started racing.

I guess I always needed a little push to get into it, but then once I did it, it just felt natural to take it as far as I could take it. I pushed myself once I was into it. But every step of the way whether it was quarter midgets to go-karts or whatever the next step was, I'd be unsure, but then I'd get in it and boom. It was the same every step of the way.

Racing isn't cheap. Was it very much a family affair, with them backing you financially as well as emotionally?

Yeah. They had a small business. They didn't have a lot of money but they had enough. They probably put too much into my racing at certain stages, but from about the age of five and a half until I was about 15 or 16, yeah, they were doing everything they could to support my racing. Once they realised that it was going to get out of their league, they had gotten me enough exposure to where other teams started to take an interest. We never had to pay anybody to put me in a car. There may have been some parts swapped, but that was never contingent on securing a ride

By the time we started to look for other teams to take me, I'd be presented as a guy who could win races and then my stepfather would just ask the question, 'Do you want to run Jeff?' So he would work as my business manager in that sense. He handled it all from team owner to driver coach to getting me on the phone with sponsors to bringing other money in for parts and pieces on the race team, to then it turning into managing my career and putting me with other teams in cars.

So for a decade or more, the sacrifice on the part of your mum and your stepdad must have been vast.

Oh yeah. As a parent now, I look back on it and I'm blown away by that kind of commitment. He believed in me more than I believed in myself. I was always, 'Yeah, you know, I'm OK. I get in the car and I do alright.' But he was always, 'You're not just this, you're going to go here and you're going to go here.'

Do you think he saw something special in you?

I guess. Certainly more than I saw in myself. I always needed a little bit of a push. I wasn't always the most disciplined when it came to stuff like that, but I liked it, I enjoyed racing and I loved competition. I was never a speed demon. I just liked the competition.

But going back to the question of sacrifice, I put my daughter in a race car recently, a couple of years ago, and it was the most terrifying thing I have ever experienced. I really thought I was going to have a heart attack. So for a parent to not only put their child in racing, but then pursue it and push it and to see the cars get faster and more dangerous, I don't know if I have that in me as a parent. But I'm thankful that they did.

We see it all the time in racing, the karting dads that end up following their kids or hanging off their kids' coat-tails through their whole careers. How difficult was it to maintain a family relationship, a father/son relationship, with that manager/driver/coach relationship and to know that behind those hard pushes and difficult edges, there was love?

Well, this is where it was quite unique for me, because it was my stepfather. If it had been my father, I don't know if it would have worked out. I think that, at some point, where you are blood-related, you have to shut off some of the business mind and aspect of it, and the emotional, family, blood relationship overrides that. I didn't have that with him. There was love but our relationship from the beginning was almost like a business relationship and I think that's what I struggled with. I didn't want to have that kind of relationship with my stepfather. I wanted a loving relationship with him, do family things together and take vacations. We didn't do that. When I talked to him it was like me talking to a business manager.

That was part of the reason why I wanted to draw the line with that, because I thought now it's more important for us to be family. And that was where I was wrong. That's not the way our relationship was.

Do you think he needed that, not being your blood father? It's so easy, I imagine, in that role of stepfather, to feel that you're an outsider in a child's life and that you're pushing too much into the life of a child that isn't your own. Do you think he maybe needed the racing as a way of forming a bond with you, and something that would bind you together in the absence of a blood tie?

You know, everybody, but especially as a parent, you want to feel needed. You want to feel like you're making a difference and helping your child through life. My kids are never going to be totally separate from me, they're always going to need a little something, and that's the relationship I have with my stepfather today. I call him, we have lunch, and I tell him what's going on business-wise because I want his opinion because he's a smart guy and I can tell he loves that. And that's what we missed in those seven years. I didn't feel like I needed him and I think that crushed him.

I guess those formative years as a child, you just want him to love you but maybe he felt as though he needed that managerial role to form that bond?

I don't know. I was just living. I wasn't thinking big picture. You don't as a kid. I just went here and went racing. Went there and went racing. But I certainly didn't worry about our relationship back then.

So as you got into the higher levels of racing, as you achieved this success, your parents were both there. Were they coming to all the races, were they a constant part of the inner circle?

Yeah. They were very involved. Mom would do the scoring, keep the times. My dad would work on the car. Even when I wasn't driving for them, they were still involved.

When I got into the Cup Series, there's not much obviously that they could do any more. Now you have a whole infrastructure of people around the car and it's a totally different type of car. Even though my dad probably wanted to help on the building side, and actually as a manufacturer he ended up designing a lightweight jack that a lot of teams still use in the Cup Series, he ended up being much more involved in my personal contracts, personal services, those kind of things. He was running my office for me.

And then you got married, to Brooke.

Yeah. We'd been dating for maybe a year.

And did your parents like her?

Erm, maybe at first. But they blamed her for pulling me away from them. So, no. And then, as ugly as the divorce was, they definitely didn't like that and what that did to their son. My mom and my dad are really good. If they didn't like her, they didn't say it. I guess because they thought if I was happy then they were happy.

Once you got married, did you notice the relationship with your parents start to change?

Definitely. It started to change because they saw me starting to change. They saw me evolving and doing different things and travelling the world, making a lot of money. I moved out of North Carolina and down to Florida and then what really became a barrier was that my wife's family became involved in all the things we were doing and my family got left behind.

So they saw that they were coming second, where they used to be right there in everything. I think they had some resentment towards her at that point and could see that she was starting to drive a wedge between me and them. My ex never said that she didn't like them, she just saw them having some control and she wanted to be the one who had control.

Did you see it at the time, or were you so wrapped up in marriage and your career taking off and living in Florida that you were blinded to it all?

I had no idea. To me at that time, my life could not have been any better. We were living life and I was winning races. My career was ridiculous, the lifestyle I was living, and we did cool, fun things. At that point the lifestyle just continued to build and build, so I was so wrapped up in that and having fun. Even as my relationship with my parents got worse, I had regrets at the time and I knew it wasn't right, but there was so much distracting me that I thought I'm going to continue down this path.

I hate that about myself. I hate that I did that. I should have been strong enough to say 'No! This isn't right.' I made some effort, you know? 'OK, your parents are coming for Christmas, so when do my parents get to come?' I'd make some effort, but not enough. It should not have been like that for so long.

I won all four of my Cup Championships with a wedge between me and my family. Maybe it wasn't quite as bad in 1995, but in 1997, 1998 and 2001 we had no relationship. I got divorced in 2002 and so they really never got to be fully engaged and a part of my championships. And I never won another championship after 2001. So when they came back on board, even though business-wise it was more successful financially because the sport and the money was getting better, and even though I had some good years on track, I never won another championship.

So, that wedge. When did it come and why did it come?

It was sort of gradual. Don't get me wrong, there were a few things on my mind too. When I got married my mom was still paying my bills. She was still balancing my cheque book practically. Those things needed to come out of her hands and I needed to be more responsible on that side of things.

From my dad's standpoint, there were some things that we needed to get sorted out where what he controlled and the things that he was in control of in respect of my affairs, allied to the fact I'm now married, really needed to be looked at. That started to become a wedge because I was thinking it, but my wife was the one acting on it. She was the one pushing, telling me I needed to go in there and say, 'You can't do this and you can't do that.'

So I suddenly started bringing these things up. 'You know Mom, we need to hire an accountant,' and she'd say, 'Well I don't mind doing it, so you don't have to pay for someone else.' And I'd have to turn around and say, 'Well, you know there are some bills coming in that are personal', and I think there was one particular moment where something was bought that was expensive and my Mom questioned it and my wife found out about that and just went off. 'She shouldn't even know about it, it's not her decision.' So, it's little things like that and it started building.

What ended up happening was I suddenly went about trying to move them to the side, and it wasn't really registering. And then one day I just said, 'OK, we have to have a meeting', and I wrote down a list of all the things they were doing that I wanted them to step away from and hire somebody else to do, and when I showed them the list my dad just looked at me and said, 'Well, you don't need me any more. Because everything on that list is what I do.'

And that's when it started to go downhill.

Was that you initiating it? Had you discussed it with your wife?

Yeah, it was me and my wife. I would have probably done it over time, and now I know, having talked to my parents, that they'd seen it, they understood. We could have come up with a plan together and phased it out over time, leaving them with the things that we still thought it was important for them to be involved in. We could easily have done that. That's the thing. It just didn't happen at a mutually agreed timeframe.

So that meeting, that list, what happened after that?

It was bad. I lived probably 30 minutes from them, and maybe we'd have a weekend off and they'd be on a Sunday drive around the lake area where I lived and they'd just pull into my drive to stop by to say 'hello', and my wife would be like, 'They didn't call, I don't understand why they're coming over.' And then she'd say, 'Don't answer the door.' Oh yeah, shit like that. It got ugly.

I think my parents, while they blamed her because I'm their son, they knew I could have done more too.

But at that time you don't see it because you're so caught up in it. You want to be a man. I'm married now and I have to look out for my family and we make our decisions together as a unit.

Right!

It's so hard! And at the same time that all of this was going on, it was 1995 and you were driving to your first championship. How did you keep focused on racing when you had this tremendous inner emotional turmoil developing?

You know, that's something I never really struggled with. I never let outside distractions affect what I did in the car. I had a very good race team and car so that spoke for itself in the performance. But even through the rest of my career, there's always stressful things going on in life. Whether your career is booming and you've got to make strategic decisions to take advantage of opportunities, be it marketing or licensing or whatever it may be, purchases, growing your business, they're all stressful but they're also distractions. If you can't manage those distractions when it's time to get in the car then you shouldn't be a professional race car driver.

No, for sure. But there are business and marketing decisions, and there's your family. There's your heart. Your soul. Or actually, are they the same? Is that just a racing driver's mentality? You get in the car, you pull your lid on, you buckle up and everything else is gone?

It was for me.

Then I guess the time when it all comes home is when you take off your helmet and you're no longer in that bubble.

Yeah. You get out and you celebrate and when you do that you want to be surrounded with the people that you care about the most in the world. You want to be with the people that worked the hardest to get you there, whether that's your team that worked on your car or your family, especially the ones that were there from the start, to see how far it's come and where it's gone to.

And so if I won a big event, I was yearning for them to be there. Especially the championship. It's the culmination of it all. They did come in '95, but there was a wedge and it wasn't the same. It wasn't the same embrace. It wasn't the moment that it should have been and I will never get that back. Just thinking about it right now, it sends shivers up my spine. It was my first championship at the NASCAR level but that moment was ruined because of these other things, personal things in my life. And I allowed that to happen. That pisses me off.

So for all the 1990s and into the early 2000s, were your family ever there again?

No. If anything it got worse through the late 1990s.

It was in 2001 that I started to recognise this wasn't right. That this wasn't the way I wanted to live my life. I think I started making a more conscious effort to include them in things, whether people around me agreed with that or not.

Do you remember that first moment you realised you had to sort things out?

Yeah, I do.

When I won the championship in 2001, I'm on stage, I'm celebrating and I'd moved to a new crew chief and it was a big personal victory for me because prior to that everyone had said that Ray Evernham was the greatest crew chief of all time and he was the contributing factor to all of my success. And, of course, in many ways that's true. Well, Ray left the team in 1999 and in 2000 we struggled so everyone said, 'Yeah, I told you it was all him.' Well in 2001 we won it all and it was a personal high for me. It was possibly the greatest accomplishment for me.

I'd already been having some issues in my marriage, but the absolute light-bulb moment for me was I'm on stage and they're handing me the trophy and I'm celebrating and we're taking pictures and then somebody says, 'OK, we'll go and get Brooke over for some photos.' I'm like, OK, great. So they go over and get her and she comes over and she's pissed off. I mean, super pissed off.

This is it, the crowning, most amazing moment in my life and she's mad because somebody else had to go get her. That I didn't come get her sooner to be a part of this moment. And I knew right then, we were done.

I thought, listen if you can't put your selfishness to one side at that one moment and realise what this moment is all about, then we truly don't belong together. So that was it for me.

She and I hardly ever fought about anything, but looking back I realised that's because I pretty much did whatever she wanted me to do. I just catered to her and spoiled her and we had this great life together because of that. And in that moment I was like, nope. That's it. I think that was the culmination of the build-up of all the other crap that was going on too, the stuff with my parents, and so when that happened it was boom, we are done.

And from that moment on, I decided to change my life. And the first person that I called was my mom. And I said, 'Mom, I need to come home, sit with you', and I went straight to their house, sat down and told her I was getting a divorce. And I am sure she wanted to just leap for joy, but she didn't. She embraced me. She was sad that it was going on and that I was hurting, but I said right then, 'You and I and John, we are going to fix this. This has gone on for too long and I know I can't take it back but I'm going to fix this.' I could tell that, even though it was a sad day, it was one of the happiest days for her.

And how about with John, your stepdad? Did it come back quickly?

Oh yeah. When that call came, he played it cool, you know, 'OK, yeah let's talk.' But on the inside he's like, 'Yes!'

And so from 2002 onwards, did you feel different? Was there a levity or an ease around you?

Oh yeah. Everyone was just like, man where have you been? You've been so, so different for the last seven years and now I was interacting with old friends and catching up on old times and just relaxed and out and about and not on eggshells wondering if she is going to be OK if I do this. It was so amazing. For my parents it was great, for other parts of my family, for friends.

Of course, I was single too. So that was fun.

And then you found Ingrid. Was it tough at that point to think, shit I really don't want to get back into the same routine that I did before, I don't want to be that guy again, let a relationship affect who I am and my relationship with my parents? Or was that not even an issue because you were aware of how bad things had got last time and how far you'd strayed from who you were?

Well, I think that I wanted to recognise those things before you take those steps. I also realised I got married really young the first time. I was too young to be married and I needed to live my life more, so I said, OK, I'm going to make up for lost time, live my life and I actually happened to meet Ingrid in 2002 when I was still going through my divorce. I met her, we dated for a short period of time, but I told her that I was in absolutely no position or place to be in a committed relationship. I said, you're amazing and I hate that I'm saying this, but I will ruin this.

She was hurt but she got it. So we went our separate ways for two years and then I ran into her in New York, I'd gone through the fun times, started to get a better feeling of who I was, what I wanted out of life and the mistakes I had made the first time, and that if I ever met the right one how I would do it differently. And once I reconnected with Ingrid it was clear we wanted the same things. It wasn't about being married or having a certificate or standing up in front of 700 people, we just wanted to have a relationship, we wanted to have children and that's what led us on our path.

And she let me be me! She was independent enough, confident enough in herself and lived her life and her own career, travelling around the world, where she wasn't trying to hover around me. I'd already said I'm going to do my own thing because I'd made that mistake the first time, but she was already down that path of wanting me to be me. I was not going to let my feelings for somebody else allow me to lose sight of myself.

Is that ultimately the lesson of those seven years?

Absolutely. I have no regrets. It taught me a lot. Sure, I wish I'd made a few different choices and decisions, but I'm happy for the lessons and the experience because it taught me so much about myself. We always say, the hardest things in life, be it racing, the bad losses or the personal tragedies, those things teach you more about who you are and how to get through life than the successes.

And as a father now yourself, those lessons become all the more valuable.

Definitely. Oh yeah. Now, I totally look at it differently. For how I want my kids to focus on being independent, to live their lives. You're going to go through these stages in your life when what you want out of it changes, who you are, what's important to you.

Just don't try to move too fast, too early. Life has a lot to offer.

Jimmie Johnson

**'I experienced the most intense internal struggle I have known as a driver...
When the crash started, I literally thought I was dead. And then to sit there, in the
dark, and to have all that time to think... I left that desert a totally different man.'**

Jimmie Kenneth Johnson is hands down one of the greatest drivers ever to have sat behind the wheel of a stock car and an undeniable motor racing legend. He is the only driver to have won five Winston Cups in a row, and with his total of seven championships (so far) he ties with Richard Petty and Dale Earnhardt for the most NASCAR titles in history. He is a four-time All Star race winner, a two-time Daytona 500 winner and a four-time winner of both the Coca Cola 600 and Brickyard 400 races. At the time of writing he has amassed more than 80 career victories and over 350 top-ten finishes at the top level. These are the statistics of one of the most sublime racers NASCAR has ever known.

Born in 1975 in El Cajon, California, Jimmie was racing before he'd left pre-school, making his competitive début on motorbikes at the age of four. Ultimately four wheels and off-road shone the brightest light for the youngster, dirt and trucks providing the adrenalin rush and competitive spur of his nascent career.

Eighteen years after his first outing on two wheels, Jimmie Johnson made the move from dirt to asphalt to mark the start of a stock car career that has rewritten the record books. He became only the second rookie in history to secure pole position for the Daytona 500 and won on just his 13th start in the Winston Cup. He took his first championship in 2006 and an astonishing five-year title-winning streak followed. He turned the sport on its head and redefined NASCAR for a new generation.

But Jimmie Johnson wasn't always so revered. In his youth he was wild, his excesses and hot-headedness making him a sketchy prospect. Far from having an assured path to the top of the sport, his mistakes left him staring at the void. At a time when he could have been learning from his mistakes, he was compounding them.

The folly of his youth left him in his most desperate state, fearing not only for his future but also for his life. In the pitch dark of the Californian desert, Jimmie Johnson faced his demons and emerged a changed man.

There was a lot going on with my career in 1995. I was 19 years old and it was a pivotal year for me, getting connected to the right team owners that ultimately helped me bridge the gap from dirt racing into stock car racing. There was a lot going on in a lot of areas.

Most specifically, 1995 ended up being so huge because of what happened to me after I crashed in the Baja 1000. I literally sat there for a day until help got to me. I mean, I yelled at myself, I'm not sure if I punched myself but I experienced the most intense internal struggle that I have known as a driver.

I'd started driving for Chevy at 15, racing their stadium trucks and then transitioned into the endurance desert racing. And man, I was fast. Prior to that day I was about as fast as it came. But I never finished. I crashed and I crashed, right up until that race. And from that day on, and I had probably another three or four years of dirt racing after that, but I have not been upside down in a car since that day.

When the crash started, I literally thought I was dead. And then to sit there, in the dark, and to have all that time to think... I left that desert a totally different man.

When you started out you didn't want to be on four wheels, right? You wanted to be on two.

I did. My grandparents owned a motorcycle shop and you know I just grew up in that space. All my heroes were definitely dirt racers and most of them were two-wheeled dirt racers. My start came in motocross and that was really my world growing up.

In California, where I was a kid, there was a huge culture for bikes with some of the biggest names. I guess they're all old now, but guys like Ricky Johnson and Jeff Ward, the guys from that Southern California area were my heroes. That was my back yard. That's where I grew up.

Was the mindset between motocross and then going dirt racing very different? Were there any similarities between the two?

Definitely. You know on motocross there are plenty of obstacles and you're off the ground a lot, line choice, tyres and then the dirt. That was very similar on four wheels. My first start on four wheels was in this little buggy in the Mickey Thompson Stadium Series and it was almost like a formula car with a roll cage. So that transition from two to four was, I'm not going to say easy, but it was a similar type of racing. Not at all like when I transitioned from off-road truck racing to stock cars and asphalt. I mean, for that I had to start over. That was a totally different experience.

In Europe kids from a young age race with slicks and wings on asphalt, but in the States it seems they often start on dirt tracks. Is there a difficulty moving from dirt onto asphalt or is there some similarity in terms of trying to find grip and choosing the right line?

The dirt really forces you to make some compromises. It's probably an arguable point, but guys that only drive on asphalt are used to a high grip level and they can really perfect aspects of a set-up and have good consistent grip. On dirt you're always chasing moisture and lines moving for all kinds of reasons, if it's holes changing and bumps, the dirt changing or whatever it might be, you are forced to explore lines and make compromises and I think that's been a big help for me. What was tough for me though is that in my form of dirt racing, we never worried about the turns. The turns are what you did after all the jumps and so my mind was very much in tune with springs and shocks and making the vehicle handle over the bumps.

So when I got into stock cars I had to learn a whole set of new terms and how to use the car from an aero standpoint. We never had that with trucks. We didn't care about aerodynamics and getting the vehicle low. It was all about speed in a straight line. In stock cars you had to incorporate turning and cross weight and the rear roll-centre height and things that are more specific to NASCAR like the track bar, camber and all the things that will make a car turn. I didn't have the slightest clue. I knew what it meant to go straight but I had to really learn stock car racing and oval track racing in general. It was quite a learning curve.

So what kind of a racer were you when you were this young buck racing on dirt tracks? Were you aggressive? Were you all about elbows out and fighting?

I was aggressive but I wasn't real big into the conflict, you know? I was always respectful to others on track. Of course, my aggression led to some mistakes and I upset a few people along the way but more than anything I was just taking too much risk and I had some huge and spectacular crashes. In the stadium trucks and the desert trucks that I raced, I mean I'd just be up front, running well and then had a huge yard sale, time after time.

Why was that?

So, when I started on four wheels I was 15 and racing in a lower division in a buggy. At the end of that year I got spotted by Herb Fishel from the Chevrolet race shop and they were looking to build a second stadium truck. They decided to put Rick Johnson in the primary truck and then develop a new truck for me. So I'm in this new truck, I'm under contract with Chevy at 16 and I just didn't know any different, you know? The racing that we did in the stadiums was a 15-lap feature on a stadium floor so the race might take five to seven minutes. I just got set on this habit of... kill. You didn't have time and you couldn't wait for something to come to you. You just had to go, go, go.

And then as that sport went under eventually, that transitioned into the endurance racing. Now I'm 19 and they give me the keys to a trophy truck, a Chevrolet factory-backed programme, the fastest vehicle on the planet to race on dirt and go around all these obstacles. In one race, I literally ripped the right side off the truck at the very first mile marker of what was a 500-mile race.

I couldn't get that out of my wiring. I just grew up in that environment. Short, high-energy bursts of racing. It took until that crash in '95, just sitting there reflecting on what was the second big wreck I'd had in that truck that year, for things to change. Because I had just about killed myself.

I'd been in the truck for like 18 hours. I thought I could solo the event, which was a mistake. I was up in the hills about midway down the Baja peninsula, up in the mountains, and I'd nodded off while driving. I woke up and realised I was in high gear and that I had a very low-speed 90-degree right-hand turn in front of me. I just went sailing off the side.

Before I left the road I hit a massive rock that set me into an inverted flip out into the darkness. I didn't know how far I was going to fall. Fortunately it was just down an embankment and it wasn't anything too severe, but I'll never forget plunging into the darkness when I was kind of shocked back to being awake and just seeing all the headlights on my truck just shooting right up into the black and feeling the truck rotating around, flipping over. I had no idea where I was going to land. How it was going to come out. So that left a pretty big impression in my mind.

You know, the day following, sitting there, was just big for me. I did a lot of soul-searching about the way I was racing and what I was doing.

That's a lot to take on board. Do you remember landing?

I do. We hit the rock on the passenger side and that ripped the front right off and stuffed it back into my co-rider. And then the first impact was on my side and it smashed the cage down on top of me and actually pinned me in the truck. As we tumbled over a couple of times, we ended up back on our wheels. My co-rider was knocked out and was making some pretty bad wheezing noises. So I thought he had broken ribs and a punctured lung. In the end he ended up just being bruised up and fine, it was just the way he was sitting in the seat unconscious that led to his breathing being like that. But I came out pretty much unscathed. Just trying to get out of the truck from the roll cage having been smashed on top of me was the only difficulty I had.

Could you get yourself out of the truck?

Once we came to a stop I could see the roll cage was pushing me towards the centre of the vehicle. My left hand was in a bit of pain as one of the bars for the window area had smashed down onto the steering wheel and cut my hand, but then as I pulled the steering wheel off and my eyes started to focus I was really worried about fire. I evaluated the situation, turned the power off, looked around and I saw my co-rider unconscious. There's a lot of space inside the truck and I was able to get out at that point.

How long was your co-rider out for?

Probably 30 seconds or so.

Were you able to get him out of the truck as well?

On his side the cage was more intact. It was more the suspension that was pushed back into the foot box on his side of the vehicle so he was able to get out pretty OK. But then we were just stuck there. It was the early days of GPS and tracking back then and the series had helicopters and aircraft there to help transmit radio broadcasts. But at night in Mexico you can't fly those kind of aircraft, so during the night they're all down obviously and we're up in the mountains. Where we crashed we couldn't get a transmission out for help. In the meantime we have a vehicle, called the chase vehicle, that follows each vehicle down the peninsula and they try and leapfrog you to assist if you have a mechanical problem or need to change a spare tyre and come help if you crash, whatever it is.

Well, my chase vehicle got into a fender bender in some small town and my guys were arrested. So as I crash and need assistance and help, my guys are trying to buy their way out of some Mexican jail and lose track of where I'm at, out on the race course.

So, once they get turned loose and get out and get going, they understand that they haven't heard a radio transmission from me, I haven't cleared the next checkpoint and they literally go to the checkpoint that I last crossed through, and they start driving down the race course itself, trying to find me. We crashed just before sunrise and it was at around sunset that those guys showed up.

We were able, somehow, to get the vehicle moving again. They had a bunch of tools and welders and all of those sorts of things. So we got the vehicle started and moving out of this area of rock and boulders that we'd come to a rest in and drove the vehicle out to the paved area where we had a truck and trailer. By the time we got it up on the trailer and to say that we're officially safe, it was damn near a full day from the crash to when the truck was put on the trailer.

When you were sitting there, then, for almost a full day, with your co-rider, did you say much to each other? Did he give you any grief over the incident? Or was it very much a time of solitary thought and consideration?

He didn't give me much grief. We were both pretty nervous about my future. As I mentioned, this was the second big crash I'd had. The first one, two months before, had almost completely destroyed the truck and then this incident happened and the vehicle was in such rough shape that as we looked at it, we thought that when somebody gets here we might just pull the engine out of it and leave the rest here. It was destroyed.

And where it was positioned, between these boulders, we weren't even sure we would get it out. So it was more quiet than anything. My co-rider is a great friend and I think kind of sensed what I was going through, the soul-searching I was going through and the concern I had for my career and what this meant, what was going to be next.

Young racing drivers think they're invincible. Did that crash give you a kick in the pants? Was it what you needed, in hindsight?

It really was. You know, for me, as an individual, the risks I was taking, I just got so comfortable over that 100 percent effort line. Vehicles, at least in the off-road days, flipping one, sure it hurts, but it's not like doing 200 plus in a Formula 1 car or a NASCAR and hitting a concrete wall. So, you know, the penalty for failure really didn't have as a high a consequence and it was really easy on dirt and in these trucks to just kind of live on the wrong side of the line.

That moment scared me so badly. Granted, it wasn't that I was pushing too hard. I simply dozed off and then woke up and realised what was going on, but it still had that profound effect even though it wasn't a typical mistake.

After that, the funding at the team I was driving for dried up and I didn't have any backing. So I had to hit the street, start selling myself and try to find my next opportunity. I still had Chevy's backing and blessing but, you know, it humbled me to have that event as my last one. Not only did that day in the desert thinking about things change me, I had to now go out and sell myself and reflect back on that moment, tell that story and try to tell owners that I'd changed, that I was different and more mature.

I actually spent much of the next year commentating in the pits for the off-road series so that I could stay current and relevant as I was trying to sell myself. And while I was out there doing the commentating I got connected with the Herzog family. I ended up spending two years in trucks with them and then they had goals of making it to NASCAR. They invested six years in me in three different series to get me up and going before I was spotted by Jeff Gordon and Rick Hendrick. So there was a long road to follow, not just after that day in the desert but before I really got my chance.

So that moment in the desert, was it a conversation you had with yourself? Did you almost have two voices talking and fighting with each other, or were you reflecting over moments of your career to that point and thinking I could have done this differently or should have done this differently?

I was much more in a reflecting space. I just kept asking, why? You idiot! Why this? Why did you do that? Why? You know? WHY?

When I was racing in stadium trucks I had multiple races where, with a couple of laps to go, whatever it might be, I'd be in the lead and make a mistake and tip it over in a turn.

Too much speed, lose the balance, onto the door and over onto the roof. Why? Why was I doing that? I should have had this one in the bag and that one, and so many races. So, yeah, there was a lot of reflecting.

And to have to then go and sell yourself. We often say that drivers are only as good as their last race, so to have to sell yourself on that basis, with a year out as well, on pit road, how tough was it to convince people that, yes, you may have built up something of a reputation but you had seen the light and you could harness what you hadn't been able to harness before?

It wasn't easy. Especially in the off-road industry there are people that compete out of a love for racing and it's more of a hobby for them than it is a profession. So first of all, to find a team with a professional mindset and a place to grow my career was really tough.

The one thing that really helped me through it all was having Chevrolet's support. They saw something and continued to believe in me and that shining light really helped as time went on. And then I met the Herzogs and got to know them. They'd been racing as independents for many years and badly wanted manufacturer support. From afar it always appeared they had big support, but really they'd been funding everything by themselves. So having Chevy's involvement and potential further interest in the team for the future was the perfect storm that came together.

We talk about support all the time and I think often people think that support is a financial thing more than anything else, but it certainly sounds like you needed emotional support and guidance from those people in those positions more than anything. Did you find that you had that from the Herzogs and from Chevrolet at that time?

Yeah, I really did. And that was one thing that really got me through. Prior to meeting the Herzogs, I couldn't get anyone to commit to funding me. I had all these great people around me, I'd learned how to network like you wouldn't believe, I had all these contacts, all this support, everyone saying you're going to make it. The energy was there. But nobody would write a damn cheque. So I was very rich with support, and I think that has helped shape me into who I am and leads me to want to help others.

I've had great mentors, you know, people who believed in me and supported me emotionally and I find myself doing that stuff now as well. There were some frustrating moments of thinking... this is all great, but where's my ride? I need a car, I need something to race.

So when you're finally making it and you have this great career and all of the success and you look back on those days as a kid, the folly of youth and the big crashes, do you view them maybe not necessarily with fondness but with a wry smile of having to go through that in order to get to where you did?

Without a doubt. My journey made me who I am. I'm very, very grateful because it has turned out in epic proportions. You know, in my early days I didn't win a lot. I was always around but I made plenty of mistakes and threw wins away. But I was moving quickly and racing against people who were much older in a professional space. I was a teenager, and I didn't really experience success until my Cup career started when I was 26. And yet all the while I had this great support from Chevy.

You think about any form of racing, and 26 is pretty far into it. But that's really when things started to turn around for me and I started to experience great success. I fell in love with this sport because of the experiences and the people and I had the right reasons in place and really have enjoyed my experiences. The success came after it.

So in all aspects I am grateful that my journey turned out as it has because I think it taught me to be much more understanding and just to come from a different place. Ultimately to lead me to where I sit now.

Without that scare do you think you'd have achieved the heights that you have?

I don't think so. Actually, I know for sure I wouldn't have. Not only that day in the desert thinking about things, but the window of time after that and selling myself and deep conversations about if I get a chance again what I'm going to do with it, how I'm going to treat it… that all happened because of that crash.

Ultimately you don't know what you've got until you almost lose it all.

Mario Andretti

'How close does it have to get... how do I just go on? All of us race drivers are doing the same thing so even after he was injured my brother understood why I kept racing. So would Ronnie Peterson... It was our brother bond.'

Mario Gabriele Andretti is widely considered to be one of the greatest racing drivers in history. In a career spanning six decades, and that continues to this day, he has competed and been victorious in everything from dirt track to stock cars, Formula 1 to Indycar, NASCAR to sportscars. If it had an engine in it, chances were Mario Andretti could win in it.

Even today, over two decades after his official full-time retirement from motor racing, his is a name so revered that it has come to symbolise the finest elements of what it is to be a racing driver.

Mario and his identical twin brother Aldo were born in February 1940, in Rina, Istria, then part of the Kingdom of Italy. Today part of Croatia, his childhood home found itself annexed by Yugoslavia at the end of the Second World War and as part of the Istrian Exodus of 1948 the Andretti family found itself homed in a refugee camp in Lucca, Italy. Mario and Aldo fell in love with motorsport as boys, seeing the Mille Miglia in the flesh for the first time in 1954 just one year before they sailed for America to begin a new life in Pennsylvania.

America's fertile racing scene proved a happy hunting ground for the two talented Italian hotshots, who raced anything and everything on which they could lay their hands. They were considered equally gifted and their reputations became as recognisable as their names and good looks, but it was Mario who excelled after two devastating crashes cut short Aldo's burgeoning race career.

Mario Andretti went on to be a four-time Indycar champion, in 1965, 1966,

1969 and 1984. He was 1978 Formula 1 World Champion. His sportscar successes included three Sebring 12 Hours victories. In NASCAR he won the fabled Daytona 500 in 1967. He was named Driver of the Century by the Associated Press.

He was, and he is, one of the very finest racing drivers ever.

To many, Mario Andretti *is* motorsport.

———————

I was fortunate in my career to almost always be moving forward. I was always making some sort of progress. Of course, there were times when things looked bleak, but I never suffered that absolute lowest point of devastation.

I think I have two strengths that have been critical all my life. One is the ability to adapt. People who adapt survive. And the other is resilience. And resilience is the quality that when you get knocked down, whatever happens, you can quickly rebuild yourself, pick yourself up and keep moving forward.

Fatalities in the sport aside, my own journey had a steady stream of disappointments from early on. I can't compare them to the death of a fellow racer or friend or close team-mate. These are heartbreaks in an entirely different compartment. There is no setback with the magnitude of a fatality.

When I talk about my stream of disappointments, I'm referring to things like in 1961 when I was trying to go from stock cars into sprint cars. I was supposed to race in a URC [United Racing Club] sprint car race at the Bedford Fair in Pennsylvania and my car didn't show up. So, I'm walking around the paddock with a helmet under my arm asking for a ride with anyone who would have me and it seemed everyone looked at my small physical stature and figured there's no way you can drive a car without power steering.

While it was discouraging, and I must say quite annoying, it just made me work harder. Mind over matter. That was me. Mind over matter, mind over everything. My rationale was always that this was part of progress and I was in progress mode. I could tell myself, OK that isn't the one but I'm evolving. The next one will be the one. Or the next one. I believed it would work, never that it wouldn't. I was so determined and steadfast and relentless. Or maybe just a dreamer. A pipe dreamer to be exact, a little Italian kid with a huge imagination and an unlikely-to-ever-happen plan. Just Hope with a capital H.

And when my manic pursuit lined up with luck, suddenly it clicked. And seize the moment is exactly what I did and what I still do.

And in my case, almost every negative eventually would become a positive.

How did you get started in racing?

I was 15 when we moved to America and I thought all our dreams of becoming race car drivers were being left behind. As luck would have it, there was a half-mile dirt track near where we lived in Pennsylvania. My twin brother Aldo and I thought it looked very do-able. But how exactly do you become a racer without a car? Well, we decided to build one.

Twin boys who spoke Italian were quite the spectacle in our little Pennsylvania town. Everyone knew about us. So we gathered four buddies and the six of us decided to build a 1948 Hudson Hornet into a Sportsman Stock Car. The plan was that Aldo and I would be the drivers and the other four guys would be the brains of the operation. To get started, each of us threw in whatever little money we had from working part-time at the gas station. Combined, we had about 500 bucks.

Then, the clever guy in our bunch named Charlie Mitch came up with the idea of buying information. Good old Charlie, the mastermind in the group. He was the one who actually understood pretty much what we needed to make the car go faster. NASCAR was coming to life and Charlie knew all about it and knew that Hudson as a manufacturer was dominating especially on the short tracks. One of the Hudson factory teams was dissolving; Marshall Teague and Herb Thomas were the top guys and they were folding up the team because Hudson went out of business, so we bought all the information like set-ups from the Marshall Teague team in the Carolinas. And that's why the car was as fast as it was.

As I said, all of us digging up every last dime we had only got us 500 bucks. And the price tag on the information was $1,000. We needed another $500, but to borrow it from the bank, you need credit, which we didn't have. Then, this guy named Jimmy Taviani who had a business in the neighbourhood and sort of liked us, agreed to co-sign a loan for us. That's how we got the $1,000. In the end, we bought more information than we needed and some of it wasn't relevant, but we bought set-ups and information about shocks, cambers, cross weight, ride heights, tilt and so on.

Because Jimmy Taviani co-signed the loan for us, we put his company name on the car and he bought the fuel, tyres and gave us a garage to work in, with all the tools. The six of us boys worked day and night on that car to get it ready for the start of the next racing season. We were *so* proud when we made our début with the Hudson. Aldo drove the first weekend and me the next. And we each won.

That's not the whole story though. You see Aldo and I were under-age, so we had to change the birth date on our entrance forms. You had to be 21 to race legally and professionally and we were 19. Everyone knew we were the twins from Italy, but it's not like there were computers to check our background. So even with our fake IDs, the local organiser asked about our race experience. We made up a story about how we used to race in Italy.

'Yeah, yeah, we raced Formula Junior,' and we gave them all these names of places we'd raced and who we'd raced against and the story took on a life of its own. Thankfully, in those days there was no way for anyone to check. Even 15 years into my professional career, I had to tell people, 'You've got to let that story go, it's bullshit! I never raced in Italy!' We made it all up just so they'd let us race that first time. Who would ever think it's that hard to erase a lie?

So, with fake IDs and a fake resumé in place, my brother and I obviously wanted to look like race drivers. We had to look like we had done this before. Aldo and I had a little money from working at my uncle's gas station, so we bought two Sala Sport driving suits from Italy with all the zippers and stuff. Aldo's was blue, mine was white, and when we showed up the locals said, 'Oh my God, here are the boys, champions from Italy.' Everyone else was there in their T-shirts and we really looked the part.

Aldo was the first to race our car and they started him last, but one by one he passed everybody and won the race. I couldn't believe my eyes. And there we go, cash in hand, $25 for the victory. And then in the feature they started him last and again I couldn't believe my eyes. Bam, bam, bam, passing everyone, and he wins the feature and $150.

Our first race was March 27th, 1959 and by July my brother and I had paid everyone off, including the bank. We were the sole owners. We had no more debt. At age 19, our dream had become reality. So, four years after arriving in America, my brother and I were both racing. One car. He would drive one weekend and I'd drive the next. In our first four races, each of us won twice. And that's how it began for me.

At that time, I thought the next step would have been sprint cars and I kept going to the track trying to wiggle my way in but couldn't even get a practice. Just rejection. So, what to do?

How did you get from there to the big time?

By age 21 I was married and looking to get into sprint cars and my wife's father agreed to buy me a three-quarter midget which was a famous deuce that Bobby Marshman and other great drivers had made their name. It wasn't that he just bought me a car because he was a nice guy, although he was. I made him a deal. I told him if he would buy the midget, I would give him 50 percent of all the money I won and when I sold the car he could keep all the money. That was a huge hardship for me, but I just wanted it so bad.

My father-in-law bought the car and I was successful. I won the biggest race of the year in 1962, the 100-lapper at Teaneck, New Jersey and who was second to me? Len Duncan, the icon of all icons in midget racing. What did that do for me? Well, all of a sudden, the Mataka brothers took notice and they gave me a ride in their full-size midget. They had a lot of good drivers over the years but they had never won a race in ARDC [American Racing Drivers Club] even though they had a pretty good car. I was the first one to win races for them.

Now in the midget world, they had all these race events all over the place… on the same day. So, it was on Labor Day weekend in 1963 when I won three midget races in one day. First I won my heat, a match race, and the feature at Flemington, New Jersey. Then I drove to Hatfield, Pennsylvania, about 70 miles away, and again won my heat, the match race and feature. A second feature was also run at Hatfield that night from a previous rainout, and I won that race as well.

After the last race that night, on my cool-down lap, the PA announcer Chris Economaki's shrilling voice said over the loudspeaker, 'Mario, you just bought your ticket to the big time!' It's one of the most memorable moments of my career. I'll never forget how much of a boost it was for me. It was incredibly meaningful because Chris was the absolute authority in our sport. As a young racer in those days, your personal stock wasn't worth much until you were noticed by Chris. If he wasn't aware of you, you simply weren't a factor in the sport. If you weren't on Chris Economaki's radar screen, you probably weren't on anybody's. Chris was that important. He was almost like a scout in that he could spot talent and was so highly respected that car owners of that era would take careful note of any driver Chris brought to the forefront. So, on that day in 1963 I won three midget races and got noticed by Chris Economaki. I'll never forget it.

So from there what am I looking for? What's my next step? Well, I'm still looking for sprint cars and USAC sprint cars. Why? Because that's where I'd find A.J. Foyt, Roger McCluskey, Parnelli Jones... all the top guys that run the maximum formula. Somehow thankfully the midgets gave me the next leap, with the bonus acknowledgement of Chris Economaki.

And then when I got to sprint cars the next question was how do I get to the next level? Well, in those days many of these situations came because of somebody else's misfortune, and that was the case for me. Chuck Hulse was hurt badly, and I was given the test to drive a Champ Car. It's sad and selfish and horrible to take advantage of someone else's misfortune, but what if Chuck Hulse didn't get hurt? What would have been my next step? What would have happened had I gone another direction? That's what happened throughout my career. One event or situation sort of presented the next one.

Of course, it's not all straight up. I had ups and downs, highs and lows. But my process was always to look back at the end of the season and evaluate how I did versus the year before. Well, maybe I won one more race, or more. That, to me, meant progress.

I had a really good go once I got to Indycars. In my first full year, 1965, I won the championship. And then you think well maybe I was lucky, but in '66 I won another championship. Then '67, '68 I lost the championship by the narrowest margin. In '69 I won another championship. So, I had a five-year run with three championships and two second places and all of a sudden I just wanted to spread my wings to other places. I wanted to diversify. In '68 I was already doing some Formula 1, which probably contributed to my slight lull in Indycars because my focus was elsewhere. That's just the way it goes. I don't think I was spreading myself too thin. My perspective was always more is more, not less is more. And in '72 or '73 when I didn't win in Indycar, I was winning somewhere else. I was winning in sportscars or dirt cars.

I don't think I ever had a moment where I ever thought, 'What the hell am I doing here?' or, 'There's no way this is going to work.' I never really had that. Maybe I'm the eternal optimist. It's been like that my entire life, quite honestly.

Maybe I'm living in a dream, in a bubble. I hope it doesn't burst. That's all I can say.

Your optimism and your inclination to anticipate the best possible outcome… you're a very blue-sky type guy. Where does that come from?

Being positive is a mind-set. It's just the belief that 'this too shall pass'. And it always does. You have to always look forward, not back. Don't become too hung up on bad stuff and don't get too hung up on your success either. Just always focus on the next thing. Keep focusing on progress. That's how I stay positive. It's not that I brush things off and don't care. It's about focus and determination.

Before coming to America, we were in a refugee camp. For me, it was from age 8 to 15. More than anything, my dad wanted to get us the hell out of there. He put in a request for US visas, but we waited a very long time before the visas were granted.

And it was in Italy that I was *really* developing a love of car racing. One of my fondest memories is the Mille Miglia. Every year my brother and I would watch from the side of the road. Then we'd talk about nothing else for weeks. And in 1954, a couple guys who owned a parking garage near the refugee camp invited Aldo and me to go to Monza with them to watch the Italian Grand Prix.

In those days, motor racing was more popular than any other sport in Italy. And the World Champion at that time was Alberto Ascari — my idol. I was only 14 years old, but I went to that race and the die was cast. I wanted to be a racer. And I wanted someday to race in the Italian Grand Prix in Monza. I told myself, I'm coming back to Monza someday. Oh my God, if this would ever happen to me, that I could grow up and race, that's all I need dear God. Just give me that.

Now all the while, my dad was still determined to move us to America. It was going on seven years since we had been in the refugee camp and he still waited for word on our visas. We had almost forgotten about it. Then, all of a sudden, our visas came through and my parents gave us the news: we're moving to America. My brother and I were devastated. We didn't want to move. We were afraid our dream of becoming race drivers would never be realised. With a lot of mixed feelings, we headed for America, leaving most of our belongings behind.

On the morning of June 16th, 1955, the Italian ocean liner *Conte Biancamano* arrived into New York harbour. That was the day we began our new life in the United States. My parents, me, my brother and my sister. My dad had exactly $125 to his name and none of us spoke English. We settled in Pennsylvania. My dad was determined to make a life for us. Two years later, we had a house and a car. We weren't rich, far from it, but I'd say my dad rode the wave of change very well. Instead of being victims of change, we became victors.

So, I guess the point is that I don't think you're born with optimism or the strength to overcome adversity. But somehow, like my dad, I was intensely driven to make something happen. Really big success is built on adversity, failure, frustration and the way you deal with turning it around. My parents could not foresee our future when we left Italy. But they had the courage and self-confidence to accept the challenge without being so sure we would succeed.

Is it true that your dad wasn't aware you and your brother had built this car and were racing it?

Aldo and I were not only under age when we started racing, we also couldn't tell our dad we were racing because he was vehemently against it. We had to build that first race car secretly. We ran an entire season without dad finding out. He would have absolutely prohibited it had he found out. The advantage we had was that my dad didn't speak very good English. Aldo and I learned English pretty quickly because we had English for three years in school in Italy before we came over, and we would hang out at my uncle's gas station in Pennsylvania interacting with people and so we would learn. And of course we were in school in America.

But my dad and my mum, my dad especially, had a difficult time learning English. So that was to our advantage. Aldo and I could talk racing without my dad knowing. We started racing four years after we arrived in America. We were winning races locally and locals would say to my dad, 'Hey your kids are really doing well,' and he thought he was being patted on the back for raising us well, but it was actually about the racing and he had no idea.

Sadly, when Aldo got hurt pretty badly in the last race of our first season in 1959, at the invitational, that's how my dad found out. He felt vindicated to some degree: 'See, I told you not to go racing.' He was very concerned, as any father would be who learned their teenage sons were doing something secretly that was, in his mind, very dangerous.

The only thing he knew about racing was that you were going to die. What would be in the news? More than anything it was fatalities. On the ship, on our way over to America, it was 1955 and the week of the 24 Hours of Le Mans. I remember seeing the headline that 83 people were killed. It was that awful accident with Pierre Levegh going into the grandstands. That was what resonated with my dad. In 1955 Alberto Ascari had also been killed and in Italy it was such big news because he was everyone's idol. So that's all my dad knew. He only understood the negatives and naturally didn't want his kids doing it. So, we had that hurdle to overcome when we started, in fact not even a hurdle, it would have been a complete stoppage. So we couldn't tell him.

As time went on my dad became the biggest supporter. Aldo and I remained very close, even when we were racing in separate events. We continued racing and Dad would always go to Aldo and ask how I was doing, then he'd come to me and ask how Aldo was doing. I guess he didn't want us to think he totally accepted us racing, but he was doing his checks and balances. Just making sure both sides of the story added up. He didn't want to be kept in the dark again.

My dad and my brother were both part of all the good things in my life and career. I remember I took my dad to the Italian Grand Prix in 1971. It was a last-minute thing and I was racing for Ferrari at Monza. He was so proud. It was just great.

How was the relationship with Aldo, your twin brother? Did you ever race against him? Or were you always sharing the car?

As you know, Aldo and I built our first race car. When we started racing in 1959, we only had that one car so we shared. We would alternate. And we only had one helmet because that's all we could afford. We shared everything. We even shared a bicycle.

In our first season we raced at three different tracks, and to be invited for the last race of the season in Hatfield, you had to be at least top three in points at one of the three tracks, and we both earned that even though we were running alternate weeks. And that's why we were both invited to that race and that's when we finally raced each other. I was driving someone else's car that weekend; Aldo was in our car. And that's the race that Aldo got hurt.

In 1960 he took a sabbatical, but then came back. When I moved to sprint cars, he kept racing stock cars.

The sad part about this story is that it didn't work out for Aldo. He had a second accident ten years later, this one more serious than the first, which was also pretty bad. As a result of the last one in 1969, he was hospitalised for several weeks and suffered such severe facial injuries that we no longer looked like identical twins.

While my career was flourishing, it was the end of racing for Aldo. He had worked just as hard as me and he had wanted it just as bad. It's hard for me to put into words how tough this was for both of us. From then on, he watched from the sidelines as I fulfilled the dream we both had.

Aldo's story isn't about this rotten, unfair thing that happened to him. It's about having the power to adapt to change and, once again, about becoming a victor rather than a victim of a situation. He became a successful businessman and for that reason I say he still has the make-up of a great driver; one who wins regardless of the conditions.

There was never any jealousy with my brother. He cheered me on every day. And the memories that make us smile now are the good ones as well as the bad. Life is not always fair. Just because you work hard, doesn't mean it's going to pay you back. Setback and defeat and dreams that don't come true are part of sharing a full existence. He and I are both optimists.

I know Aldo recovered, but having that first big accident in 1959 and then repeated a decade later, ultimately ending his career, must have been tough. As I understand, Aldo's second crash happened in a car that you'd bought for him.

Yes, I owned the sprint car he was driving. He had come out of stock cars and he wanted to get into single-seaters as well. He was driving some stuff that I didn't think was very good, and I was able at that time to provide him with a good car. In fact, the sprint car that he had was fitted with a double overhead cam Ford engine. He had all the latest stuff. He had a good car under him. And the accident wasn't his fault. The champion, Pete Folse, I don't know what happened, but he'd spun and was pointed across the straightaway and Aldo T-boned him and ended up in the grandstand. The catch fencing really did a job to his face because he was wearing an open-faced helmet. That was the end of it for Aldo.

When that happened to your twin brother, someone with whom you'd shared every moment of racing and your life, did that ever place a question mark in your head over your continued participation?

You know, probably for a moment. But I don't really remember it. I don't know what it is. There were so many things like that happening. Going through the midgets, we used to have two or three guys at least, maybe four or five guys, killed every year. That was something that was almost accepted. It *was* accepted, in fact. If you're going to be hung up on that then you might as well stay home. You almost had to just put it out of your mind.

When Dan Wheldon was killed in the Indycar race in Las Vegas, in 2011, there was a debate between the drivers about whether they should continue or not and I stood up in front of all of them and said, you know, this unfortunately is part of our business, part of our world. But what is the point in *not* racing this week if you're going to be racing next week? As a race driver, the only way you can honour Dan Wheldon is by going on and whoever wins the race dedicates it to him. Dan himself had done that a few years before in Homestead when he won and dedicated the race to Paul Dana who'd been killed earlier that day in the warm-up.

But, and I almost took some offence to this, my good friend Dario Franchitti said, 'Mario, you know, you're used to these things.' And it really hit me. I said, 'What do you mean I'm used to it?' You never get used to a fatality. I'm a human being. I have the same feelings. You never get used to it. There's always going to be someone missing. I lost friends. Jud Larson was a very personal friend. Billy Foster was a very personal friend. Ronnie Peterson. These are team-mates that were really, really close to me.

Are things ever the same? No. Never. It's a loss forever. But if you're going to be in the business… it's hard to explain, but if you dwell on it then you're in the wrong business. That's all I can say. If you don't think that this can happen, you only have to hope that it won't happen to you, but again if you dwell on that negative then you're a danger to yourself in my opinion. You'll be tentative, and you will be doing a lot of things that are the wrong things in a race car.

It's hard to really explain how you put it out of your mind. How close does it have to get? My twin brother was affected, so how do I just go on? All of us race drivers are doing the same thing so even after he was injured my brother understood why I kept racing. So would Ronnie Peterson. So would Dan Wheldon.

It's loving what you do. Like going to war or being a coal miner or a roofer or a police officer, the risks are inherent in the venture. It's my calling and I could not imagine doing anything else and being happy. The danger is built into the calling. If it's a rewarding profession to you, and you followed your calling, then I don't see quitting as the way to deal with it. Quitting makes it worse. You quit and then what?

And if you're a top earner, how do you take care of your family? There's always something that justifies what you do. How do I justify taking the risk? It's love of my calling and making good money. Overall, when you do something with risk, it's not foolish risk, but calculated risk. And explaining it that way makes the positives outweigh the negatives.

You're responsible for one of the most memorable quotes in motor racing on this very subject and the ultimate mortality of racers, when you talked about Ronnie Peterson's death and you said, 'Sadly, motor racing is also this.' It's a very famous line and is an absolute truth about this sport. In preparation for this interview I had a chat with Freddie Petersens, the Swedish Formula 1 journalist who I know you know and who was close to both Ronnie and fellow racer Gunnar Nilsson, who died very suddenly of cancer, and he told me you didn't attend their funerals because, in his words, you were so close to them. You've talked about not dwelling on the past and I have to ask if that is why you didn't go to their funerals? Were they so close to you that you couldn't allow yourself to dwell on their passing?

Unfortunately, yes. The answer to that is yes. I figure if I am immersed in a negative, it's going to affect the way I think. I will mourn respectfully in my own way and it has to be that way. It's the way that I handle situations like that.

You know what? I don't want to be inappropriately funny or callous when you ask me a serious question, but it was back in 1965 and there had been a fatality at one of the races. And my good buddy Jud Larson, who was killed the next year in 1966, I said to him, 'Are you going to go to this guy's funeral?' He said, 'Hell no! He ain't goin' to mine!' Isn't that terrible? But you had to have that thick skin.

It's hard to explain. Only a fellow driver would understand that kind of talk. It's a coping mechanism, I suppose. Does it mean you're not mourning and hurting inside? No. Things will never be the same and you, forever, will be mourning a friend. But you were in it together, playing in the same arena. So, we talked that way about each other within our own company. Never publicly. It was our brother bond.

I still feel something when I see a picture of me and Ronnie Peterson. But am I regretting that I never closed up shop and quit? No. While quitting is an option for some, it wasn't an option for me. I can't even explain how I feel when I see pictures of my friends and I'm immediately back in that place where we did shit together and the stupid things we used to do together outside of our work. All of that is still alive in my heart. It's just that I didn't allow it to deter work and my life. You know what, in my place they'd do the same. That's the way to think. They would understand.

Is that how you were able to race for so long? Because you're still driving that Indycar two-seater! I remember when I took a passenger ride with you and you were still on it, still getting the back end out and hustling it around the track. You still have that love, that fire, that passion. Did you ever lose that or has every day been a joy?

There's no-one on this planet that loves the sport more than I do and loves driving more than I do. As I got older, I feared the moment I had to be realistic and say it's time to stop. I pressed the envelope as far as I could. I was still healthy at 54 and driving Indycars. My last endurance race I was over 60. It was hard to let go. But I've been blessed throughout my career. I feel almost guilty in some ways. Why was the sport so good to me and for so long when so many other careers were ended before so much could have been accomplished? Believe me, I know I'm lucky.

But I was driven by pure desire when I was 19 and had the same desire at 60. All the way to today. I have fun driving the two-seater, taking journalists and sponsors and celebrities for rides. I get my satisfaction from doing the settings and every time still trying to go faster. Driving has been my life and still is my life and I count my blessings every day that I was able to do it for so long and if there is a way to do it until they put me in a box then I think I'll do it.

You've narrowly avoided the bullet on many occasions. But you famously came out of retirement back in 2003 to test Indycar for your son Michael's team after Tony Kanaan injured himself. There was a chance you'd be called to qualify the car for the Indy 500. But at this test at Indy, you hit debris and the car went skywards. After so many decades of racing, of competing and as you say, avoiding that bullet... when the nose of that car went up and the car started to lift, what went through your mind?

I'll be very honest with you. I thought that might be it. I'd never experienced anything like it. Just going up in the air like that, flipping over and over. I expected the worst. My luck had run out and my life was over. And then all of a sudden, I landed on my wheels and had barely a few scratches. That's when I looked around, looked up to heaven and was thankful for another day. Death is inevitable, but none of us write our own ending. Mine wasn't that day.

What happens at that moment? After so many years, to finally have that thought, even if just for a second, that this is it?

It happens so fast, quite honestly. I'll tell you one thing though. I used to own a suite above Turn 2 at Indianapolis and as the nose of my car went up, I thought that's where I was going to end up. And then as soon as my car landed after flipping end-over-end, honestly I was ready to go back out again. Sure, people were going to say, 'Oh you should have learned your lesson and quit while you're ahead', but no. I was ready to go. Same day if necessary. What made me go airborne was not my mistake. If it had been my mistake, maybe I would have been less anxious to go back out. But it wasn't. Things like that can happen, and I got away with it. If they had needed me to qualify the car for Tony the next day, I would have done it. Nothing had changed in my mind.

I guess my love for driving supersedes everything else. It supersedes even reason.

Mika Häkkinen

'My troubles gave me experience. I learnt. I grew. Without mistakes, you don't learn. Mistakes make you stronger. I have five children and I am so proud to tell them to make mistakes. Do mistakes and you will learn.'

Mika Pauli Häkkinen is a two-time Formula 1 World Champion and a racer who, in his decade-long career at the top of his sport, finished on the podium in just under a third of the Grands Prix he entered.

Born in 1968, the 'Flying Finn' began karting at the age of five, achieving success at every level before stepping up to open-wheel single-seaters in Formula Ford and Formula 3, then rapidly ascending to Formula 1. He made his début for Lotus in 1991, his exploits catching the attention of Ron Dennis at McLaren, the team to which he moved as test driver in 1993. Häkkinen didn't stay on the side-lines for long: when full-time driver Michael Andretti walked away from Formula 1 mid-season, the Finn was called up to replace him and to race alongside the legendary champion, Ayrton Senna.

In their first race as team-mates Häkkinen outqualified the mighty Brazilian. He had arrived.

With Senna's departure at the end of 1993, Mika became team leader, guiding McLaren through a dip in form as it forged an alliance with a new engine partner, and having himself to come back from the terrible injuries he suffered in a death-defying crash in qualifying for the 1995 Australian Grand Prix.

In 1998, the McLaren-Mercedes combination proved the class of the field, and the Finn took his first World Championship, backing it up the next year by successfully defending his crown. After two further seasons, Häkkinen announced he would take a sabbatical from the sport. But he never returned.

Mika Häkkinen was one of the fastest and toughest racers of his generation, and a driver regularly listed among the all-time greats. A World Champion and a legend in his field, perhaps one of the most telling compliments bestowed on him is that he was, so it is believed, the only driver that the great Michael Schumacher ever truly feared.

It's very interesting for all of us to understand how to overcome these bad situations. You know, people who are reading your book in the future and listening to these difficult moments for people, like me, who have achieved certain levels of success in motor racing, I think it can maybe help or be a lesson.

I would tell the readers that maybe before you get to these difficult places, try to make sure that you don't end up in these situations. Of course, sometimes in life you cannot choose. Shit happens, let's put it this way.

I'm going to be 50 soon, so of course in my life I had many, many different situations where I was looking in the mirrors and saying, 'Mika, what is going on here? How do I get out of this trouble?' But again, even today, I'm happy of those troubles. Simply because they gave me experience. I learnt. I grew.

Without mistakes, you don't learn. Mistakes make you stronger.

I have five children and I am so proud to tell them to make mistakes. Do mistakes and you will learn. And they look at me, head on the side, all confused. 'What is Daddy talking about?' You know? But I tell them, 'Don't be afraid.' Of course, don't jump off a cliff and do something crazy. But there's nothing wrong with making mistakes.

In motor racing I had many situations where I felt really down because I made some silly mistake.

One example of a stupid mistake that I made in motor racing was in Monza, in Italy. But it's not the one you are thinking about. Everyone remembers when I spun in the race. But this was something else.

I was going flat out in testing many years before. We had a four-day testing programme and Monza is a not so exciting circuit: very long straights, chicanes and temperatures over 30 degrees. Really hot. And just driving, driving, lap after lap, testing, testing. It's not so much fun. On the straight you can relax a little bit, but for the corners and those chicanes you need all of your energy. It's really maximum attack.

Then you go around the chicane or corner and then again, it's another a long straight. So after a couple of days when I was testing there I relaxed a little bit too much on the straight line. And on the start/finish straight in Monza there is a bump. You always hit it. You always know it is coming and the whole car is affected. You have to remind yourself that you have to hold the steering harder, to make your body stronger and then once you get past the bump you can relax a little bit again.

One time I didn't concentrate. The bump came and I hadn't prepared for it and my leg bounced up. On the back of the steering wheel is a quick release and my knee hit it and the steering wheel came off in my hands! It came off!

Now at this point I'm doing maybe 340 kilometres per hour and the steering wheel is in my hands and not connected to the system. So you can imagine that the feeling was quite scary. Well, it's really scary. So I grabbed the steering column. I tried to hold it, but obviously it was impossible. It was too hard to control it. And I just pressed the brake pedal as hard as I could. With both feet. Full on the brakes. And I slid hundreds of metres.

I walked back to the garage, back to the engineers and the team manager and I felt so stupid. I asked them, please can I have the rest of the day off? At that moment I felt really quite down, you know? Because whatever you do with your life, you must always focus. Always focus. Because it can be like this when things go wrong.

It's like when you go to school and you're sitting there in your classes and at one moment you say, I don't want to listen to what this teacher is telling me and you switch off. And it could be just the most important moment. And you miss it. Focus! When you go to bed and take a book and you read, then you can chill out. Then you can relax. Until then, stay focused.

The more you do it, the more you learn.

Is that where your lowest moments came from, then? Times where you reflected on yourself, where you beat yourself up because you'd lost your focus?

Like I said, I have a massive number of situations where I really felt like I could just walk away. With so many situations. But that was just one of them.

One moment that really hit me, going back to motor racing, was in Melbourne in 1998 when I won the World Championship and I was leading the Grand Prix and I knew this year is the year. If I don't do it now, I'm never going to do it. So I put all my energy for that. And Melbourne was the first Grand Prix, the car is fantastic, I'm leading the race, my team-mate is not far behind and just before I went past the pit entrance I hear something on the radio. And I thought they said come to change tyres. And it was not that message.

So I went into the pits. The team saw me. And they were all confused. What the fuck are you doing?

So I went back out and I had lost the lead of the race. And at that time I felt really down. Really down.

It's that concentration thing again, isn't it?

Yes. The focus. It is concentration and being all the time at the top of your performance.

But of course I had a bad accident in Adelaide in 1995 when I cracked my skull and I lost part of my hearing. It's a decent excuse! So the radio, the messages and this and that, I couldn't get the message correctly in my head, in my brain. So that was the situation.

Did that affect you for the rest of your career. Losing some of your hearing?

Definitely. It's more tiring when you have to focus on someone if they speak to you. If your attention is on hearing correctly because you don't hear very well, then it takes away from your complete focus. It's why I made a marketing agreement with a hearing aid company because I have to tell you that as soon as I had my hearing aid fitted, it changes all your life. The quality of your life increases. Because you no longer have to look at people's lips when they talk to you. For the first time again you hear what they say. And it raises the quality of your life so you enjoy yourself more. You can hear!

Did your crash in 1995 affect you as a driver or as a person? To have such a big accident and, as you say, to come back but to have done so much damage to yourself physically.

In that case, you know, after the accident, after a couple of months, when I made a decision to come back to racing I just turned off the brain. I pushed that accident, that moment, that terrible thing to the side. And I just focused on motor racing.

I said, don't think about it. I'll be really selfish. I'll just think about motor racing. That's it. That's my focus. I said, 'Mika, finish your mission and what you've been working on for all your life.' And then when I did win a World Championship a couple of times, I thought to myself. 'Oh shit, you know, don't push your luck further. You've now done a few times the World Championship. Don't try three times or four times or five times. Now come back to life and concentrate on other things. This thing is dangerous and there is more to life than motor racing.'

Is that why you walked away after the two championships?

It definitely affected my decision.

Do you understand why Nico Rosberg walked away after his World Championship?

I fully understand. I fully understand. He was fighting for so many years to be able to win his first Grand Prix, then winning a World Championship, being next to Lewis Hamilton who is kicking-ass quick. So Nico realised that if I need to sacrifice again my life to be able to win a championship, it takes too much of me. It's too much energy. It's too much of who you are and what you can give.

You said you had to switch your brain off to come back to racing after the accident. Do you remember much about the accident?

I do. I do indeed. The really bad moment was after. It's quite a lonely situation when you are in that moment. You cannot move. You cannot walk.

Everything is out of time. Doctors are moving around you. You cannot live a normal life. You are just lying in a hospital, in a bed, non-stop.

Those kind of moments you don't want to experience. Of course, the accident itself, yes I remember small parts of it but not the whole thing.

One thing I remember about the accident was definitely that when I tried to get out the car I could not. I said, I cannot move. So I realised... shit. Now it's something really badly wrong. And I just thought to myself, OK, don't try to do anything. Just relax. But it was hard because I could not breathe and I was losing consciousness.

And then the doctors came so fast and Sid Watkins cut a hole in my throat to enable me to breathe and then I went to sleep and fell into a coma.

Talking again about switching the brain off to come back to racing... something I've heard a lot in researching this book is drivers saying that when you pull the helmet on and close the visor you can change, you can switch. Is that something that as a racing driver you just have that innate ability to be one person out of the car and to get in and become so focused and so channelled on this one thing?

No, not only racing drivers. Anybody can do that. Sport generally helps that. If you do sports and you want to be successful in sport then you have to switch off. When you have to do any certain type of activity like a sport you have to give it your full focus. You can't be thinking how is the weather when you are doing something extreme. The more you practise that, the more you learn how to do that switch and your process of thinking becomes second nature. It is something that you learn with time.

But motor racing is extreme. Motor racing is so dangerous that if you don't do it right, you will have a bad accident. So you need to really put all your energies to enable you to balance that way. OK, now it's free time and I can relax or now it is race time and I have to make everything perfect. You learn to handle this kind of situation.

Maybe switching off is the wrong way to describe it. It's not switching off. It's just moving your process of thinking for certain areas so that in that way you can control your path to performance.

Do you think you ever achieved the maximum of that or is there always another level you can go to?

Oh yeah. For me, I did. But that's the danger when you do a sport like Formula 1. Because you constantly have to do that. You have to be at the maximum of your focus. But the danger is that then you carry these kind of emotions with you into the real life. I mean real, real life.

This isn't real life. We are not living real life. Today we are sitting on a boat in Monaco, drinks on the deck. This is not real life. But when you are with your kids and your family, everyday life, it can be quite hard if you start using the mentality that you have in racing in real-life situations. It can be dangerous.

Even if people understand you. You turn yourself into a very selfish person when you are focused as we are in racing. People start to look at you in a strange way. They ask what is he doing, why is he behaving like that?

Did you struggle with that?

I had to learn. I had to figure out how to step back from that world and I think my accident helped me. It taught me not to be so serious. To realise there was life outside Formula 1.

The need for that selfish streak... Again, I guess we are discussing that channelled focus. How did you learn to be one Mika in the car and another Mika at home?

I believe what I have learned is that the people who you are hanging around with, people with whom you communicate and who you are working with, the companion that you choose in your life, all these elements affect who you are and how you handle your life. When you look in a mirror you might say, 'Oh I'm so good looking and I'm such a fantastic guy', but you really need to live in reality. What is happening out there when you're driving a racing car isn't reality.

People can change you, but the people who are around you, you have to select them very carefully so that they change you in a good way. Not in a bad way.

You need to have an inner confidence in the first place. And I was very fortunate because my family, parents, sister, were all the team around me when I was a kid. They created such confidence that whatever I faced in the world when I got older, I was always prepared to go through these troubles. Thanks to them.

Be confident in yourself. Focus. And surround yourself with the people who bring only good things into your life. With this you will find the way out of even the most terrible moments.

Niki Lauda

'I went to the funerals. I went to a Thai funeral where the last 25 unidentified people were buried, which was really hard... I spoke to as many relatives as I could... From day one, I promised that I would find out what had happened.'

T he story of the fiery crash that almost claimed Niki Lauda's life in 1976 and his astonishing comeback just six weeks later is one of the most awe-inspiring tales in the history of all sport.

Andreas Nikolaus 'Niki' Lauda was born in Vienna in 1949 into a wealthy family, but one that did not approve of his desire to race. Regardless, Niki continued, achieving some levels of success in junior formulae. In order to move up the ladder, however, Lauda was forced to use his family's good name in the business world to secure bank loans to fund further progress. His dogged, single-minded determination and clarity of purpose eventually took him to Formula 1 and to the mighty Ferrari team, with whom he won his first World Championship in 1975.

His fight with James Hunt for the 1976 World Championship and the accident and injuries he suffered at that year's German Grand Prix are known even to those who have never watched a lap of motor racing. Lauda was administered the last rites by a priest, so close did he come to death, and yet a matter of weeks later he drove through unbearable pain to finish fourth in the Italian Grand Prix.

Despite souring relations with Ferrari, brought about in part by Lauda's refusal to race in the 1976 Japanese Grand Prix and in part by the team bringing in Carlos Reutemann to replace him after his accident, he won the championship for the Scuderia once more in 1977 before retiring at the end of the 1979 season. He returned to the cockpit in 1982, winning his third and final title in 1984 for McLaren before retiring for good at the end of

1985 to focus on his many businesses, including his airline, Lauda Air.

While many might expect that 1976 season to have been the toughest period of Lauda's life, the Austrian himself, in one of his final long-form interviews before his death in 2019, insisted it was not.

On May 26th, 1991, Lauda Air flight 004 crashed north of Bangkok, Thailand, killing all 223 passengers and staff on board. The thrust reverser had deployed unexpectedly on the number one engine, causing the Boeing 767 to spiral out of control. Lauda took personal charge of the investigation into the crash, for the next eight months dedicating every waking moment to discovering the truth of that flight, and to clearing the name of his pilots.

I was running my airline very hands on. I was flying these planes myself and I was in charge of safety and all of these kinds of things, which is logical. We had very high standards and took care of everything.

The first I heard about it was at quarter to ten one evening. Austrian television called me and said, 'One of your aeroplanes has disappeared on the way out of Bangkok.' Well, they had called me a couple of weeks before when I had been in a restaurant and said, 'Thank God we are speaking to you, we've just had a message that you were killed in a car accident.'

So I said, 'What is this bullshit? I'm sitting here. I'm not dead.'

So, my first reaction to the call about the plane was to say that this was the same kind of bullshit. You know? Why would my plane crash?

But then it came through that it was so. And then I went to the office, got the main people there at about midnight and discussed with them what we could do. The first thing they said was for me to stay in Austria and worry about everything we would have to deal with the media and the aftermath. But I said no way. I had to go down, straight away, and take a look at it.

So I did. I flew down there straight away and I was taken by the authorities in a helicopter to this place in the middle of nowhere on the border between Thailand and Bangladesh. As we got closer, I saw napkins and other things on the ground which was very hard. You see, in the beginning I was looking down and thinking why is there so much paper everywhere, in this jungle? And then I saw the Lauda Air logo on them and I realised what I was looking at.

Because the plane flies in one direction, the further you walk and the closer you get to the final crash site, the larger the debris gets. The landing part comes down earlier and the bigger parts later. Eventually I ended up basically where the airplane's cargo was lying there as one piece, as long as the room we are sitting in now. And the rest was spread around.

I took the Boeing representative from Vienna with me and I asked him on the way down, 'Have you seen a crashed plane before?' and he said yes. So I said, 'Give me some advice for what we will see.' But nothing prepared me. As we walked around the site, there was the smell of burnt bodies. I saw children, adults, taking rings from the dead bodies lying in the jungle. This, I will never ever forget... the situation we were in. For some time I just wandered around.

But I looked at as many details as I could, taking it all in, making notes in my mind.

Then we finally found one engine, which was almost completely destroyed, lying somewhere. And then two kilometres away we found the other engine. Then I said to this Boeing guy, 'Why is one thrust reverser deployed and the other one is not?' He said, 'Things come down from 28,000ft, that's just the way it is. That's the way the crash is.'

I stayed there for two or three hours. I asked the authorities for the flight data and voice recorder and they said they'd found them and identified them and they were now in a little place. So I asked them to show me and I saw how damaged they were. I said, 'What are you going to do now?' They said they had to carry them home and send them somewhere. 'Sure,' I said, 'but when? You leave them here for another three days? What are you guys going to do?'

So then we took them with us and I asked the authorities to find a place to review them as quickly as possible. That place was in Washington, because the NTSB [National Transportation Safety Board] took over to look at the recorders. This maybe took only three or four days because I pushed hard, and then I went to Washington myself.

They didn't want to show me by myself because it was my plane. And the annoying thing was that these flight data recorders were ready to look at but the Americans said we can't start before the Thai authorities are here. And the Thai authorities messed up which floor of the building they were supposed to be on, where they should go to and — I'll never forget this — we waited one hour before they turned up.

When we finally looked at it, the flight data recorder was completely destroyed unfortunately because it was aluminium tape in there which was so badly burnt that there was no result on it. Normally this should never happen because it is approved for up to 900 degrees, but it was lying in a place where there was the big fire and it was sitting there too long. It was completely destroyed. Nothing on it.

But the voice recorder we could listen to. I could hear my crew's voices speaking. Everything was normal until you could hear there was a huge rattle in the cockpit. The pilots did not speak any more with each other which normally is never happening, you know? They are usually running checklists or whatever. And then you could hear from the microphone, the captain, the co-pilot, he said, 'God damn it', then he said, 'We are upside down' — and then after 18 seconds it all stopped. And that was it. It was the only information we had.

So then I said to myself, well, it must have been something completely surprising that happened so quickly that these two human beings couldn't do anything about it. This was my first impression.

It became clear quite soon that the problem had been with the thrust reverser but nobody knew why. The result only came out eight months later. Boeing had been testing the thrust reverse system in Seattle and eventually discovered that the directional control valve, which keeps the thrust reverser closed in the air, had failed. An O ring jumped out of its position and the thrust reverser was thrown out. In the air.

But this only came out after testing and testing and testing at the Boeing factory. Up to then, for eight months, nobody knew what happened.

As I understand it, you took a very active role in the investigation.

I did one good thing in the aftermath. I have to say now it was difficult but I did it. I said right from day one, if officially this is my fault or Lauda Air's fault then I have to close the place down. I have a responsibility. I had *the* responsibility. So I had to do it.

That freed me on the other side to be really aggressive against Boeing and everybody, to find out what the hell went wrong. It took eight months before they found out because of this complicated testing of the thrust reverser. Had we had the flight data recorder it would have been easier.

But then the cause became clear. I went over there, to Seattle, and I flew the simulator. I put in all the information, and I believed that nobody could fly it in these circumstances because the thrust reverser stalls the left wing 75 percent, the plane turns upside down and crashes. It was completely uncontrollable.

How many times did you run the simulation yourself?

Ten times. And I always said I'm going to get it, I'm going to get it. And I never did. The test pilots at Boeing said none of us would be able to get it either. You can do whatever you want, fight the problem, even if you know when it is coming. You won't save it. The error system was so disturbed by the thrust reverser blowing under the wing that even that couldn't hold it.

Did Boeing accept that?

Sure they did. They all accepted it and all thrust reversers worldwide had to be changed.

But not immediately? I heard that you'd offered to take them up in a 767 and rerun the simulation for real if they didn't believe you.

When I came out of the simulator I said to them that now we know what the issue is, you have to say what caused this crash. But they said it wasn't so easy because of lawyers who had to write a report and all this. I said, I don't care. It has been eight months and I have the death of 223 people on my back. I have the responsibility. But if it is your fault then you have to tell the world. If it was my fault, you would expect the same.

They said, 'Yes, yes, we know Mr Lauda, but we have to be careful because of this and that and lawyers and backwards and forwards.'

'I do not care.

'So you will go. Now. Take yourselves up with two pilots to 28,000ft, throw the thrust reverser out and then if you still land afterwards then I want to be on board too, to take a look at it and how you did it.'

'No we can't do that,' they said.

'Why not? If you believe this isn't the cause, what's the problem? Do the test.'

And then they gave in. They said, 'Yes, you're right. Tomorrow we will issue a first statement about the possible cause of the crash.

You knew the pilots. Was there a personal mission for you to clear their names?

Yes. Of course. And for us as an airline, too. It could have been a technical problem. If your maintenance is wrong and the thrust reverses, this could also have been a cause. It was for all of us important to really find out what happened.

What did those eight months do to you?

I went to the funerals. I went to a Thai funeral where the last 25 unidentified people were buried, which was really hard. There was a grandmother with a little kid, and this little kid threw marbles into the grave and there was this huge noise as the marbles fell so far down and hit the top of the coffins. I went to ask the grandmother, and she said these were the marbles that the parents had bought the child on their last holiday together. They were both dead.

For me, this was the worst time in my life.

I spoke to as many relatives as I could. And they were always free to call me. And I remember one guy, who was the boyfriend of the purser of the plane, he was just completely finished and told me he was going to kill himself because he had nothing to live for any more. I talked him through all this. But even with the pain and the loss, I have to say that nobody really attacked me personally. And maybe that was because, from day one, I promised that I would find out what had happened. I had to.

You'd come through so much in your life up to that point. We live in a motor-racing world and your story is so famous, from having the last rites read to you in 1976 to coming back to racing six weeks later. Was there anything from your past that, in those weeks and months, gave you that strength to persist and to push against all the odds?

I simply said to myself, 'This is my responsibility. I have to clear that thing up.' That was the only thing that was black and white to me. And so it wasn't so difficult to push it all the way through.

Did you ever lose faith that the truth would out?

No. The timing pissed me off. How long it took. Because there was no data available and this was the problem. If the data had been there we would have known in a few weeks. So that was hard. The uncertainty for such a long time.

When Boeing finally admitted their responsibility and made the changes to their planes, did you feel peace with it, or was it something that still sat with you?

No. It was peace for me because an airplane, after that experience, will never ever crash again because of a thrust reverser system. And it never did. They had to add another mechanical lock to the hydraulic, electric-driven thrust reverse system. Every single plane has the same system now. Worldwide. So at least, with the long fight, there came a solution to it and it can never happen again.

It's impossible to say, I know, but if it hadn't been your airline, if this had happened to someone else, do you think they would have fought as tenaciously? Do you think those same changes would have been put in place?

In the end, yes, because Boeing had to do something. You cannot let these things fly without it.

But, you know, the only other annoying thing was that I was too naïve.

I picked up, two or three weeks after the crash, a replacement airplane in Paris, a UTA [Union de Transports Aériens] 767, and took it on a test flight to Vienna. Then I flew with this plane, the first charter flight to Rhodes, 240 people in and 240 people out. And when I flew the plane I said, shit. I'm sitting in the same airplane that I've just seen 223 people die in, all over the jungle, and nothing happened. The same engines, the same airplane.

Then when the passengers came with the bus, they all went in front of the engine and said, 'Mummy, Daddy, take a picture of the thrust reverse system.' Human beings! I said, 'Fuck me. This is the way that it is.'

It took a long time to realise the problem and then to change it.

Did you ever need counselling after this? After what you'd seen in the jungle, after going to the funerals, dealing with the families and fighting for so long? Is it something you still think about?

Yes, I still think about it. I can tell you what it smelt like. You never forget this. But I never had counselling. Because I was working my way through, and in the end I could fix it. With the help of Boeing.

So the investigation was your therapy?

I didn't need therapy. I was faced with a problem and you have to fix it. It's not so complicated. It is just hard work. First you have to tell yourself, honestly, if it is my fault I go home. And if you take that decision, the rest is easy. Because then you fight with an open book.

You know who it is. Me, or them. And it was them.

So for me, then, it was over.

———————

Andreas Nikolaus Lauda
22 February 1949 – 20 May 2019

Rick Mears

'Too much of anything is too much. No matter what it is. Too much of a good thing becomes too much. And believe me I've done too much of a lot of things over the years as well. I don't always listen to myself as well as I've listened to race cars.'

R ick Ravon Mears is one of only three drivers to have won the Indianapolis 500 on four occasions, stands alone as a six-time pole sitter at The Brickyard and is a three-time Indycar champion. Today, in his mid-60s, he is among the best-regarded and most influential driver coaches and advisers in American racing, and one of Roger Penske's most trusted allies. There are few men in the Indycar paddock more revered than 'Rocket Rick'.

Raised in Bakersfield, California, Mears learned his craft and first made his name in off-road racing. But it was in open-wheel and Indycar where he excelled. His brilliance behind the wheel and consistent race-finishing pedigree in far from exceptional equipment brought him to the attention of 'The Captain', Roger Penske, whose number one driver Mario Andretti was splitting his time between Indycar and Formula 1. Penske needed a stand-in and signed Mears to fill the gaps when Andretti was overseas.

The part-time ride became full-time, and Mears was crowned champion in his very first season. Methodical, intelligent and gifted, with an innate ability to drive a car on his fingertips, Mears was never more a force than on the mighty speedways and superspeedways of American oval racing.

But just as his ascendant star was shining its brightest, an horrific accident at Canada's Sanair circuit very nearly cost him everything. But he survived, recovered and returned. Although he never quite recaptured the championship-winning form he had displayed before his life-changing accident, his speed never left him.

But unknown to many, even to the man himself, Rick Mears was struggling with inner turmoil. Beneath the confident exterior of the mighty champion, demons toyed with him, making manifest in illness and addiction.

I've been so fortunate that it's hard to really recall rock bottoms. Life has been great and everything's been ten times better than I ever dreamed. Obviously when I did my feet in at Sanair, that was the worst time of my career: not knowing if you're even going to be able to walk again, let alone drive again. But fortunately I've always been the type of person to live by the old saying, 'Don't cry over spilled milk'. It doesn't do any good, it's a waste of time and you need to be looking forward, so in that instance, every day, you just say, well, it could have been worse. And that's what you do to get through the bad times.

The healing process took so long. You'd take a couple of days, take the steps forward and then take a step back and when you get knocked back you've just got to say, hey, it could have been worse. You know, you look down and your feet are both still there. I mean, it could have been a lot worse. And that's kind of what helps pull you through it.

The big blessing was that I was with the team and the people at Penske. And having that is what basically saved my feet. Roger and the doctors made a decision to get me back to the States because up in Canada, where the crash happened, they were going to take both feet off. The doctors up there said, 'There's nothing we can do with him'. But fortunately Roger said, 'Hey, no, no. Time out. We've gotta try something else.' And he and Dr Steve Olvey were standing there and they got it figured out and got me loaded on a plane back to Indianapolis, got a hold of Dr Terry Trammell and they started working on piecing my feet back together.

So I was that close to not having any feet, period. Right off the bat, when you realise that's what happened, that tends to help get you through it.

That's it. It could always be worse.

But then also the fact of being with Roger Penske and the type of man he is. He came in to take the pressure off me. That guy never put a day's pressure on me since I've been with him. He just told me to do what the doctors told me and not to try to hurry anything as it may do more damage than good. He said, 'Just do what they tell you. And don't worry about it, your seat will be there when you're ready.' And that just allowed me to relax and focus on getting better and getting well and getting back into the car.

So, yes, it was bad. But there was a lot of good in it too and it makes you stop to smell the roses a little bit, you know? Prioritise some things. You've got a lot of time to think when you're laid up like that. You learn to appreciate what you have a little more.

You attracted Roger's attention early on in your Indycar career. What do you think it was about you in those early days that really brought you to his notice and led to his lifetime loyalty to you?

Well, at first I wondered that too. It was as big a shock to me as it was to anybody. When we had the first conversation he said he had something in mind and to give him a call before I made a deal with anybody else, and I think I probably fell over. But after being with Roger for so many years now and seeing how he operates, I know that he's a long-term guy. What was interesting is that everything I had done before I got into an Indycar was not something that he was around, like motorcycles, motocross locally, the little Formula Vee and Super Vee for a year and a half, and a couple of SCCA races. There wasn't much that he had actually seen. I first came into Roger's sights when I ran my first Indycar race in 1976 with Bill Simpson in an Eagle-Offenhauser.

The desert racing I had done before that had taught me so much. All racing teaches you. You learn from everything. If you don't, you're crazy. Everything applies somewhere to something. Everything you do. The desert racing taught me early on to not outrun the equipment. You know, when you've got eight hours to go down in Baja, or over in Vegas in the desert and somebody blows by you, you've got to listen to your car. A car tells you if you're hurting it. And back in those earlier days we didn't have the equipment that we have today where you could just basically qualify every lap.

You had to listen to the car and listen to what it was telling you. So that taught me a lot. When someone went by you'd go, 'OK, I know I can run him back down.' But the car's telling you that it doesn't want to do much more than this if it's going to last another eight hours. So, sure enough, down the road you'd see whoever it was that went by you, upside down with a corner torn off. And so there you go. OK. I did the right thing.

So you learn to listen to the car and listen to the equipment and I applied that to everything I ever got in. When I first started driving Indycars, in my very first race at Ontario, a 500-mile race, I was in a four-year-old car and qualified mid-pack. I said, 'OK, what are my best options here? I can make sure I get to the end. And the longer I run, the more guys I'll outlive and the more experience I'll get.'

First of all I wanted to get a full 500 miles under my belt. That's experience. Secondly if I get the full 500 miles under my belt, I'm going to beat more guys that have fallen out or have trouble, because I knew I couldn't outrun them. So it's not brain surgery.

And that's basically what I did. That's the kind of approach I took in every race.

I also learned in the desert that the only way you can win a race is to finish. To finish first, first you have to finish. If you don't get to the end you can't do anything, period. Again it's not difficult to figure out. So that was always my approach. Plus I really didn't like pain. That was a good incentive to not make mistakes.

And you know what? The fewer mistakes I made, the more laps I got under my belt, the more experience I got, the more I learnt, and the better I got. And that's the approach I took. Finish, finish, finish, finish.

I ran the last couple races that 1976 season with Art Sugai and then a couple more early in 1977 and went up to Indianapolis. There Bobby Unser, who I'd met at Pike's Peak when I was running there right before I got into Indycars, he helped me out, showed me around, took me out in a rental car and ran me around the track. That kind of thing. Before that, the first professional I'd ever met was Parnelli Jones out in the desert. He'd already retired from Indycars but he was racing in Baja, I'd met him and we'd become friends. So, both guys were kind of helping me out.

After Indy, Art Sugai decided to get out of the business, but Bobby got me my next ride for another half season with Teddy Yip in an M16 McLaren, which again was an old car but decent equipment and I took the same approach to get to the end.

I think what initially caused Roger to look at me was what I was getting out of the old equipment, plus the fact that I hadn't bounced it off the fence. It's a little easier to take somebody like that and say, 'Oh, maybe I'll give him a shot.' You know the odds are pretty good so far, it looks like he's not going to destroy my car. And I think that's what really caught his eye initially.

And the results you guys had were almost instant. You did a part-time season in 1978 and then in '79 you jumped in full-time and you were champion at the first time of asking.

Yeah, I mean it's all about the people, the team, the equipment. Indycar just seemed to suit me and the faster the track the more it seemed to suit my natural driving style. The slower ones I had to learn. I had to work on that. The tracks I had to work hardest to figure out were street circuits, because you needed a good solid grip on the steering wheel and to start shaking the thing around, just manhandling it. And I always tended to drive more on my fingertips, not the palm of my hands. That was very suitable for a speedway because the smoother you are, the closer you can get to the limit without stepping over it. I remember the very first test with Roger at Phoenix and I got in the car and when I started running it just clicked. I thought, oh, this is what it's supposed to feel like!

I did everything exactly the same as I'd been doing in the other cars and the only thing that was different were the numbers. All of a sudden the lap times were coming down because it was better equipment, everything was more in place and more up to date. So, that came from everything I had learned in the other cars, all the way back to the first sprint buggy my dad had pieced together with a Volkswagen stock 1,600cc motor. He'd always said that if you can just learn to be competitive and run up front in this and keep finishing races, then we will get the money and get a better motor in it and you're going to be long gone. It all just fell together.

You said you didn't like the idea of pain. Was that a big thing in terms of how you approached your driving? Did that come into your mind driving street courses as opposed to driving the speedways? Did the walls and speed on the narrow street tracks feel a bit close?

No, no. I was a lot less worried about pain on street courses than I was on the speedway. It was just the driving style that was different.

You really had to manhandle the car. There was a lot more room for error on street courses. You get out of a car on a street circuit and you're physically worn down. You get out of a car on a speedway and you're mentally worn down, you're mentally exhausted because there's no room for mistakes and you're holding your breath every corner, every lap. I could take two or three percent off and it wouldn't be a problem. But if you're going to run quick, you've got to be on the limit, you've got to be out on the right rear, you've got to have the thing freed up and you've got to be ready for it to go at any second. You're basically qualifying every lap. So the feeling of that and to know that if you make a mistake it is going to be a big one... it is mentally exhausting.

But the streets are good. The difference was, for me, I had to get more animated in the car. I was used to trying to do everything very smooth, very precise, very fine and for the streets I had to learn to over-drive. I had to learn how to manhandle the thing, but also to let it go. You can hit a corner and get into it too deep and wait for it to jump out and catch it. You can reflex drive on a street circuit. On a speedway you have to learn to drive off a feeling that the car gives you just before it happens, because if you wait until after it happens, it's too late.

So tell me about Sanair and the crash in '84. It was a short oval, right?

It was a little less than a mile long, a three-corner track like Pocono, and it was brand-new. That was part of what did a lot of the damage to me, because the guardrail that I hit was set in gravel and not in good solid dirt. There was too much of a gap underneath the guardrail on the bottom rungs and it allowed the nose to get under and then being set in gravel that allowed the post to lift up.

So the car basically went under the guardrail and the guardrail came through the top of the car and caught the back of the pedals and forced my feet back against my shins.

So, it was a brand-new track but it was a little bull ring. It was a fun track, mind you. I just made a mistake. I got over-anxious and made a mistake. The biggest mistake was that I did it in practice. You know, the same scenario in the race, I'd have done the same thing and been fine.

What exactly happened?

After the last race I think we were tied for the lead of the championship on points with Mario Andretti. With Sanair being a new track we'd gone up there for a test while a lot of the other teams hadn't, and so we'd wanted to try to hold onto that advantage as you go through the weekend, stay that step ahead that you got in testing.

I've always been one of these guys that needs to see speed on the watch, you know? I can tell if I'm quicker or slower, but I need to see it on the watch, I need to put the lap down and have the evidence. But with Sanair being such a short track it was very difficult to get a clear lap and set a proper time.

So we're in practice and I was trying to get a clean lap and I was behind a couple cars. I thought, once I get by this guy there's a gap ahead and that'll give me a clean run. I had a good run coming off turn three and just as I dove to the inside to go by him, to the left I see another car warming up down alongside the guardrail on the front straight. So I jumped to the left of the car ahead, I had my right front inside his left rear already and I saw the car warming up coming from the far left, and it's just one of those split-second timing judgements you've got to make. I'm looking at the gap closing down and I'm already committed.

I could tell that the gap was going to still be open enough when I got there, so now I'm focused on the left rear of the guy ahead and my right front, staying as close to him as I can as I'm going by to utilise as much of the gap as I can. And as I go by the car warming up, he goes completely out of my sight and I thought, OK, I'm good. And just as I thought that, I felt a hit on my left rear and it just turned me head-on into the guardrail. I'm watching the guardrail coming at me and that's the last thing I remember.

It was the impatience that led to the mistake. But then also I learned later that it would never have worked out. Back then when you warmed the cars up you'd come on and off the throttle. He'd picked the throttle up just as I was passing which ended up keeping the gap and it not opening up like I thought it was going to. So, it was a timing thing that just didn't work out. In a race you wouldn't have a guy warming up.

I chalked it up in the book. I screwed up.

So what's the first thing you remember? As you said, you saw the guardrail coming towards you and then what?

It was just bits and pieces after that. The first thing I remembered was hearing somebody saying, 'Rick, do you know who I am, do you know who I am?' I looked up and it was Roger. They already had me on a stretcher on the infield and he's talking to me and I said, 'Yeah.' That was kind of the first thing I remember, but from then it's just bits and pieces.

The next thing I remember I was in hospital, laying in a bed, my feet just killing me. They had everything packed in ice and I'm screaming to get the ice off me because it felt to me like it was making it hurt more. I remember a guy in a bed across the room in the corner, an older gentleman, and I just have this memory, I don't know why that sticks in my mind, but it's like he was raised up halfway like he was doing a sit-up, and just sitting there. I remember thinking how can you sit like that for that length of time?

The next thing I remember was laying on a stretcher on the outside of a helicopter. You remember M*A*S*H, the TV show? Just like that. I was on the outside hanging on the running gear on a stretcher with a sheet over me and it was blowing all over the place. And they're flying me out of there to get me to an ambulance to try to get me across state lines to switch ambulances. I don't remember all of that. But that was Roger organising to get me out of there, get me back to his plane to be able to get me back to Indianapolis.

And then, again, it's just remembering moments in Indianapolis before the whole process started with Dr Trammell as far as piecing the jigsaw puzzle of my feet back together began.

And the Canadian doctors had wanted to amputate your feet.

Yes, they said that. When I looked down the first time, my feet looked like two footballs on the end of my legs they were swollen so bad, and five little footballs on the end of it that were my toes. Basically the accident had crushed every bone in the right foot, half of them more than once. They said the right foot was basically a bag of mush and the left foot had more than half the bones in it broken and it tore off both Achilles tendons.

They said there wasn't anything to do for me and they'd have to take them off. That's when Roger stepped in and said, 'No, no, no, wait a minute.' And he got me home. Terry Trammell, who was a new young doctor at the time studying a lot of the new ideas and new ways of reconstruction and everything, took the bull by the horns. It was this that basically introduced him to the racing industry and he's still involved with it today.

Roger did that. And it was Terry that put me back together.

My wife was talking to Terry's wife about this some years later and apparently he'd come home that night after the surgery and half destroyed his kitchen at the house because he thought he had lost the right foot. He didn't think it was going to make it because the circulation was so poor. Even though he'd pieced the bones back together in that big puzzle. But it ended up surviving. Thanks to him.

Was there ever a doubt in your mind that you would get back into a racing car when you woke up and you knew what had happened?

No. When I looked down and saw both feet were there, at that point I knew I was going to be in a car again. The only doubt I had was, having been in a hospital for five months, how long it was going to take me to get back to where I was at. This whole sport is about how do I improve the next corner over what I did the last time through it? How do I make it better for the next race? How do I make it better than the last time? That's the way it works.

So the only doubt I had was how long it was going to take me. And, after being laid up this long, I had to learn to walk again. I didn't have any balance, I didn't have full movement of my ankles, no side to side in the right ankle and only about a quarter of the up and down motion. The left one was closer to normal but still restricted. So how long was it going to take me to get back to where I was at before, in order to be competitive? That was the only real question in my mind.

And how long did that take? For most of us it is hard to imagine what it must be like to spend those five months in a hospital bed, and to be sitting there with your own thoughts every day and to have to deal with that.

That's where the 'it could have been worse' thoughts come back. That's a mantra that I had to use. You have to remember how lucky you are and you have to keep saying it could have been worse, it could have been worse. And, again, we can go back to not crying over spilt milk. It's the same way in a race car. In later life I've found my place on the pitwall, and I'll be listening to guys on the radio and somebody would have cut them off or done something to piss them off and they'd be screaming on the radio for two laps and I'm sitting thinking, how the hell are you driving the car? You know, I can't scream and yell on the radio and drive at the same time and get everything out of it. It's just a normal deal. If someone cut me off in Turn One and it made me mad, I had to be over it by Turn Two if I was going to get the most out of it. My focus had to be back in the car, not on him.

You get over it. You go forward. And it's just a slow process. You just try to go forward every day. You ask how is today going to be better than yesterday? Just like the next corner. How are you going to take the next corner? Always look ahead.

A lot of help at that time came from the doctors and from Roger and the support from my wife was incredible. But the best therapy throughout the whole time, and what helped get me closer to what you feel will be normal, was the first time I got back in the car at Phoenix. That was right after I got out of the hospital. I couldn't even walk yet. Simpson made me a special pair of shoes with some padding in them and I was basically on crutches. They just kind of wheeled me out in a wheelchair, picked me up and set me down in the car. I'll never forget it.

I got in the car and went out, just did the install lap, came in and checked it out and then I went out and started leaning on it for a few laps. I got up to speed a little bit and got a feel for certain things, and when I came in all the guys jumped down on the top of the car, stuck their heads in and asked, 'How was it?'

I just said the car's a little tight in the middle of one and two and a little free coming off four. And they just died laughing.

They said, 'You've got to be kidding me. No! How are your feet?'

And it dawned on me that this was the first time in five or six months that I hadn't been thinking about my feet. My head had just gone straight back to the car. It was the first opportunity I had to get away from the pain, not thinking of my feet hurting and all of that. I was back in my office. And I remember thinking, wow, this is great. It had got my mind off my feet. I was focused back on the car again and it felt like home. And so we ended up running the test, and by the end I was quicker than my team-mates so I thought, 'Yeah, OK!' I wasn't back, I knew I wasn't back yet by any means, but it got me over that first hump of, well, how rusty am I going to be?

You lay off of anything for six months, swinging a golf club or whatever it is, and it takes time to get back. But that test showed me I could make my feet work well enough on the pedals and I hadn't lost the feeling in my butt of what the car was telling me. The car was still talking to me. I could still hear it. So all that stuff was still there.

Now it was a matter of refining and retuning and getting the strength back. I couldn't run very many laps. I was falling out of the seat because I didn't have any strength from being laid up for so long. But it was going to be OK. That test eased my mind. I knew I would get back and now it was simply a matter of how long it was going to take to get physically fit enough.

And how long did it take you?

I don't remember exactly. But that was the first time basically in my life that I ever really had to work out. I'd worked out a little bit from time to time, but I grew up running two different classes on motocross bikes, sitting in an off-road car for six, eight, ten hours at a time without getting out. I rode water skis, motorcycles in the desert for fun and relaxation and so when I first got into an Indycar, four hours was a snap. It was smooth, no holes, no dirt, no dust. I mean, it was nice, you know?

But when I did my feet, the combination of being older and being laid up, I had to physically start working at it more seriously. I had to get a routine, go in and work and get myself back to the best I'd ever been. And I can't remember what race it was, but I had a realisation a few races after I came back that I was almost there, because for a while in the first races I'd be on the radio all the time asking how many laps I had left to run.

Well, this race in particular, all I remember is that whatever race it was, it was really long, and it seemed like all of a sudden here was the white flag. And I hadn't even asked how many laps we had to go. I hadn't even thought about it. I was having fun doing what I was doing. It made me realise I was getting closer to where I needed to be.

That comeback season in 1985 — do you think you were properly ready for the first time you went back to race?

Well, it depends on how you want to look at it. Was I at 110 percent? No. But I needed it mentally, to get back in the car and get going. I mean even in May at Indy I was still rusty. We qualified 10th or something. Now, I've never been one for records or stats. If I'm doing my job, the records will take care of themselves. I don't change anything I do because it might be a record, because what I've done is what got me here. And if I start doing something different, it might be wrong. And that's just the way I've always looked at it.

But recently I had to go through my stats for a book that we were doing at

Penske, and we were going through my biography and one of the PR girls said to me, 'Did you know that in the 14 years you ran at Indy you were on the front row 11 times?' And I thought, wow, you know, I hadn't even thought about it. And to me that is the kind of stat I like because it showed a consistency, which is what I always tried to do.

So to be down the order at Indy, when you look at my record there, I knew I was still rusty. With another year under my belt I wouldn't have been 10th that day. I was still sneaking back up on the limit and refining and tuning my feeling and the whole thing. And at the speedway it's all about small steps. You can take bigger steps, but the odds go up of stepping over the limit.

But once I got into the race and got back up to speed and dealt with the turbulence and chasing the track and working with the guys and getting the car where we needed it, all that kind of thing to be ready for the shoot-out at the end, that's when I started to feel like we were back.

I really felt I could have won that race. I ended up setting the fastest lap. So, OK, I was in the ballpark now. I just needed to position myself for the shoot-out. And then the gearbox failed. And that was that.

That must have done so much for your confidence, because you got a top three next time out at the Milwaukee Mile.

Oh yeah. It was the confidence, the seat time. You can test and test until you are blue in the face, and I've always told rookies that you can be the fastest man alive in testing but you're going to learn more when the green flag drops than you ever thought you could because you're into situations that you would never do in a test whether it be turbulence, traffic, being forced up into the grey, forced down over the apron, eight cars in front of you instead of one and somebody behind you at the same time. There's so many scenarios that you cannot reproduce in testing that you're going to learn from. So you may think you've got it together but you'd better be open-minded and ready to learn when that green flag drops.

That's also part of the getting back up to speed; working yourself through those scenarios, refining that feeling back to where it needs to be. And it all came back together pretty quick again. That speed came fairly quick, it was just the longevity and the physical fitness to do what you needed to do throughout the whole day and throughout the whole weekend. That took a little longer than the speed coming back.

You would go on to win races after your return, but do you think you were ever as good again after your accident?

Yeah. Yeah, I think so. Because I would have retired before I did if the speed hadn't been there.

There's always another level and it's all about getting there. And that's one of the early things I learned, after about two or three years of running in Indycars and winning races. I remember one year thinking I'm kind of getting this figured out now, and then I ran another year and looked back at when I thought that and I realised, damn, I really didn't know anything about it, you know?

And so now I thought I was getting a handle on it. And I ran another year and I looked back and, damn, I still didn't know. I just thought I did. And then it finally dawned on me that there is no end to that. There is no end to how much you can learn and how much you can improve yourself. And if there is then you'd better get out of the car. It's all about learning and there's always another level to go to. You may think you're at the top and at that last level but you're not.

So it's all about how do I keep going forward and making it better? And basically when I retired that was the reason. The desire had gone away and I wasn't willing to recommit, refocus and do the work that I was going to need to do, to go to the next level. And that is why I got out.

So I felt that, even after the accident, I not only hit the levels I had beforehand but that I got better. Taking the win at Pocono was big, mentally, for me. I felt like I was pretty well back before that but I didn't have the win under my belt. To stand it in concrete. It's like having to see that lap time on the clock. Ultimately it is just validation. I know in my heart I've done a good lap but I want to see it.

I knew I was back but until I got that win... you know? That stamped it for me, mentally. I was back. And that was an important victory.

You talked about those constant improvements, getting to the end of each season and looking back and realising that the season before you thought you had it sussed but you hadn't. And I guess that has a lot in common with what you were saying about your recovery and looking at the way you approached racing, in that there's always the next corner to attack, the next braking point and apex to hit. Is that the way you approach racing and life? That whatever is done is done, and there's always that next challenge?

Yeah, pretty much. I mean that's the fun part, attacking the next corner, the next race, the next challenge. And how do I improve it? That's the fun part. It's like I always enjoyed working with the set-up of a car and even back in the old motorcycle races or recreation on the weekends riding bikes over the sand dunes with the three wheelers or whatever we were playing with at the time when we were growing up. I never went back to the desert or back to the dunes or back to where we were going the next weekend with the same equipment. I had spent the whole week after work modifying things, changing something, because that was the fun part. Going back to see if I made it better, you know? And plus, working on the chassis and the set-up of the car, as far as how I approach life, well I've always been basically lazy. That's why I chose a job sitting down.

I realised early on, the better that car works, the less I have to. I've worked a lot harder in a race running third than I have winning, because the car wasn't right and I had to carry it more. On any given day you have to try to get the most available out of the car.

It's like tinkering. I like to tinker with things and work on them with my hands and it's just the way I grew up. I never had any schooling for engineering. It was all seat-of-the-pants trial and error and what you learned every time you got in a car. That was the important part about making changes and learning what the change did. And when I got into Indycars I didn't think I did anything differently to anybody else. I thought I was way behind the curve until even at the end of my career in Indycars when I started to realise, wow, they don't all necessarily think about it the same way I do.

You have to understand that when you change A, it may not be A that made the difference. It may be what A did to B and C that actually made a difference. So then you've got to look at B or C and find out what A did to each one of those that made the difference. And then, whatever they do, start digging deeper into that because that affected what you were looking for. And it's that same scenario throughout, whether it's aero, mechanical or a combination of the two. Toe, rake, ride height, camber, pressures… all of that. They all work together and changing one thing might make a change that you feel, but it may not be what you changed that affected what you're feeling.

I've always enjoyed just taking more time with that stuff, even the balance for a slot-car chassis when I was eight years old and trying to figure out how to make it work better. I've just always enjoyed that kind of thing. So I think that really helped me in racing — figuring out how to build a better mousetrap.

I remember working with Paul Tracy and he always had a mindset with his crew of, 'Get it close and I'll do the rest.' He didn't realise how hard he made it on himself by being that way. I remember there was this one race where Emerson Fittipaldi was quicker than he was and Paul was getting flustered and frustrated and he came in yelling at the guys saying, 'You've got to give me the tools!'

So I remember going to pull him aside and I said, 'Paul, you've got to give *them* the tools first before they can give you the tools you need. Quit running at 110 percent every lap in practice. Back it down to 90 percent. If you're running 110 percent in practice, you're so busy saving your life that you aren't listening to the car. Back down! Listen to the car! Get consistent! Give those guys the feedback they need. The only reason Emerson is outrunning you is that he's built a better mousetrap than you. That's what he does.'

Emerson and I spoke the same language. I could always count on what he said. If he said he'd made a change and it had done X to the car, you could take it to the bank. I knew exactly what he was talking about. I knew and I could trust exactly what that change was going to do with the car. And I could feel comfortable in doing it before I went out to qualify. Because I knew what to expect. He was great at it. There are 'feel' drivers and 'reflex' drivers — and he was a real 'feel' driver.

I enjoyed doing it. And you always work harder at something you enjoy. Your team-mate is your yardstick and I think one of the main things that really helped me early on with Penske was that Roger has always had a team. There's always been a team mentality and a group of people who have worked together as a unit. A lot of teams started approaching the team concept and getting the drivers to work together but they still didn't utilise them as a team like we did. I mean, it's hard and it's difficult. I didn't realise it at the time but I fit the mould perfectly in that respect because I grew up racing with my brother and we'd go home at night and pick each other's brains because we knew that if we could help each other to the next level and get an advantage on everybody else, all we had to do was race each other. That's the team concept in a nutshell. But it's such an individual sport that it's hard to get a lot of these drivers to come around to that.

I've dealt with a lot of them. I went through a lot of team-mates in my years with Roger and you always knew that they were your yardstick, the guys you've got to beat. If they beat me, it makes me dig deeper. If he beat you or he's quicker, well, OK, I'm leaving something on the table somewhere. Where is it? I've got to go find it. You elevate each other.

That's what the team concept is to me. It's up to me to do a better job and beat everybody else with the same equipment. That's my job and that's what I want to do. As long as you don't change the equipment and try to get equality in a way that takes the driver and his skills out of it. That's wrong, dead wrong. When you start taking my tools away by trying to equalise, that's wrong. Just make the equipment the same and I've got the same tools to work with to do something different than the other guy.

So I guess, going back to that mantra and what you said earlier about listening to the car... from your earliest days of driving, and I guess then even more so with the recovery from the accident, is it important to listen to yourself as much as it is to listen to the car, to know that at all times you're doing what's right for you, as you are what's right for the car?

Oh yeah. Yeah. But I tend to not listen to myself as well as I listen to a car sometimes. The car is more obedient.

I've never liked routine. That's why I like racing. It is always different. I've jumped around a lot of different hobbies because you do them for a while and you get to a certain level but I get to a point and think, OK, I'm not learning as much and gaining as much as I was and so I start losing interest and I go on to try something else. I may come back to it. But racing was the only thing I ever stuck with. It kept my interest over time because it was always different.

Where there's a track condition shifting from one day to the next, it is all about change. Every corner of your lap the fuel load goes down and the tyres are going, the wind is changing. Qualifying at Indianapolis was always my favourite thing, because you've got four laps and you've got to be absolutely on the money and that means adapting in every corner. Those four laps may look identical but I'd never run one corner the same way twice. You've got to be open-minded and be ready to adapt and change and listen to what it tells you. It's just an ongoing thing. And then the race is the same. Five hundred miles of change.

So, it's listening. It's listening and adapting. But in terms of listening to your body, sure, you have to listen, you have to adapt. You have to work out and you have to eat right. Again, when Emerson came to the team he had his own chef with him, cooking him certain things to eat. I'm not saying that's wrong, it just wasn't for me. I remember Phoenix one year and I'd out-qualified him and I was in the truck with a quarter pounder with cheese or a Big Mac or something and he walks through the door and his chef is right behind him and he looks at me and he just points at me and says, 'See!'

We were just laughing and joking about it, but that was kind of me. If you listen to your body it may say, OK, I want some salad. You don't have to stick to some regimen. Your body tells you what you need if you're listening to it. Some people lean towards salad and vegetables and when I listen to what my body is telling me, I might need salad and vegetables too. But there are also times when my body is telling me it needs some steak. My body is telling me it's had enough salads and so it's ready for something different.

But too much of anything is too much. No matter what it is. Too much of a good thing becomes too much. And believe me I've done too much of a lot of things over the years as well. I don't always listen to myself as well as I've listened to race cars.

And that's something I think it's important to talk about here. You asked me, right at the start, about my hardest moment in life. And, well, I ended up drinking too much after I got out of the car. It was starting to kick my ass and I had to sober up. I got away from it.

That was a down time in my life. I've never tried to hide it. But I've never tried to announce it either.

If you'd be willing to talk about it, how did your problems begin?

All I can do is kind of go by what I've learned through getting sober and attending Alcoholics Anonymous and all of that.

We're all wired differently and I've got an addictive personality. It's probably why I work so hard. You know, that car set-up thing? Anything I do, I try to do it as much as I can and as good as I can. I guess I tried to drink as good as I could drink. But I had no idea of the disease of it. I never had a problem with it until after I got out of the car because the car unknowingly kept it in check. You have to stay physically fit. I wasn't thinking about keeping it in check, it was just something I never even thought about.

I didn't feel like I drank any more or any less than most people. I never really even thought about it. But when I got out of the car and retired, it was like, OK, I can relax a little bit now. You know, I don't have to work out. I've been doing it for years and years and years and now I can kick back a little bit.

But at some point you cross a line and you never know when or where that line was.

Fortunately I realised, and again this was part I guess of listening to my body, because I've seen how many people struggle with not realising or admitting to themselves that there's a problem.

Did it take retirement, crossing into the real world, for you to realise that this was a problem?

Not having that something to keep it in check, the driving, the physical fitness, all those kind of things... that allowed it to progress quicker.

I've never been someone who really enjoyed going to a function or the cocktail party beforehand or whatever. And believe me, getting up on stage scares me to death. I tell people that and they say, 'Yeah, right, that bothers everybody. It's everybody's worst fear.' And I'm like, you don't understand, it *really* bothers me.

Even back in grade school I was one of those kids who hated being late to class because you open the door and everybody looks at you. I can tell you my first experience of not getting up on stage was in grade school and everybody had to give an oral report. The teacher was going through all the students, 'OK you're next, you're next, you're next', to get up and give a report. And it came to my turn. I stood up and said, 'Give me an F.' And I sat down. That was my oral report.

You couldn't have dragged me to the front of that class with horses. It has never been me. And then I end up getting a job where, for 30 years, I had to stand up in front of people and be the centre of attention.

A good example of how much I hated getting up in front of people was my fourth win at Indy. Michael Andretti and I have our shoot-out, our battle. I get the lead back and I start getting away. I've got about 10 laps to go. And now it's like qualifying. Hit your marks. No mistakes. You got to go. It's show time.

And what am I thinking instead of hitting my marks? I'm thinking, 'Oh, man, if I win this thing again I'm going to have to give an acceptance speech.'

True story.

But a couple of beers at a cocktail party would help settle the nerves. I'm not saying that's an excuse for drinking, but it gets away from you before you know where you are with it. And before you realise the progression it is taking, and that's where I said listen to your body, listen to what it tells you. Being open to listening helped save me.

I remember getting to a point of thinking, uh-oh, this is a problem. Once you know it has progressed to a certain stage, that's when I did something about it. I went and got the help I needed, to do what was needed to not do it.

And that's when I started to learn, because I was beating myself up. I consider myself to have a little self-discipline. You know, with the job I had and the things I've done over the years, you've got to have a little self-discipline to do what you do. But this was starting to kick my butt and I started beating myself up. I've always wanted to take things on myself. And it was a real awakening of, hang on a second, what is going on here? I should have more discipline than this.

That realisation and admitting it to myself took me away from the denial part of it long enough to realise that maybe I had a problem. That is what got me in the door to get help.

A lot of people struggle with the denial part of admitting to themselves that they have a problem. To say, 'I am an alcoholic.' You know, a lot of people just really struggle with it. As soon as I got in and started getting the help I needed and the disease concept was explained to me, it was such a weight off my shoulders.

Now I understand it's not that I didn't have the willpower. It is a disease. And there is a medication for it, and that medication is doing what I need to do to not do it. But I could quit beating myself up for it, for not having the willpower, for not being able to pull myself up by the bootstraps.

The education was what I needed. And it goes back to that racing mindset again. The program gave me the tools. The tools are basically your medication.

It's the best thing I've ever done. And that was 15 years ago.

But listening to my body, just like listening to the car, was part of what helped. Because, again, and we are going to go full circle here, it could have been a lot worse.

It's back to that same thing I said right at the start. There's no point in crying over spilt milk. I've been very fortunate in my life. It could have been a lot worse.

Sébastien Loeb

'My philosophy is that I am very happy with what I achieved... to be able to still live in this world and continue my passion, I think it's just chance... I'm lucky to have this opportunity... But I don't do it for the image. I do it because I like it.'

Sébastien Loeb isn't just a rally driver. He is *the* rally driver. The most successful man to ever enter the fray of the most diverse and challenging discipline of global motorsport, the Frenchman has won the World Rally Championship an incredible nine times. He has won more rallies than any other driver in history, has more podium finishes than any other driver in history and has won more rally stages than any other driver in history. Even more astonishing is that he achieved all of these records in just a decade of full-time competition.

Born in the Alsace region of France in 1974, the young Sébastien marked himself out as a brilliant gymnast, winning at local and state level. After school he became an apprentice electrician, but driving fast cars was now his real passion. With confidence in his burgeoning abilities, he left his full-time employment at the age of 21 to concentrate on motorsport, and soon came to the attention of Citroën and its sporting boss, former rally ace Guy Fréquelin.

Loeb won the inaugural Junior World Rally Championship in his first year. So impressed was Fréquelin that he offered his young charge the chance to step up to the full WRC that same 2001 season, for a one-off attempt at the San Remo Rally, and Loeb finished second.

From there, Loeb was chosen to head Citroën's assault on the WRC, taking part in seven events in 2002 before a full season the following year. Loeb came second in the 2003 championship. By a single point. He won the next nine.

But Loeb's desire was never going to be quenched by rallying alone. He has competed at the Dakar and come close to winning. He finished second in the

2006 Le Mans 24 Hours. He has raced and won in the FIA GT Series, the World Touring Car Championship and rallycross. He has also tested Formula 1 machinery and proved fast. So fast, in fact, that he was due to contest the 2009 Abu Dhabi Grand Prix for Scuderia Toro Rosso before a full Formula 1 switch in 2010, until politics and red tape scuppered what could have been one of the most audacious cross-over attempts in a generation.

Sebastién Loeb's records may never be broken. He has redefined his sport into the new millennium. And yet even he, at his very lowest ebb, questioned aloud whether he would ever get to live his dream. The greatest of all time very nearly didn't make it at all.

The worst moment for me was when I was a young driver. It was only my second year of racing. For me, when I started, I didn't have any money and I only really got a break because some guys believed in my driving.

I did Rallye Jeunes, an operation made by the French Fédération and Peugeot at this time, and the goal of this operation was to let everybody drive. It was for 15-year-olds and you did a selection in every region of France. Then the best of each region went to the national final and the winner gained a season in rally. So that was, for me, the only possibility to start rallying because I didn't have the money.

And so I did this and in the first year I nearly won. I was the best, the fastest and everything, but the judges decided it was the second-placed guy that would win. That was a disappointment for sure, but then I did it again the next year and then I was again leading but I made a mistake. But after that some people called me and they had a little organisation, they were doing some rallies themselves just for fun. And this guy wanted to help me to start in rallying. He knew a bit how it works and everything so I started my first season with them in the French promotion formula in a Peugeot and then the next year after they bought a car, which was a Citroën Saxo kit car, we entered the promotion formula with this car. So everybody was driving the same car and it was just the driver who made the difference.

And this was something where the manufacturers looked at what happened. If you have a young driver who tries, is beating the reference guys, then, yes, maybe you have a chance to get some help from the manufacturer and to go forward like this. At this time it was only my second season but I was the young driver who people were speaking about for the future.

And in this championship, in the middle of the season, I crashed the car in the last stage of a rally. The people who were helping me were really disappointed and not happy from what happened but, OK, it's racing and we had insurance that helped because these people didn't have a lot of money either. They had invested their own money in the story. So the car was broken but we had the insurance and we were able to go on.

Finally the car was ready for the next race, completely new, but I had to drive a little bit with the car before the race to check if everything was OK. We had no insurance when I was driving like this. And I broke the car. In the test.

That car was worth a lot of money that I didn't have at all. And the guys who owned the car also didn't have the budget to build the car again. And suddenly I went from being the young guy climbing and looking to be the next champion, and suddenly it was finished. I had no car any more. I had no money. And there was nothing I could do. I couldn't go to the next race.

So for me I was starting to believe that my career was finished and I was only just really dreaming about being a driver. And I knew that I had the potential to be. So it was a terrible situation for me.

And we decided with the guy who was the owner of the car, Dominique Heintz, who is the guy I am associated with now in Sébastien Loeb Racing, we made our own team and we helped some young driver to run in rallying or racing and so on, well he told me the only thing we can do is to try to find sponsors to build the car again and for that maybe it's good that as you are the young star we go to the next rally. But you go to work there and then you just cross paths with people and to meet them and explain to them that you need some help to continue. We did that and I went there and finally we found a sponsor, a guy who was a Citroën dealer, who listened to our story. He gave us some money to start to rebuild the car. And from that, finally, we were able to be at the next rally.

But something was not right. I started this rally and on the first stage, in the first seven kilometres, I must have lost at least 20 seconds. I was really too afraid to break the car and to do a mistake again. I was really down in my head with no confidence at all. But then, stage after stage, I built again my confidence and at the end I caught up the gap I had and I won. When you won this rally you received some bonus payments from the manufacturer to help you to do the next rally and pay some tyres, and so finally we came back and I won again the next rally and we came out of this really difficult moment.

So even though we came out of it in the end, this for me is the worst memory that I had in my career because I was just beginning to dream to be a top driver and to have a future in rally and suddenly everything was finished. It was a hard moment, really.

What took you from gymnastics to rallying?

There was nothing that took me directly from gymnastics to this. I stopped gymnastics when I was 15 because I preferred to hang out with my friends in the street than to be in the gym. That was the first thing why I retired from gymnastics. And then I was always enjoying to drive my moped. I did some little competitions in France with mopeds but I did only two or three races because I didn't have the money to race more, but my friends had their own mopeds and when they were not available I did the races for them and I was always the star of the show.

Then when I first got my driving licence and my first road car I saw that I was much better than my friends at driving and I had all this passion to take the perfect corner. I was always in the field with my car and trying to practise. I didn't know why I was training and practising like this, but I always enjoyed trying to brake late, to turn, to slide and to control it and the passion came from that. Then I saw this operation which was Rallye Jeunes for the young drivers and I entered it.

How did you meet Dominique Heintz?

After my first Rallye Jeunes there were some things written about me because I was the young guy coming from nowhere, arriving and beating everybody, even the guys who were already racing. There were two categories: non-racing people and the racers, and I arrived from nowhere, no-one knew about me, and I beat everybody, set the best time. But it wasn't just about the time. That was part of it but there was also a judge, well, a jury and the jury decided that, OK, I was fastest because they couldn't say anything else, but they decided to choose the other driver because the judges had the last word to decide and this guy was known in the area of the rally.

So I paid for that, but what I'd done in that first competition and the way the winner was decided created a story that came out in the newspaper, that this young driver from Alsace was basically screwed by the jury even though he was the best. And Dominique Heintz was a guy who lived in Alsace, had a passion for motorsport and he called me and said, 'I understand what happened to you. Maybe we could meet. Maybe I can help you.'

And so I went to meet him but at the time we didn't yet agree to do something together. The next year I did again this Rallye Jeunes and I was again ahead of everybody but I made a small mistake in the last race in the final. You have 15,000 people entering this event, every year. Dominique ended up thinking that if for two years in a row this guy is the fastest out of 15,000 people, then he could be something special. So, with his friend Rémi Mammosser, they decided to invest in a little car to help me to begin in rallies.

Dominique was a military captain and Rémi was a businessman selling home heating, so we're not talking about billionaires. But they had a little association, Dominique was racing a bit sometimes, in fact he had done the Dakar on a bike, and so the idea to call me came from the fact he'd only been able to do the Dakar because he had the help of some people, some motorbike dealers that gave him the opportunity with some money to help him. He always thought that one day maybe he can give something back to someone because without the help he'd been given, he never would have done the Dakar. And so he saw my story and he started to help me.

So it's all going well until you have that first crash, then rebuild the car, then crash it again in that test, without insurance?

Yeah, it was a little private shakedown. I did a mistake. It was in the night. Dominique and Rémi hadn't arrived at the Rally and they let me drive the car. We had two mechanics, me, my co-driver. We blocked the road and we tried to test the car.

I was maybe a bit young and a bit stupid because I didn't think enough that it's possible to break the car.

Did you know that there wasn't any insurance on it?

I didn't even think that far ahead. Normally we should just do a few runs, but something was a bit wrong. The engine wasn't correct, there was a misfire and so the mechanics worked on the car, the night came, and so we put the headlights on the car, still continuing to do some runs, and finally I went offline, I touched the gravel on the side and I flipped the car onto the roof and that was it. Upside down. I knew immediately that it's very bad because then it suddenly came into my head that the car was not insured in the test, because when this situation arrived I felt in my stomach that it was really bad, what I did.

I remember I called Dominique and I told him, 'The worst thing just happened.' And he understood what I was speaking about.

And how old were you at that time?

I was 23. I started in racing late.

So you've got your whole potential career in front of you, you're the hot-shot talent and all of a sudden this terrible thing happens. Did the realisation dawn that night that it was going to be a pretty major problem for you?

Yeah. I knew that we were in a complicated situation because even before that, to be at the start of this race was complicated because, OK, we had insurance but we had no money to pay the excess. I don't know how much it was but that made it already complicated to be at the start of the next rally. We needed to find some sponsors and we found a guy who paid for my tyres for the rally, so that was a big help to be able to be there. And then I made the mistake.

Those things make you grow up pretty fast, don't they?

Oh yeah, for sure. But that was stupid, to take some risks without any insurance.

And then to have to walk around without a car and having done this very silly thing to have to plead with people to back you — did you find that hard?

For sure. At this time, talking to people was not the thing I was the best at because I was always a bit shy. And so it was not easy for me to do this job. But like you said, at the end it makes you grow up and understand things.

Having made that mistake, as you said you were 20 seconds off when you got back in the car. Did you have to kick yourself at that point and say, 'Come on, what am I doing?'

Yeah. But it was mentally very hard. What I had to do was to forget about what happened, to get confidence again and to concentrate on the road. The problem is that if you are afraid to crash the car then in the corner you don't see the road, you see the tree, you see the bushes. You look at what is around you instead of being concentrated and focused 100 percent on pushing your car. So that's something which is not easy to be able to put away and to say, OK, now it's gone.

But then, what's always helped me is that I get a feeling with the car and as soon as I have this feeling I know I'm able to go nearly on the limit and I don't have the feeling or the need to take big risks because when I take too big a risk, I can't control everything that I do. And when I arrived in this situation, when I found that feeling with the car again, I started to forget what had happened and to be sure of myself and confident again. I came back into a rhythm.

So driving within yourself?

When you drive in rally, and also in racing, for me it takes one hundred percent of my concentration. It happens all the time that sometimes I'm driving I feel like I have too much brake on the front, I want to turn the button to change the bias, but I don't have the one second that I need just to say, OK, this will go this way or that way. You listen to the notes, you concentrate on the road to anticipate what is coming and it takes so much of your concentration that I'm not able to have one second to think whether I turn the dial right or left.

And so I think this is the same when you crash and you're still thinking about it. If you have in your mind the thought of, 'I'm not allowed to crash, I have to be careful', then your mind is not completely on what you have to do. It's important to just forget about everything to allow yourself to focus everything on your driving.

How important do you think it was to have such a big lesson so early in your career?

I had some other lessons also. This one, for sure, was when I was like an amateur driver so I understood that the money is something important. After this the next year was again complicated because I won this formula and then the guy who helped me had taken all the bonuses and just sold everything. And then it was finished, again. And then I found myself another sponsor, who helped me to do the first event of the gravel French championship. And I won.

Citroën immediately started to tell me, OK, now you have to continue. I said I don't have the money to continue, and they gave me an engine. Then I did the rally and I won again. Then I needed to get another sponsor, and so on, until the point where everybody started to work together. And from then on, Citroën put together their own programme, I joined it and from that point I didn't have to pay any more.

But going back to what we talked about, that crash, from that lesson I learnt that it is important to concentrate and think about everything you do because you can lose a lot from only a small mistake.

Another lesson I had a bit later was in 2003 when I did my first full World Championship and I finished second by one point. One point! And that was a lesson. Because when I was thinking back to the season I know that I lost this point in many places.

Sometimes you secure a second place because, OK, you've got some good points and it's OK. But from that point on I said every point I can take, I take it. That was also a lesson and, then also to say, OK, I won't let anything to the side affect me. I need to optimise everything to get every point I can get.

That's a huge lesson to learn. Do you still look back and rue that one point?

No. I won nine championships after that, so in the end it wasn't so bad. But at that moment, yes, because I didn't know if it was the only opportunity I will get. It's not every day you can win a World Championship so, maybe I lost my opportunity to win the title at this point. At that time, not knowing what I know now, yes it was very hard. But then after what happened in my career, after that, I have no regrets.

It was really quite incredible to be able to fight for the title in the first season.

So take me to 2006. You broke your shoulder while mountain biking and missed a huge chunk of the season.

Four rallies.

Right! And yet you were still champion because you'd come out at the start of the season and you'd been brutally dominant, taking, as you said, every point that you could.

I think the lesson from 2003 helped me to win the championship in 2006. I had so much lead that even with a broken shoulder and sitting out four rallies, it was enough.

We sit here today and you've just come back from a Dakar you desperately wanted to win but it slipped away from you. I guess the question I have is about success and whether it is easier to accept when you don't get the result you want because you have achieved so much already, or whether that taste for success is so great that not achieving it becomes harder to accept?

It doesn't make it harder.

Today, for me, my philosophy is that I am very happy with what I achieved in rally and today to be able to continue to drive in some different disciplines like Dakar, like Le Mans, like WTCC, to be able to still live in this world and continue my passion, I think it's just chance. Good fortune. I'm lucky to have this opportunity.

So I did some racing, some rallycross, Pike's Peak, Dakar. For sure I prefer to win. But in racing there are a lot of parameters. You cannot control everything. Dakar is complicated. I know I have the level to win it. I'm able to drive fast enough. I'm able to be quite safe and not to take too big a risk. But, yeah, you need more than that to win Dakar. You need a bit of luck too.

But, for sure, I'm still the same person. I like to win so when it doesn't come it's frustrating. At the end for sure some people might think, OK, he doesn't win any more... blah blah blah... and I know that for my image and my reputation, to continue competing is a risk.

But I don't do it for the image. I do it because I like it and it's my passion. I continue to race because when I'm fighting for something I feel alive. I have been given the opportunity to race in different disciplines and to keep challenging myself. And it is the greatest gift.

Tom Kristensen

'If I'd have known there would be so many obstacles, would I have set out on this path? Maybe not. But that is the good thing about life… When you get through the obstacles, it means more. It means your heart is really there.'

Tom Kristensen is widely regarded as the greatest endurance racing driver of all time. With nine victories at the Le Mans 24 Hours, he is the most successful driver in history at La Sarthe and has come to be known around the world as 'Mr Le Mans'.

The Dane got his break at Le Mans by chance, with a last-minute call-up to the Joest Porsche squad in 1997. He arrived at the race with no prior testing or knowledge of the car or track. And yet he won, on début. Thus began his staggering career in endurance racing and the birth of a motorsport legend.

Besides sportscar racing, where he was also crowned champion of the American Le Mans Series and won the Sebring 12 Hours six times, Kristensen turned his hand to numerous other styles and disciplines of motorsport over his career. From karting, he went into open-wheel racing and became a champion in Japanese and German Formula 3, and a race winner in Formula Nippon and Formula 3000. He also won races in British and German touring cars.

His greatest successes came comparatively late in life. His first visit to Le Mans was just a few weeks before his 30th birthday. His final Le Mans win and crowning as World Endurance Champion, in 2013, came when he was 46.

But the truth of his incredible history in motorsport is that Tom Kristensen very nearly didn't become a racing driver at all. For all of his success, the plaudits and the adulation with which his undeniable talent is met around the world, for three years after graduating from go-karts the Dane had no seat, no drive and no future. For 1,000 days, one of the greatest drivers in history was preparing for a life not behind the wheel, but behind a desk.

I was home born in 1967 in Hobro, a little town in Denmark. My dad ran a Shell petrol station and my mum was working on the cash desk and helping to fill up the cars as it wasn't self-service in those days. I was brought up on the first floor of that gas station.

My dad was actually a racing driver and did a lot of dirt racing and some on asphalt, all without much budget, but always with touring cars. He was a good driver and competed in the Paris–Dakar and stuff like that later on. So, from the beginning, I was always interested in racing.

When I was young I always looked at karting when we went to race tracks but it wasn't until I was close to nine years old that I actually got to race a kart for the first time. I got an old kart with like a chainsaw engine, really old school, and it wasn't very reliable. I was always working on it and learning about engineering in that way.

The years went by and karting became good for me. I started gaining some success and won all the championships you could win at club level, at national level and then at Scandinavian level. I won the Scandinavian Championship in 1985 against some good drivers like Mika Häkkinen, who I had a big fight with for the win that year, changing the lead eight times in the final between us.

The 1986 World Championship was in the States, in Jacksonville, but the track was clearly never going to suit the Europeans. It wasn't at the CIK [Commission Internationale de Karting] level.

I started in cars in 1987, but just a few races here and there in Formula Ford 2000 with a Danish team, only with a Formula B car which was a year or two years old, because I really had no money. So the CRG team called me up and asked if I wanted to do this one-off comeback in karts for CRG Kali Kart in the world championships. I came second. The year before I was far stronger and maybe could have been champion.

At the same time, I was getting an education because my mum always pushed for me to study hard. I went to business college but missed a lot of lectures through racing. Even so, I applied to work at a local bank and became a junior trainee. This was always a back-up, because my dream was to race. But as things would work out, this was to be where I would end up for the next three years and through what I can describe as the hardest period of my life.

I had wanted to leave go-karts and go into single-seaters. But I had no money at all.

Nowadays we see karting as quite a direct route into Formula cars. Was it the same in the 1980s?

There were a lot of guys who stayed in karting and earned a good living in those days. We weren't in a hurry like the guys today. Today everyone is in a rush.

We didn't have nearly the same amount of track time as kids do today. They have so much testing, so much running, and simulators too these days! We didn't have any of this. It was a different dynamic. Probably there was a bit more of an unknown in those days when you were going and exploring, and actually I found that nice.

Was karting a bit of fun or did you race with an eye on it becoming your life?

There was never a long-term plan. I was always looking year to year. I was also pretty OK at soccer. As a matter of fact, my dad was too. I played soccer the year I was confirmed into the church, and it was at my confirmation that a guy told me he had found a kart for me and that I could use it for the upcoming season, I just had to help him on track. Without that happening, I would have ended up playing soccer.

So, in 1987 you're second in the karting world championships, and then you get into 1988. You want to be racing. It doesn't happen. What stopped it?

The dynamic was basically money. I called so many people to try to find budget but there was nothing. And this is what started a period I now refer to as 'The 1,000 days'. This was the period between being second in the world in karting until I signed with Bertram Schäfer Racing with Volkswagen motorsport in Bitburg in Germany in 1991. I would have signed whatever he put in front of me. But he said, 'OK, you have to live here, you have to drive when the engine has to be renovated, you have to drive to pick up parts, you have to do this and that, go to the UK to Ralt to pick up whatever.' So I signed that and I won the first race of 1991 in Zolder and went on to win the German F3 championship the year after Michael Schumacher, against guys like Karl Wendlinger and Heinz-Harald Frentzen.

So for those three years, 1988–90, you want to race, you want to be in a car, but you're not. How did it feel to watch guys you'd raced against move up the ladder while you're sitting there not racing?

It motivated me. Of course they were getting experience, they were racing all the time. But what was amazing was the respect that they still gave me. Guys like Mika Häkkinen and Alex Zanardi, if I ever came to a race they welcomed me, they introduced me to team bosses. The guys I raced against and who I rated very highly, still remembered our fights from karting and were very friendly towards me. That motivated me to never give up.

In one way, it led me to think, well, if they can do it then I can do it. But on the other side, it gave me on some occasions a satisfaction that even if I felt defeated because I wasn't racing, I knew that at least I had beaten these guys once upon a time. But these guys are the ones who, all through my career, have always picked me up and tried to do things for me. Some others have tried to protect themselves, but the good guys, they supported you and said positive things about you which eventually led to a test here and there. And eventually to that F3 chance in 1991.

So what were you doing for those three years?

I was driving, but not what you think. I was working at Himmerlandsbanken, driving a bank bus. If you imagine a mobile library, well imagine instead that you have a mobile bank. The guy who used to drive it had left, and they knew that I'd done karting and was a racing driver, so they just said, 'Hey, this guy will do.' And so I drove this mobile bank to small villages that had no bank branch.

I was a junior in the bank and so I'd been put on different departments. I liked the foreign transactions or dealing with stocks and shares, but at the same time I liked speaking with people and being the cashier on the desk. When I was put in the driving seat of the bank bus, that wasn't really my idea of banking. But in a strange way, maybe it was pushing me back behind the wheel, back where I was supposed to be.

I would travel to as many races as I could. I would speak to everyone that I could. And when I did, I would give them my office number because it looked professional. But that number was the number for the bank bus.

So sometimes I'd be driving between tiny places you'd never have heard of like Vebbestrup to Rostrup to Astrup, suddenly the phone would be ringing. I had a lady with me who was a senior at the bank, and she would run back in the bus to answer the phone and if she ever answered the phone in English or German I would hit the brakes and stop the bus because I knew that call was for me. I would run down, speak to whoever the team was, and just hope.

Did you ever approach the bank to sponsor you? Maybe to give you a loan like Niki Lauda had done to finance his career in the early days?

It was never in my mind. I was respectful for my future. I would never put myself in debt to race. That was always very clear for me. I never raised a lot of money because I never wanted to owe people. I raised a small amount to pay for travel or a test. But never more. It was always something inside me, something I needed to do for myself, that I needed to prove to people at the teams that I was good enough for them to take a chance on me and to do things this way. That was the right way for me. But of course it took time to win people around to give me a go... 1,000 days actually.

So how do you do that when the only thing you're regularly driving is a mobile bank?

One thing in these years is that actually I did some testing. One of the guys I tested with was Franz Tost, who today runs the Toro Rosso Formula 1 team. He was running an F3 team called Eufra, but he needed funding back then. Still, he called me to test a few times. He was one of the few guys who already rated me at that time even though I was maybe a few tenths slower than their regular driver. But the fact I could jump in just like that and be close I think impressed him. He knew my determination and grit.

So did Siggi Müller. He gave me a non-championship race in Opel Lotus at Zolder. I don't know why. It was a new championship and I think either David Coulthard or Rubens Barrichello won that day in 1989. I was in 15th or 16th or whatever, but I'd just jumped in and raced. It gave me experience and the building blocks for racing.

I had gone over and done a bit of testing for TOMS in Japan with Jan

Nilsson, the Swedish F3 champion, and a few other drivers, and that gave me some other experience, and would actually form the basis from which I would go to drive for them in 1992.

But these 1,000 days were very hard, and, yes, I could have given up very easily. But that was never really on my mind. I was disappointed many times. And if you could see how many letters I had written to sponsors, how many times I tried. It's amazing. I became so disappointed in constantly coming up against them saying 'no', but I used it to stay motivated.

My dad always believed in me. He's not around any more unfortunately, and I think he was a bit embarrassed that he couldn't help me more than to give me his emotional support. But that was enough for me.

And what about your mum?

In a way she was happy that I was working in a bank. She had been through it already with my dad.

So every time you got the one-off drives, was she supportive or was she happier when you weren't racing?

To be honest I never noticed. Actually, the first wake-up call for me came over Christmas many years ago when people were making jokes that when I raced at Le Mans, every year, she didn't sleep well.

So when the opportunity came to race full-time in 1991, was it a relief, or after all of those years out was there ever a worry that this could be your one and only chance and you couldn't blow it? Did you have any doubt that you still had what it took?

No. Every day I was living what I had always wanted to do. Throughout my career I have always been so grateful to the people who have believed in me and given me a chance. I constantly mention these people because they gave me this career.

What type of car do you think suited you the best, when you started racing properly?

I had to adapt to whatever I got in to. But, again, I am grateful for that because I think that versatility is a key to having a long career. Being motivated and always going in and being curious to how the car works and how it reacts. Yeah, changing to many types of car is a good thing to do for any driver.

When I went to Japan in 1992 I drove a lot of different cars and we still won the F3 championship in 1993 even though I was also racing Formula Nippon, touring cars, sports prototypes. And I started to earn a good amount of money, which was important for me to be able to tell my family that the choice I had made was the right one.

What I enjoyed the most, though, was sportscars. They gave you the combination of the power, very good aerodynamics, but a little bit of weight too.

You were German F3 champion in 1991, in your first season in formula cars. What did you learn that year?

I won my first race in the 1991 season, and from then on I drove quite protectively because I wanted to ensure I won the title. I didn't go balls-out because I was always looking at the title. I think I only won four races in the whole season, and that included that very first race. In the final race at Hockenheim, I was already champion, and so I could go balls-out. I beat the Häkkinen and Schumacher records from the year before and that motivated me as well. And that was really the time where I realised that I had it. Or at least had something.

Winning one race at the start is all good. But to combine that with a championship and then, when you don't have to worry any more, to go out and deliver and beat those records, and then you look back to a time when you didn't know if you would get a chance, and to know that I had taken that chance and done it well, that was very important. Driving free allows you a very different nature, a very different mindset. That year taught me a lot. Bert Schäfer had quite the temperament as well and that taught me a lot, and I had a lot of respect for him and the team.

We've already touched on Frentzen and Schumacher and those guys, so I guess the big question is that while they went to endurance with Mercedes and then to Formula 1, did you hope for the same progression? Was the move to Japan a sideways one for you, or were you just glad to have a seat again?

I'd tested in Formula 3000 at Mugello with Giuseppe Cipriani's Il Barone Rampante team, that Zanardi had raced with, and again it was Zanardi pushing for them to give me a shot after he moved on. They'd already signed Rubens Barrichello for 1992 and so there was only one car left and lots of us testing for the seat. Of course, I needed money, but he was very fair to me and it was not so much. At the end of the day I was fast, but Luca Badoer had been the fastest and he went on to sign with Crypton and won the championship.

I went off to Macau and had a good first race and from there I went to Toyota in Japan. There weren't two chairs to fall between in Europe, and there was a certainty in Japan. They had been impressed when I had tested a few years before and so now they offered me a good contract and I couldn't say 'no'.

As I said, it allowed me to drive a lot of cars, and crucially it gave me my first proper taste of a Le Mans car when I drove Toyota's TS010 in the Japanese Prototype championship. I remember the first time I drove it, the test car at the Yamaha test track. It was high-revving, a lot of downforce, and we were running on a very dangerous track, I think probably because the more experienced guys were a bit reluctant.

You had a lot of success in Japan. What brought you back to Europe?

I inherited Eddie Irvine's car at the Cerumo team in Formula Nippon and touring cars because we'd had the same engineer. I finished second in the championship in 1995 and at that point I'd been in Japan since 1992. I loved it there but, you know, there were many factors pulling me back to Europe, not least family and my girlfriend.

So I came back, raced in F3000 in Europe whilst at the same time commuting to Japan for GT races. It was a bit of a mess. I had some success in F3000, but I had more poles than wins.

Then, four days before the week of the Le Mans 24 Hours in 1997, I got a phone call. Joest Racing had wanted to run Bernd Schneider in their Porsche but Domingos Piedade at Mercedes wouldn't allow him out of his contract. Joest had asked Mercedes who would be a good replacement and so Piedade suggested my name. He was big with AMG at the time and their DTM team used Bridgestone tyres. As a result, he'd been out in Japan a lot and had seen a little bit of my racing. So he said to them, 'You have to take Kristensen.'

Everyone, of course, questioned it. I went out, I was immediately fast and, sure, I had only done 17 laps in testing, but I think my first stints in the race were reasonable. It was at night when I really came alive though. It was then that Ralf Jüttner, the team manager, apparently said, 'Fucking hell, you know, we can win this.' We weren't cruising, we were a few minutes behind and pulling in.

In the third stint, I did the fastest lap of the race and a little bit later I got a clear lap. And I tell you, in 18 years at Le Mans I can't count ten clear laps I've ever had around there. You know? A lap with no cars to pass at all? And I had one on my début, which was so important just to figure everything out in a clear, perfect way. And then I made the lap record.

Michele Alboreto was ready to get in after my third stint, but they asked me to do a fourth. They pulled him back and told him to hold off, but I think that motivated him too. I was only told this later, but apparently Michele had looked at the screens and said that the track looked like it was getting quicker, and Ralf had replied, 'Well, at least it is for our car.' That was nice to hear.

But Michele and Stefan Johansson had embraced me so well as my team-mates. That dynamic, when you are driving at Le Mans, taught me a lot. They had nothing to lose except for the fact that they wanted to win that race. They gave me everything I asked for, and they never bossed me around. They never pulled me in and said, 'You must do this, and you must do it like that.' No, no, it was never like that. They were very respectful of my racing in Japan and treated me not as the young kid but as really a part of the team.

There are a lot of good people behind every story. And that story ended with us winning at Le Mans. It was my first race there and my first victory.

Today you sit here as 'Mr Le Mans'. When you were driving that bank bus, having a dream, did you ever, for a moment, imagine that you would achieve so much?

Of course not. Not in those days. I'm just so grateful to have had friends along the way who could feel my frustrations, who motivated me to do other things when I couldn't be in a car, who came with me to push me on when I did get a chance. Some of the kart races, we were always on a shoestring budget and other racers would help me out. One time there was a race at Zaragoza in Spain and someone couldn't make it so they said Tom, you have to go instead of me. They gave me their mechanic and he drove 33 hours so we could race and we finished on the podium.

It's things like that.

If I'd have known there would be so many obstacles, would I have set out on this path? Maybe not. But that is the good thing about life. You don't know they will be there. That's why, when you get through the obstacles, it means more. It means your heart is really there and that you have really worked for it.

And for me, so many times in my life, the thing that has pushed me to achieve has been to return the belief and the kindness that other people have shown to me. You want to repay the people who have taken a chance on you.

Is that why you think you've achieved so much?

I think perhaps it is because I care. I have always performed better when I've had a good dynamic at the team, too. Let's say at Le Mans, you have to have a good relationship with your team-mates and with the team. I have spent a lot of energy trying to create that dynamic. And that has worked for me and has been very important.

And that support from family, friends, is that what got you through and made you so appreciative?

Yes. But I don't want you to think it was all nice. Sure, I took many of these dark moments for motivation. But in other moments there has been a lot of anger. But that has come when I felt that someone has said something or has written something that I don't feel is correct. If you have been wronged or people have insulted you, when things have been said that are not right, then when things go against you because of that, it can create a lot of anger.

But those are the times when you have to take that anger and turn it into determination. You can use these moments as the coal on the fire that burns inside you to achieve.

But the positive that has flowed throughout the good times and the bad are the people who have been there for me at these fundamental moments. When

I had that anger burning in me, they helped me turn it around.

One moment was when I won the German F3 title, my first championship. I won it in the way I needed to which was simply by finishing where I had to in the points, nothing too flashy. Just do the job. And I remember this older Danish driver who was commentating on the race, and he was saying it was a shame the way I was driving because I didn't show that I was a great champion. I was so angry with him.

But, in another way, I guess, that inspired me to go and do what I did at that last race where I broke all the records and finished the season with the biggest win of the year.

Did you ever have a moment, then, in those days in the bus, when you thought about giving up?

Oh yes. I couldn't quit racing because I had nothing to quit. I wasn't racing. But giving up? Yeah.

It's very easy to say 'no'. There were many moments when I found myself doing something completely different and perhaps seeing that maybe this was now going to have to be my life. But I was always drawn back to the race track. It was clearly the path and the route of my life.

I was dreaming of driving as a professional driver. In anything.

So to be standing there, in 1997, your first time at Le Mans, on the top step of the podium. The champagne, the cheers from the fans, from your rivals. It's almost 10 years exactly after your 1,000 days began. When you were up there, looking out over everything as a Le Mans winner for the first moment, did you ever think back to those times in the bank and think of how far you'd come? How much you'd achieved?

Not just that. I told you how in the dark moments I used the thoughts of people who hadn't believed in me to fire me up to achieve more.

Well in that moment I can tell you I didn't think about them once. I only thought about the people who had believed in me. That I had done something to make them proud.

And I was so happy.

Acknowledgments

E ric Verdon-Roe and Mark Hughes have, in Evro, created a company whose stated aim was to produce only a very select list of motorsport publications. To thus see my first book fall under their guiding hand, and my name placed alongside so many writers whose work I have for years admired, provides me with no small amount of pride. It truly is an honour to work with you both and with your incredible team, not least Rebecca Leppard and Judy Stropus, who have worked tirelessly to push this body of work out into the world.

Mark, in particular, I wish to single out. A decade and a half ago I was a young, inexperienced writer. Mark believed enough in me to take interest in a book I pitched on the adventures of a young freelancer chasing his dream. The book that I began, however, I was never able to complete as personal tragedies over the course of the year affected me far more than I perhaps realised at the time. There is thus a kismetic quality to the fact that, so many years later, it should have been he who called with an offer of publication. Now, as then, thank you for believing in me.

This book was only ever going to work with the time, openness and — crucially — the consent of the drivers who agreed to take part. As such, my unending thanks must go to each and every one of the drivers contained within the pages of this book. Without their incredible honesty and without their personal faith in this project, *My Greatest Defeat* would not exist.

But drivers have tremendous teams behind them, teams who have to contend with hundreds of requests similar to mine every single week. Without their belief in this project and without their grace and willingness to accommodate my (lengthy) interview requests into already busy schedules, we never would have got off the ground. As such, I am forever indebted to Helen Bramley, Ed Hassard, Bradley Lord, Rosa Herrero Venegas, Felix Siggemann, Patty Reid, Matt Bishop, Fernando Paiva, Aurélie Donzelot, Vanessa Reffay, Nicolas Todt, Sophie Ogg, Carlos Oñoro Sainz, Ben Wyatt, Christina Gaither, Aurélie Lehe, Stephanie Protet, Sami Räisänen, Inga Stracke, Allard Kalff, Jan Würgler, the aforementioned Rebecca Leppard, Jon Edwards, Amy Walsh Stock, John Lewensten, Shon Sbarra, Merrill Cain, Nicki Shields, Emma Donaldson, Steve Shunck, Ann Bradshaw and Danilo Coglianese.

I would also like to thank the people with whom I discussed the project, both drivers and the teams around them, who ultimately decided that this concept was not for them. I have nothing but the utmost respect for them and their reasons and hope very much to include their stories in any potential future volumes of this series that may lie ahead.

Although I began this journey in 2017, it was completed in 2018, a year in which I started a new professional direction working for Formula 1 in an official capacity. As such, tremendous thanks go to Frank Arthofer for his understanding and permission to continue with this project alongside my work and commitments for him in Formula 1.

To that end I'd also like to pay homage to my agent Robert Lazar for having my back.

Over my career, my focus has predominantly been on Formula 1 and so I want to take a moment to thank Marshall Pruett for his invaluable help in providing contacts and nudges for many of the American racers I'd never met when I began the book and wrote up my wish list and for being such a firm believer in this project throughout.

Gary Miereanu is a name that won't be familiar to many in the racing world, but is your go-to man for all things in the animated world of Warner Bros. He's also a massive motorsport fan. It's down to him that I was introduced to Giuseppe Camuncoli.

I couldn't have believed when I started out on this project that it would eventually have the look and feel that it does, and that all lies in the beautiful illustrations created by the deft artistic touch of the aforementioned 'Cammo'. More used to penning for Marvel than for motorsport, the time he has spent dedicated to drawing the legends included within these pages, not to mention his complete faith in the merits of this book, have stunned me. I'm honoured to have his name and his work included on these pages.

Over the past 20 years I've been given some amazing opportunities that have had a huge influence on the way in which this book has turned out. By far the biggest eye openers have come through my work in the United States, and I'd like to pay tribute to Rich O'Connor, Frank Wilson, J.F. Musial, Kaare Numme, Dan Shutte, Drew Devine, Paul Pfanner and Mark Glendenning for everything that working with them taught me over the past decade. Jean Michel Tibi, Alex Chiari, Dan Kidner and Steve Jones have been there on the other side of the camera throughout and have all played a huge role in the manner in which I express my love for this sport.

Matt Franey and Hans Seeberg taught me some of the greatest lessons in feature writing and were instrumental in allowing me the freedom to develop a writing style and my own voice. Jonathan Nicholas allowed me enough rope to hang myself in my earliest days in the commentary box. I'm forever indebted to them all.

I'd also like to thank Maurice Hamilton, Mark Hughes, Joe Saward, Tom Clarkson, Tony Dodgins, Andreas Troll, Freddie Petersens, Jon Noble, Ted Kravitz, Ben Edwards, Holly Samos, Max Loong, Mervi Kallio, Matthew Marsh, James Moy, Russell Batchelor, Stuart Roach, Luca Colajanni, Pierre Guyonnet-Duperat, Jonny Reynolds, Lawrence Barretto, Matteo Bonciani, Kate Walker, Jay Ward, Violet Cruz and many others in and around the sport who have helped me along the way, shown genuine interest in this project and who have, through advice or just taking the time to ask and listen, helped this book to its conclusion.

Leigh Diffey, David Hobbs and Steve Matchett — your wisdom and passion continue to drive and inspire me.

David Tremayne has, for the better part of the past two decades, been my mentor, my guide and most importantly my friend. It was he who gave me a break, he who gave me my first job and he whose initial reaction to this project I most valued. I owe my career and everything that has come my way in this sport to his faith and belief. Without his original belief in me, this book would not exist.

Jason Swales has, from a professional and personal standpoint, had one of the most profound influences on me as a broadcaster, writer and as a man. He'd hate me getting overly effusive in my praise of him as a producer or my respect for him as a friend, but at the points at which I've found myself edging towards despair he's been there to pull me back. And when I've pushed things too far in the other direction, he's been there with a reality check. I owe him more than I'll ever tell him.

For my friends: the people I care about the most and the ones I get to see the least, thank you for holding me up when I've stumbled the furthest. And for not forgetting what I look like.

Pip and Henry, my sister and brother. You are thoughtful and kind, calm and considerate. I never tell you how deeply I admire your limitless strength.

Sophie, my world. Everything I do in this life is to try to better myself as your father. To be everything that you deserve. Now and always.

V. My present and my future. My solace and my joy. Thank you for putting up with me. I can't wait to build our life together.

And finally, Georgie... my mum. This book is about discovering strength through the hardest times. When we lost Dad, I didn't know how you would cope. I didn't know how we would cope. But I learnt something incredibly fast.

All my life I thought that Dad had been the strong one, that Dad had pulled us through the difficulties that life had thrown at us. And it suddenly dawned on me that, actually, it was you. It had always been you. You bind us together and give us strength. You always have.

While I dedicate this book to the memory of my father, the lessons it represents are those manifested in my mother. And I'll be forever grateful to have had them both as my guides in this world.

Glossary

Aerodynamics — The study of how air flows over a vehicle. The aim of racing car aerodynamics is to make best use of that airflow to improve the car's performance, and involves the use of complex wing shapes.

Baja 1000 — An off-road race that tracks a course winding down the treacherous roads of the Baja California Peninsula in north-west Mexico. The race allows various vehicle classes to compete on the same course in a similar fashion to the Dakar Rally.

Champ Car — See 'Indycar'.

Dakar Rally — 'The Dakar' is one of the most notoriously difficult, arduous and treacherous rallies in the world. First held in 1978, it originally ran from Paris in France to Dakar in Senegal, but due to the increasing number of security threats the route in recent years has moved to South America. An off-road endurance event, it is open to numerous classes of vehicle, including motorcycles. The terrain involved is considered by many to be the toughest challenge in motorsport, with drivers and riders encountering everything from dirt and asphalt to rocks, sand dunes, mud, camel grass and deep water with stages reaching up to 500 miles per day.

DTM — Deutsche Tourenwagen Masters. For many years, this German championship has been considered the most technologically advanced, competitive and thrilling form of touring car racing in the world.

FIA — Consisting of 246 member organisations in 145 countries, the Fédération Internationale de l'Automobile represents the interests of motoring organisations and road users on a global level. One of the largest campaigners for road safety in the world, it is also the sanctioning and governing body of many of the world's premier racing championships including Formula 1, Formula 2, the World Endurance Championship and the World Rally Championship.

Formula 1 — The highest class of open-wheel racing sanctioned by the FIA. Established in 1950, the Formula 1 World Championship is viewed by many as the pinnacle of global motorsport.

Formula 2 — With Formula 1 sitting as the supposed pinnacle of global motorsport, Formula 2 has, for much of the past 70 years, been seen as the final step on the ladder to the top of the sport, featuring cars less technically complex, less powerful and therefore less expensive to run than those in Formula 1. The series has also been known as Formula 3000 and GP2.

Formula 3 — For many years, Formula 3 has been seen as the first step for young racers on which to make a name for themselves as they begin their ascent to Formula 1.

Indycar — Tracing its roots back to the start of the 1900s, America's highest level of open-wheel racing has taken many forms and many names over its life. The term 'Indycar' stems from the championship's main event, the Indianapolis 500, which runs in May every year and is one of the biggest sporting events on Earth. A national championship has been run in the USA since 1905 with a sanctioning body, the United States Auto Club (USAC), created to oversee the racing as it increased in popularity through the 1950s. Growing dissent led to the creation of Championship Auto Racing Teams (CART) in 1979 and saw a civil war erupt in American open-wheel racing that raged into the 2000s, its final battles waged between CART (by then also known as Champ Car) and the IRL (Indy Racing League). Indycar exists today as a unified and united championship displaying some of the most enthralling racing in the world.

Kart (go-kart) — The first point of contact with motor racing for many children, karting is today the single largest entry point for racers. The proliferation of rental karts has made grass-roots motor racing widely accessible worldwide, and at their sporting height karts form one of the closest and most competitive forms of racing in the world. Almost all open-wheel champions of the past 25 years began their careers in karts.

Le Mans — Les 24 Heures du Mans is the oldest active sportscar race in the world, first run in 1923. Held every year on the roads around the northern French city of Le Mans, this 24-hour endurance event is one of the single most important and prestigious races on Earth and forms part of the unofficial Triple Crown of global motor racing.

Midget car — Similar to Sprint cars, Midgets have a high power-to-weight ratio and form an early step on the United States racing ladder. Quarter Midgets are, as the name suggests, quarter the size of the full car and race on tracks a quarter of the length. As such, the Quarter Midget is seen as the perfect entry-level race car for children wanting to start out on the oval racing scene.

Modified/Super Modified — If Stock Cars need to have something in common with production road vehicles, then the notion of the modified racing car was that an individual was able to take a stock car and modify it to draw out increased performance. Crossing the lines between the limitations of stock car racing and the freedoms inherent in many forms of open-wheel racing, there are numerous sanctioning bodies for Modified and Super Modified racing cars, although their popularity is predominantly limited to the United States.

Open-wheel — An open-wheel racing car is often also referred to as a Formula car or a single-seater owing to it having just one seat. The term 'open-wheel' is derived from the positioning of the car's wheels outside the car's main body. These cars are built specifically for racing and, given the high level of engineering and technical development that goes into their creation, are often viewed as some of the most advanced in the world.

Oval — Oval tracks are predominantly the domain of the American racer, accounting for 900 individual race circuits in the USA, and are so named for their shape. They are raced in one direction, usually anti-clockwise. Ovals are classified by their size, surface and shape and can range in size from just hundreds of feet to the largest at 2.5 miles. Short-track ovals are less than a mile in length. Often involving a dirt surface, they are where many US racers cut their teeth. Mile Ovals are, as the name suggests, a mile in length, usually constructed from asphalt and are often flat. Speedways are banked asphalt racing circuits from one to two miles in length, although the name is usually reserved for tracks over 1.5 miles. Superspeedways are tracks over 2.0 miles long, the most famous being the Indianapolis Motor Speedway, which is 2.5 miles.

Pike's Peak — This is the highest summit of the Southern Front Range of the Rocky Mountains, located 12 miles west of downtown Colorado Springs, Colorado, USA. The highway to the summit has been the scene of one of the world's most famous and treacherous hillclimbs for over 100 years, its first running having taken place in 1916. Known as the 'Race to the Clouds', the event is a time trial beginning at Mile 7 of the Highway and concluding 12.42 miles later at the summit at 14,110 feet. The track has over 156 turns and until recently featured gravel sections as well as tarmac, and sheer drops at the road's edge.

Rallying — A form of racing that takes place on closed public and private roads. Rather than side-by-side competition, rallying takes the form of a time trial, or 'point to point', with drivers and their co-drivers starting at intervals and tasked with setting the fastest time they can over individual stages. The cars at their disposal are modified road-going cars, set up for the rigours of the type of surface of the rally — snow, gravel or asphalt... or sometimes even all three.

Roll cage — A tubular steel structure within a closed competition car designed to protect the driver and any co-driver in the event of a big impact, especially one that involves a car turning upside down. For an open car, this method of protection more commonly takes the form of a roll hoop to protect the driver's head.

Single-seater — See 'Open-wheel'.

Speedway — see 'Oval'.

Sportscar — Enclosed-wheel racing cars with two seats, Sportscars fall into two main categories; Grand Touring (GT) road-going cars and Prototypes. They are most usually involved in endurance racing such as the World Endurance Championship and Le Mans.

Sprint car — High-powered race cars, designed solely for the purpose of running on short-course dirt ovals. These cars have incredibly high power-to-weight ratios and are the proving ground for young American racers, with many champions of both Indycar and NASCAR having used Sprint cars as early steps on their career ladders.

Stock car — Born of the prohibition era in the United States when moonshine runners had to outrun the authorities, stock cars were and are essentially regular cars that have been modified into racing cars. Today, the most famous and highest-ranked stock car racing championship in the world is NASCAR (National Association for Stock Car Auto Racing). Established by Bill France Sr in 1948, the initial requirement was that all cars entered should be made of parts available to the general public and that over 500 units had to have been made available for sale to the public. Today known as the 'Monster Energy NASCAR Cup Series' the highest level of NASCAR racing was, for over 30 years, known as 'The Winston Cup'.

Superspeedway — see 'Oval'.

Touring car — A touring car is a modified road-going racer usually based on a family hatchback or saloon (sedan).

World Endurance Championship — The title used nowadays for the world championship for sportscars, first run in 1953. Featuring multiple classes of Prototype and GT cars, its centrepiece event is the annual Le Mans 24 Hours.